THE PYRENEAN HAUTE ROUTE

ABOUT THE AUTHOR

Ton Joosten grew up in the Netherlands, and in 1986 visited the Pyrenees for the first time. The range captured his imagination, and since then he has returned every year. In the 1990s he made a series of long backpacking expeditions in the Pyrenees and started to write walking guides. This, Ton's sixth guide, is about the long-distance route that he considers to be the most difficult, but also the most rewarding, walk from the Atlantic to the Mediterranean Sea: the Pyrenean Haute Route.

Ton has walked all stages of the GR10 (through the French Pyrenees), the GR11 (through the Spanish Pyrenees) and the Haute Route. He has walked every stage of the Haute Route more than once, all the stages in the high mountains at least three times, and has walked all the variants in the guide over the years. To date he has spent over 900 days in the Pyrenees, and the magic isn't over yet!

THE PYRENEAN HAUTE ROUTE

by
Ton Joosten

2 POLICE SQUARE, MILNTHORPE, CUMBRIA LA7 7PY
www.cicerone.co.uk

© Ton Joosten 2004
ISBN 1 85284 426 4

A catalogue record for this book is available from the British Library.

Dedication

This book is for Kev Reynolds, whose books on the Pyrenees, especially *Classic Walks in the Pyrenees*, have helped me discover what walking in the Pyrenean mountains is all about. For me, his writings have been a constant source of inspiration.

Advice to Readers

Readers are advised that while every effort is taken by the author to ensure the accuracy of this guidebook, changes can occur which may affect the contents. It is advisable to check locally on transport, accommodation, etc, but even rights of way can be altered.

The publisher would welcome notes of any such changes.

Front cover: Pic du Midi d'Ossau from the Lac d'Ayous

CONTENTS

Preface 11

Introduction 13
When to go 14
How to get there 15
Essential things to take 16
Food and water 20
Maps 20
Maps and profiles in this book 22
Insurance 22
Spending the night in the Pyrenean mountains 22
Note on the weather 23
Grading and timing of walks 25
Ten classic summits 26
Two 'consolation walks' 27
Useful books on climbing in the Pyrenees 27
Mountain safety and first aid 28
Rules for walkers in the Pyrenees 29
National parks 31
Wildlife and flowers 33

The Pyrenean Haute Route 39
Section 1: Hendaye to Lescun 39
Day   1: Hendaye to Col de Lizuniaga 43
Day   2: Col de Lizuniaga to Arizkun 48
Day   3: Arizkun to Les Aldudes 53
Day   4: Les Aldudes to Roncevalles 57
Day   5: Roncevalles to Egurgui 62
Day   6: Egurgui to Col Bagargui 67
Day   7: Col Bagargui to Refugio de Belagua 72
          Variant: Col Bagargui to Ardanne via Larrau and the Col de Jauregeberri ...77
Day   8: Refugio de Belagua to Lescun 80

Section 2: Lescun to Gavarnie 87
Day   9: Lescun to Refuge d'Arlet 93
Day 10: Refuge d'Arlet to Candanchu 96
Day 11: Candanchu to Refuge de Pombie 101
          An easy summit: Pic d'Ayous (2288m) 107
Day 12: Refuge de Pombie to Refuge de Larribet 108

Day 13: Refuge de Larribet to Refuge Wallon 114
    Variant: Refuge d'Arrémoulit to Refuge Wallon...................................118
    Ten classic summits – 1: Grande Fache (3005m) from Refuge Wallon......121
Day 14: Refuge Wallon to Refuge de Baysellance..122
    Ten classic summits – 2: The Vignemale (3298m) from the Refuge de
    Baysellance 126
Day 15: Refuge de Baysellance to Gavarnie 129
    Ten classic summits – 3: Le Taillon (3144m) from Gavarnie.....................133

Section 3: Gavarnie to Salardu...136
Day 16: Gavarnie to Héas 141
    Ten classic summits – 4: Piméné (2801m) from Refuge des Espuguettes ...145
Day 17: Héas to Parzan 146
Day 18: Parzan to Refugio de Viados 151
Day 19: Refugio de Viados to Refuge de la Soula 155
Day 20: Refuge de la Soula to Refuge du Portillon 159
    Ten classic summits – 5: Pic Perdiguère (3222m) from
    Refuge du Portillon..163
Day 21: Refuge du Portillon to Refugio de la Renclusa 164
    Ten classic summits – 6: Pico de Aneto (3404m) from Refugio de la
    Renclusa 170
    Haute Route escape route: from Refugio de la Renclusa to
    Bagnères-de-Luchon..171
    Variant: Hospital de Venasque – GR11 trail 172
Day 22: Refugio de la Renclusa to Hospital de Vielha 173
Day 23: Hospital de Vielha to Refugi de la Restanca..179
    Variant: GR11 from Estany de Rius to Refugi de la Restanca 183
Day 24: Refugi de la Restanca to Salardu 184
    Ten classic summits – 7: Montardo d'Aran (2826m) from
    Coll de Crestada..188
GR11 from Viados to Hospital de Vielha (three-day variant)................................189

Section 4: Salardu to l'Hospitalet-près-l'Andorre 195
Day 25: Salardu to Alos de Isil...199
    Variant: to Alos de Isil via the Montgarri dirt road 206
Day 26: Alos de Isil to Refugi Enric Pujol..208
    Ten classic summits – 8: Mont Roig (2868m) from Refugi Enric Puyol 212
Day 27: Refugi Enric Pujol to Refugi de Certascan 213
    Variant 1: via Tavascan to Pla de Boavi 217
    Variant 2: Noarre via Camping Masia 'Bordes de Graus' 218
    Ten classic summits – 9: Pic de Certascan (2853m) from
    Col de Certascan..219

Day 28: Refugi de Certascan to Refugi del Cinquantenari 220
Day 29: Refugi del Cinquantenari to Étang de la Soucarrane 224
    Ten classic summits – 10: Pica d'Estats (3143m) and Montcalm (3077m)
    from Refugi de Vall Ferrera 227
Day 30: Étang de la Soucarrane to Refugi de Sorteny 229
Day 31: Refugi de Sorteny to Camping d'Incles 233
Day 32: Camping d'Incles to l'Hospitalet-près-l'Andorre 238

Section 5: l'Hospitalet-près-l'Andorre to Banyuls-sur-Mer 243
Day 33: l'Hospitalet-près-l'Andorre to Refuge des Bésines 248
Day 34: Refuge des Bésines to Barrage des Bouillouses 251
    Variant: GR10 avoiding Pic Carlit 255
    Consolation walk 1: From Chalet-Refuge des Bouillouses to
    Pic Carlit summit 256
Day 35: Barrage des Bouillouses to Eyne 257
Day 36: Eyne to Refugi d'Ull de Ter 261
Day 37: Refugi d'Ull de Ter to Refuge de Mariailles 266
Day 38: Refuge de Mariailles to Mines de Batère 270
    Variant: The GR10 from Refuge de Mariailles to Chalet-Refuge
    des Cortalets 275
    Consolation walk 2: The ascent of Canigou from Cortalets 277
Day 39: Mines de Batère to Amélie-les-Bains 278
Day 40: Amélie-les-Bains to Las Illas 282
Day 41: Las Illas to Col de l'Ouillat 287
Day 42: Col de l'Ouillat to Banyuls-sur-Mer 291

Appendices
Appendix 1: Useful addresses 297
Appendix 2: Glossary 301
Appendix 3: Facilities list 304

Index 311

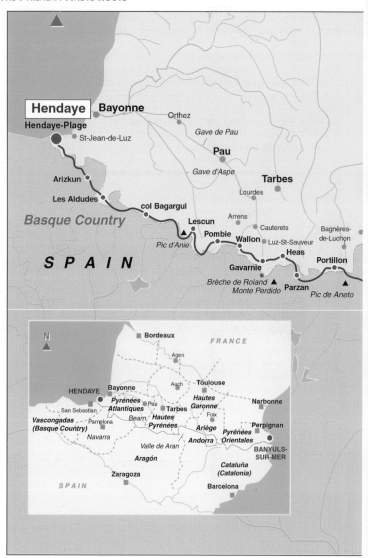

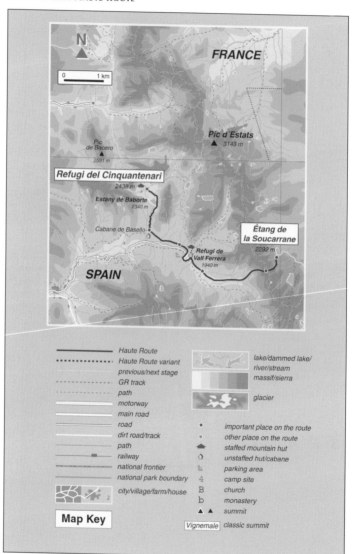

——————— Haute Route	lake/dammed lake/ river/stream
··············· Haute Route variant	massif/sierra
previous/next stage	
------------ GR track	glacier
------------ path	
═══════════ motorway	• important place on the route
═══════════ main road	◦ other place on the route
═══════════ road	⬣ staffed mountain hut
═══════════ dirt road/track	⬠ unstaffed hut/cabane
path	ⵥ parking area
——■—— railway	ⵄ camp site
——————— national frontier	B church
——————— national park boundary	b monastery
city/village/farm/house	▲ ▲ ▲ summit
Map Key	*Vignemale* classic summit

PREFACE

In 1986 I visited the Pyrenees for the first time, and since then have been back every summer. Armed with a heavy rucksack I have walked, over the years, through the Pyrenees for more than 900 days and have gradually fallen under the spell of these mountains. Now, over 15 years later, my passion for the Pyrenees is as strong as ever. People often ask me if it isn't time to visit another mountain region. My answer is always that for me the magic is still there, and as a result I cannot think of visiting another region.

I must admit, however, that in moments of weakness I ask myself what in heaven's name I am doing. In 25 visits to the Pyrenees I have walked all the stages of the Pyrenean Haute Route at least twice, completed the GR11 and GR10, visited practically all the staffed mountain huts, explored every possible region (some many times) and climbed over 100 summits (including more than 40 3000m summits). I have visited the famous Brèche de Roland 12 times, the Ordesa national park 15 times, the Parc Nacional d'Aigüestortes I Estany de Sant Maurici 8 times and made countless visits to the French Parc National des Pyrénées Occidentales.

And still I have a burning desire to return to the Pyrenees because these mountains are so special. There is one long-distance trail during which the walker is guaranteed fall under the spell of the Pyrenees: the Pyrenean Haute Route. In the end, there can be only one coast-to-coast route in the Pyrenees!

Ton Joosten

One of the alpine sections of the High Route: the Portillon region with Pic Perdiguère (3222m) on the right, seen from Pic Gourdon (3034m, day 20)

INTRODUCTION

What is the Pyrenean Haute Route (known in French as the Haute Randonnée Pyrénéenne)? It is a long-distance footpath from the Atlantic to the Mediterranean that follows the main ridge of the Pyrenees. The Haute Route is not itself waymarked, which means that there are all sorts of marks along the trail: paint flashes in various colours, GR waymarks (red–white), cairns, border stones and sometimes no marks at all. In fact the Haute Route is not a trail as such, but rather an idea. As a result Haute Route walkers often have a choice of routes, and there are numerous variants that allow walkers to avoid difficult sections of the Haute Route's main track.

In summer, from mid-July until the end of August, very little mountaineering equipment is needed. Only the third section of the Haute Route contains a few stages that may require crampons and ice axe. There is, however, a three-day variant in this guide (from Viados to Hospital de Vielha, after Day 24) that enables you to avoid these difficult stages. Should you follow this alternative route, it is possible to complete the Haute Route without any mountaineering equipment.

Having said that, the Haute Route is suitable only for experienced trekkers. Those who undertake it must have wide experience of walking on all sorts of terrain, including steep scree slopes,

Lac Gentau and the Pic du Midi d'Ossau (2884m)

boulder fields and snowfields. They also need to know how to navigate in the mountains, even in difficult conditions (mist). The Haute Route leads sometimes through untamed, remote areas where there are no waymarks or paths. The ability to read the landscape is necessary; a good intuition of how to walk (which comes with the years) is useful; and knowledge of how to use map and compass (or GPS) is indispensable.

This guide describes the Haute Route from west to east in 42 stages, divided into five sections:

- through the Basque territory (8 days)
- highlights of the Parc National (7 days)
- Gavarnie to Salardu (9 days)
- Salardu to l'Hospitalet-près-l'Andorre (8 days) and
- through the Eastern Pyrenees (10 days).

Each section begins with an introduction that contains useful practical information (accommodation, telephone numbers, maps, access to walk start points, food supply points, information on villages and internet sites).

Throughout the route there are numerous variants – alternative routes that allow the walker to avoid a difficult section should weather conditions not be in your favour. But even if you take the variant on every possible occasion, the Haute Route is still a tough trek that can only be completed successfully by experienced, well-prepared mountain walkers. More than 800km of walking and over 40km of climbing (and descent) isn't a piece of cake. The variants are certainly not meant as an

invitation to walk the Haute Route 'the Dutch way', avoiding every difficult section. Don't forget that a choice for the Haute Route is also a choice for challenge. Walkers who seek to avoid all obstacles set by the main track of the Pyrenean Haute Route are not quite ready for the toughest, but also the most beautiful, coast-to-coast walk through the Pyrenees.

WHEN TO GO

The best months to walk the Pyrenean Haute Route are July and August. In June most mountain passes in the high mountains of the Pyrenees (between the Vallée d'Ossau and Carlit massif) are still covered with snow. June, however, is an excellent month for both the first section (through the Basque territory) and, from mid-June on, the final section (if you take the variant to avoid Pic Carlit). During July most of the snow will disappear in the high mountains, though some snowfields will persist on a few high passes. Should you want to walk the entire route, then my advice is not to start before the end of June.

July and August are the best months for a long walk in the Pyrenees. They are the driest and warmest months of the year, and the weather is generally settled. August can be extremely warm, however, and thunderstorms are an everyday concern!

Late August and the first days of September often experience a short period of extremely bad weather, with thunderstorms, torrential rainfall, hail and possibly some snowfall in the high mountains. It's an indication that

Solitary bivouac near the Col d'Arrious (day 12)

summer is ending and winter is slowly on its way. Once the weather recovers, the first half of September can be exceptionally beautiful. Temperatures drop significantly in the second half of September, and there will be frost at night on a regular basis from then on. Snowfall in the high mountains is not uncommon in September.

It is always dangerous to generalise about the weather. Snow conditions vary to a certain extent from year to year, depending on the amount of snowfall in spring and the temperatures in April, May and June. Each year has its anomalies. I have experienced long periods in the mountains with beautiful, settled weather, but there have also been weeks in which the weather was totally unpredictable and changed dramatically every day. I have witnessed the most severe thunderstorms, some unbelievable hail showers and,

occasionally (even in July and August), a fair amount of snowfall. Be ready for anything in the Pyrenees!

HOW TO GET THERE

By Car

For Haute Route walkers this is certainly not the best option, as it means that you will have to leave your car at the start of the route for quite some time and travel back (by train) at the end of the trip. There are autoroutes through all parts of France, so each area of the Pyrenees can be reached easily by car. Most autoroutes are toll roads, and it's up to you to decide whether this is the best way to travel.

By Air

Flying is a better option. Ryanair has cheap air fares from London Stansted to Biarritz, on the Atlantic (train service to

Hendaye, where the Haute Route starts), and Perpignan (train service to Banyuls-sur-Mer, where the Haute Route ends) in the east. Perpignan airport is situated around 5km north of the town, and there is a bus service from the airport to the town's centre. The only other direct flights from the UK to the Pyrenees are the Ryanair flights from London Stansted to Pau. There are services from Paris to Pau and Lourdes. Air France have daily flights from Paris to Biarritz, Pau and Lourdes.

An alternative is to fly from the UK to Barcelona: British Airways have daily flights from Heathrow and Gatwick to Barcelona. Iberia has a daily service to Barcelona from Manchester and Heathrow. EasyJet has cheap flights from Newcastle, London Stansted and London Gatwick to Barcelona.

There are no direct flights from countries outside Europe to any Pyrenean airport. The only option is to fly to Paris and from there take a flight to one of the airports in the Pyrenees.

Airline information
Air France: www.airfrance.com
EasyJet: www.easyjet.com
British Airways:
www.britishairways.com
Iberia: www.iberia.com
Ryanair: www.ryanair.com

By Train
This is another practical option for the Haute Route walker. Paris can nowadays be reached easily and quickly by Eurostar. Trains arrive at Gare du Nord in Paris, from where there are several options. From Gare de Montparnasse (you have to take the subway from Gare

du Nord to Gare de Montparnasse) there are high-speed trains (TGV – *train à grande vitesse*) to a large number of destinations: Hendaye, Pau, Lourdes, Toulouse, Perpignan and Banyuls-sur-Mer. Reservations are required. If you leave London early in the morning you will arrive at Hendaye the same afternoon.

My personal preference is to take the subway from Gare du Nord to Gare d'Austerlitz and to travel from there by night-train to one of the many Pyrenean destinations – Hendaye, Pau, Lourdes, l'Hospitalet-près-l'Andorre and Banyuls-sur-Mer. The night-trains have the great advantage of arriving very early in the morning (usually between 06.00 and 07.00), which is ideal for walkers who want to make an immediate start!

Railway information
Eurostar services: www.eurostar.com
Other European railway services:
www.raileurope.com
French railways: www.sncf.fr

ESSENTIAL THINGS TO TAKE
Walkers of the Pyrenean Haute Route, being experienced trekkers, are likely to know what essentials to take with them. However, the following may be useful as a checklist.

- A solid **rucksack** of about 65 litres capacity and around 1500g empty weight. It has to be a rucksack without a metal frame and it should have a few external zip-up pockets for essential items such as water bottle and snacks.
- An ultra-light small **day-sack** of

about 25 litres might be handy in case you want to do a day-walk or one of the climbs mentioned in this guide.

- **Sleeping mat** (whether this is a classic foam mat or a self-inflating mat is a matter of personal choice) and **sleeping bag**: a three-season bag should be sufficient in the summer season.
- **Mountain boots**: make sure they fit well and have Vibram soles. Because the Haute Route passes through all sorts of terrain light-weight boots are not suitable. Take an extra pair of boot-laces with you! Make sure that the boots will take gaiters (I never use them in the Pyrenees, but I must admit they can be useful at certain occasions) and that it is possible to wear crampons with them.
- **Climbing gear**: crampons, rope, ice axe. These items are necessary for the

ascents of the Vignemale, Pic Perdiguère and Pico de Aneto. Crampons and ice axe are useful on a few sections of the Haute Route: days 12, 13, 20, 21 and 22. There are variants described in this guide to avoid the potentially difficult sections. Should you take all these variants, then the Haute Route can be completed without any climbing gear.

- **Extra footwear**: sandals, flip-flops or lightweight trainers allow your walking boots to air after a hard day's work! Staffed mountain huts generally provide some kind of footwear that can be used inside the hut.
- Three changes of **socks** and three changes of **underwear**. Thermal underwear can be useful sometimes, especially in late or early season or if you decide to bivouac at high altitude.

Border stone on the Port de Larrau, with Pic d'Orhy in the background (day 7)

- **Shirts, shorts and trousers:** take three T-shirts (use one only for travel and in the evening). I always use shorts for walking, except on cold mornings, and save the trousers for the evening.
- **Warm gear:** a windproof fleece jacket, long-sleeved shirt or sweater/pullover, woollen hat, gloves. Bear in mind that temperatures can drop significantly sometimes, even in July and August. Gloves and woollen hat are necessary!
- **Sun hat.**
- **Sunglasses** for the ascents of the high summits described in this book and for the sections on snow.
- **Waterproof jacket or a poncho.** On your way to the Mediterranean you'll have a few rainy days, so you will need something to keep your belongings dry and safe. I have always used a poncho (cheap, light and good enough to do a proper job). Make sure the poncho is large enough to cover you and your rucksack.
- **Toiletries:** toothbrush, toothpaste, small bottle of shampoo, toilet paper, soap, towel.
- **First aid kit** and an **aluminium bag** or blanket to be used in case of an accident.
- **Navigation instruments:** maps, guidebook, compass, GPS, altimeter.
- **Small useful items:** (head)torch, spare batteries, lighter, whistle, sewing kit, diary, pen, water bottles, plastic bags (to take rubbish down to the valley and to keep things separate), string (clothes line), address book, pair of binoculars, GSM, watch, lip balm.
- **Camping equipment:** tent (3kg should be the maximum for a two-person tent), cooking gear, fuel, knife, fork and spoon, Swiss army knife that has a corkscrew and bottle opener, plate, plastic cup.
- **Cash, travellers cheques and credit card.** Take plenty of Euros with you. In mountain huts, *gites* and on campsites credit cards are not generally accepted. The normal way to pay the bill is with cash. Cash dispensers and banks are mentioned in the practical information at the start of each section of the route description and in the facilities list (see Appendix 3).
- **Passport or identity card**, membership card of any mountaineering club, insurance card, small card with your name and address and the names and telephone numbers of relatives and friends to contact in case of an accident.
- **Camera**, spare batteries, films. The best thing to do is to bring enough films with you, although films are available in the villages in France and Spain.

While not essential, the following items may be useful.
- Swimsuit – only for courageous walkers. The water in the lakes and streams is very cold!
- Walking stick or extendable ski-poles.
- Set of cards.
- Book on animal and plant life in the Pyrenees.

The Haute Route sometimes runs through alpine terrain (day 20)

FOOD AND WATER

On a route such as this you will need cooking gear, fuel and food. Take a good look at the section of the Pyrenean Haute Route you have set your mind on, because not every day ends at a staffed hut or in the civilised world. You will have to cook your own meal sometimes, and you'll have to carry food supplies for several days.

There are only few places where you can replenish food supplies! This guide has a facilities list (see Appendix 3) that tells you where you'll find a shop, campsite, village, bank, cash dispenser, post office and (staffed) hut. Many Haute Route walkers choose not to spend every night in a hut, a choice that has often to do with money. Spending (and eating) each night in a hut or gite would make the whole traverse rather expensive.

Lightweight dried meals are available not only in outdoor shops but also in supermarkets (including pasta and rice meals, and mashed potato). Start each day with a solid breakfast and eat something at least every three hours, such as biscuits, chocolate, muesli-bars, dried fruit or dried sausage. Start every evening meal with a large can of (instant) soup. Always take at least one emergency meal with you and don't forget tea, coffee and milk powder.

Camping gaz cylinders are available almost everywhere in the Pyrenees, though buying methylated spirits can sometimes be a problem in small villages. Remember that you cannot take gaz cylinders and methylated spirits on aircraft.

On my backpacking expeditions in the Pyrenees I have always found that

one water bottle that holds no more than 1 litre of water is enough. However, it is advisable to take at least 2 litres of water, especially in the summer. Refill water bottles at every possible occasion and don't forget to take purifying tablets with you. There are animals grazing everywhere in the Pyrenees, even at high altitude in places where you might not expect to find cows, horses or sheep. As a result water in the Pyrenees isn't always pure. Water in villages and piped water (check it to be sure!), however, should be of a decent quality.

MAPS

The French maps produced by the Institut Géografique National (IGN) have a reputation for being accurate and reliable. Although there are 1:25,000 maps (Serie Bleue) that show more detail, the 1:50,000 maps (Carte de Randonnées) should generally be sufficient for Haute Route walkers, at least for the French sections. On some 1:25,000 maps the Haute Route is not shown at all! The IGN Carte de Randonnées (11 maps) cover the entire French Pyrenees and some parts of the Spanish Pyrenees (both national parks) and Andorra.

A useful supplement to the French maps are the so-called Mapa Excursionista/Carte de Randonnées that are made by the Institut Cartografic de Catalunya. These 1:50,000 maps have recently been produced, and show not only the Spanish Pyrenees but also a significant part of the French mountains. The maps are beautiful and are as accurate as the French IGN maps. To date

(2003) the Institut Cartografic de Catalunya has produced six (numbers 20–25) of these Mapa Excursionista/ Carte de Randonnées (though they don't cover the entire Pyrenees). These maps are sufficient for the High Pyrenees, however, so for this section you don't have to use any other Spanish maps, such as the Editorial Alpina and the Spanish Military Survey maps. In my opinion both the latter sets of maps are of a relatively poor quality, and for walking the Haute Route you should only use the best maps available! There is also a fine map of the entire Pyrenees, produced by the IGN (1:400,000), which might be handy.

Note: Guidebook and maps by themselves will not always be sufficient to keep the walker on course. A compass or GPS can be a useful, as the Haute Route sometimes passes through isolated, untamed mountain areas

where you won't find a path (and only a few waymarks). A compass or GPS can also be useful in case of poor visibility (in France, especially in the Basque territory, mist will be your worst enemy). A GPS is certainly not strictly necessary, but always have a compass with you (and the skill to use it effectively).

You'll need the following maps to complete the entire Pyrenean Haute Route:

- IGN Carte de Randonnées, 1:50,000, no 1: Pays Basque Ouest
- Editorial Alpina, 1:40,000, Alduides Baztan
- IGN Carte, 1:25,000, 1346 OT: St Jean-Pied-de-Port
- IGN Carte de Randonnées, 1:50,000, no 2: Pays Basque Est
- IGN Carte de Randonnées, 1:50,000, no 3: Béarn
- Mapa Excursionista/Carte de

Situated on a grassy bluff: the hamlet of Unha (Vall d'Aran, day 25)

Randonnées, 1:50,000, no 24:
Gavarnie–Ordesa
- Mapa Excursionista/Carte de
Randonnées, 1:50,000, no 23:
Aneto–Posets
- Mapa Excursionista/Carte de
Randonnées, 1:50,000, no 22: Pica
d'Estats–Aneto
- IGN Carte de Randonnées,
1:50,000, no 7: Haute Ariège–
Andorre
- IGN Carte de Randonnées,
1:50,000, no 8: Cerdagne–Capcir
- IGN Carte, 1:25,000, 2249 ET:
Font-Romeu
- Mapa Excursionista/Carte de
Randonnées, 1:50,000, no 20:
Puigmal–Costabona
- IGN Carte de Randonnées,
1:50,000, no 10: Canigou
- IGN Carte de Randonnées,
1:50,000, no 11: Rousillon.

As you can see, the maps required
are the IGN Carte de Randonnées, the
Mapa Excursionista/ Carte de
Randonnées, two IGN maps at
1:25,000, and the Editorial Alpina map.
(For further information, contact: Institut
Cartografic de Catalunya: www.icc.es;
Institut Géografique National:
www.ign.fr.) In the UK, maps are available from Stanfords (www.stanfords.
co.uk, tel: 020 7836 1321).

The relevant map is always given
at the beginning of each day's
route description.

MAPS AND PROFILES IN THIS BOOK

The maps in this book are, of course, not
meant to be used as walking maps, but

are intended to help walkers find the
Haute Route trail on the walking maps.
In the introduction to each section of the
Haute Route the relevant maps are
listed, and at the beginning of the route
description for each of the 42 day stages
a note of the relevant map is given.
Height profiles are found on each map
in this guide, and they also indicate the
time taken to walk the route. They therefore allow you to see in a glance what
you can expect from the walk.

INSURANCE

Make sure that your travel insurance
covers the risks of mountaineering activ-
ities before you head off to the Pyrenees.
Most standard travel insurance policies
don't, and calling a rescue service is
extremely expensive! It might be a good
idea to become member of a mountaineering club, as most of these clubs
offer adequate (and not too expensive)
insurance for mountain walkers. An
additional benefit is that, as most of the
mountaineering clubs enjoy reciprocal
rights with other countries' clubs, mem-
bers receive considerable discounts on
overnight stays (but not on meals and
drinks!) at mountain huts on either side
of the watershed.

SPENDING THE NIGHT IN THE PYRENEAN MOUNTAINS

Walking from hut to hut is becoming
increasingly popular in the Pyrenees.
Particularly in the French Pyrenees and
in the Aigüestortes region, huts become
overcrowded in summer season, and
there may not be places available when

Seasonal spots for a bivouac are to be found along the Haute Route trail (day 8)

you arrive. The best thing to do, should you wish to spend any nights in a hut, is to make reservations in advance. This guide provides a facilities list (see Appendix 3) with all staffed mountain huts and *gites* you'll pass on your way to the Mediterranean. In addition, at the start of each section of the route description, contact details are given for huts along the way.

Most of the French huts have an *aire de bivouac*, a designated area close to the hut where walkers are allowed to pitch their tent for one night. Camping is not allowed in the French national park (Parc National des Pyrénées Occidentales), but outside the park camping is allowed in general. Bivouacking (pitching a small tent for one night) is allowed in the Parc National to a certain extent: one should not pitch the tent before 7pm and the tent should be down at 9am. A bivouac is allowed only at designated places or

when you are at least an hour's walk from any paved road.

In the Spanish Pyrenees camping is not allowed, but bivouacking is tolerated in most areas (although the tent must not be pitched before 8pm and must be down before 8am). In the Ordesa National Park a bivouac is allowed only in various areas at certain altitudes (bivouacking is forbidden in the canyons), and in the Aigüestortes National Park bivouacking is strictly forbidden.

The Haute Route has a few sections where you can spend a night in a hut or *gite* (sections 2, 3 and 5 in this guide). On the other two sections it is sometimes necessary to pitch the tent and wild camp or to spend the night in an unstaffed hut.

NOTE ON THE WEATHER

An everyday concern for walkers in the Pyrenees is the weather. The Pyrenean

Beware of occasional snowfall in summer
(mid-July, Lac d'Arrious, day 12)

Haute Route always stays close to the main ridge of the Pyrenees, where weather conditions can change rapidly and dramatically. In general, summer weather in the Spanish valleys is hot and dry, while (due to the influences of the Atlantic Ocean) the air in the French Pyrenees is much more moist and brings more clouds, mist and rain.

However, there is always a danger in generalisation. A beautiful, cloudless morning doesn't mean that the weather will be fine all day long. Thunderstorms, which can be violent, may form very quickly and sometimes come with little advance warning. Always keep an alert eye on the weather and try to gather as much information on the weather as you can (from newspapers, guardians of mountain huts, tourist offices, campsites, weather forecast services). The telephone numbers of weather forecast services are always given on walking maps.

Remember that safety always comes first! Leave summits and exposed ridges if a thunderstorm is threatening and go down to a safe place (a hut or *cabane*), or go down to a valley and pitch your tent in a place that seems to be safe.

GRADING AND TIMING OF WALKS

A grade has been given to each of the 42 day stages of the route, and an explanation of the grades is given below.

3   There are only three days that have been graded with a 3. These days involve very short, easy walks on well-worn paths that have been waymarked. These walks are suitable for anyone.

2   The second category is what one might call the classic Pyrenean Haute Route day. This category involves a full day's walk with a fair amount of climbing and descending. Most of the time the route uses paths that are reasonably well way-marked and can be followed easily. There may be some rough sections that have to be negotiated. Under normal summer conditions these walks contain no serious obstacles. Most of the day sections of the route are graded 2.

1   The few walks that have been graded 1 are suitable only for experienced, well-trained mountaineers who are accustomed to very strenuous days. These walks are often very long and demanding. There is a lot of rough terrain to be tackled. The days involve long climbs, long sections without path or waymarks (orientation could become a serious problem in poor visibility), some exposed sections that require care and snowfields that have to be crossed.

E   The E stands for Exceptional. This category contains some very demanding and difficult walks with steep and potentially dangerous exposed sections that require great care on the part of Haute Route walkers carrying heavy loads. Here and there some moderate scrambling is necessary, and steep snow slopes and glacier remains have to be crossed. The E-walks often enter remote areas where path and waymarks are not to be found. Your

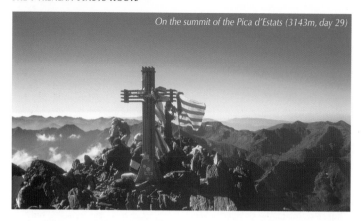

On the summit of the Pica d'Estats (3143m, day 29)

navigation capabilities will be put to a serious test! There are only three E-days.

Take a good look at your abilities as a mountain walker and at the difficulties of the various sections of the Haute Route before deciding which section(s) to undertake. Remember also to take into account the variants that allow you to avoid most of the difficult sections.

Although the Haute Route contains a few very long walks (at least nine hours), most of the days will take around six to eight hours. The box at the start of each day stage gives an (estimated) time taken by a fit walker carrying about 15–20kg. These times do not include any pauses and breaks, not even short ones. The timings given in bold in the route description are cumulative and apply under normal weather conditions. In adverse conditions (mist, rain, storms, exceptional heat), additional time (around 25%) should be added.

You would be advised, even when undertaking a short walk, to start very early in the morning in order to benefit from the relative coolness of the morning. Most days start with a climb, so most of the hard work will already have been done by the time the heat, on a hot summer's day, becomes unbearable.

TEN CLASSIC SUMMITS

It's certainly worth taking a day off here and there to climb a mountain. Along the way the guide describes the ascent of 10 classic Pyrenean summits.

- **Grande Fache** (3005m, day 13) provides a classic ascent from Refuge Wallon to a 3000m summit situated on the French–Spanish border that offers stunning views, especially of the Balaitous massif.
- **Vignemale** (3298m, day 14), the Vignemale is the highest mountain on the frontier ridge.
- **Le Taillon** (3144m), one of the many summits of the Cirque de Gavarnie – the walk, which

contains the crossing of the famous Brèche de Roland, is a two-day excursion.

• **Piméné** (2801m, day 16), the Piméné is a mountain of relatively modest height that has become famous because of the superb views of the Cirque de Gavarnie.

• **Pic Perdiguère** (3222m, day 20), the Perdiguère is the highest summit of the Cirque de Portillon, which contains about a dozen 3000m summits – the walk offers the possibility of adding an exciting walk on the frontier ridge, crossing three other 3000m summits.

• **Pico de Aneto** (3404m, day 21), the highest summit of the Pyrenees is a must for every Pyrenean walker.

• **Montardo d'Aran** (2826m, day 24), just like the Piméné this is not a high mountain, but the summit offers excellent views, especially of the Maladeta massif.

• **Mont Roig** (2868m, day 26), there is a short, rough climb from Refugi Enric Pujol to this frontier-summit.

• **Pic de Certascan** (2853m, day 27), the highest summit of the vast region between the Mont Roig and the Pica d'Estats.

• **Pica d'Estats** (3143m) and **Montcalm** (3077m) (day 29), the highest summit of the Catalonian Pyrenees and the highest summit of the Ariège.

None of these climbs is technically difficult: grade F or F+. Climbing gear in summer is needed only for the ascents of the Vignemale, Pic Perdiguère, Pico de Aneto and perhaps the Pica d'Estats.

TWO 'CONSOLATION' WALKS

Sometimes, if weather conditions are

USEFUL BOOKS ON CLIMBING IN THE PYRENEES

Pyrénées, Guide des 3000m (April 2003, SUA Edizioak), a very fine guide that contains over 400 routes to the 3000m summits of the Pyrenees. Written by Luis Alejos, who has climbed all 212 3000m summits. Excellent route descriptions. ISBN 84-8216-147-4. Internet: www.sua-ediciones.com. This book is a French translation of the original Spanish.

Walks and Climbs in the Pyrenees (2001, 4th edition, Cicerone Press), by Kev Reynolds. This book contains numerous climbs in France and Spain and has generally been recognised as one of the classic guides on walking and climbing in the Pyrenees. ISBN 1-85284-328-4. Internet: www.cicerone.co.uk.

100 sommets des Pyrénées (2001, 3rd edition, Rando Editions), a very good full-colour guide describing the ascent of 100 classic Pyrenean summits. Written by the inventor of the Haute Route: Georges Véron. ISBN 2-84182-129-3. Internet: www.rando-editions.com. In French.

not in your favour, you may be forced to follow an easy variant instead of the Haute Route's main track, thus avoiding a difficult section but also missing a spectacular part of the Pyrenees. Walkers who have set their mind on the difficult sections, but are forced to take the easy way, might find some consolation in the extra walks presented in the guide.

Walkers who have avoided the hard climb to Pic Carlit on day 34 and followed the GR10 to Bouillouses can make the classic climb of Pic Carlit (2921m) from Bouillouses (see day 34) the next day (without heavy loads!), an easy but very fine walk that includes a lovely circuit along a dozen lakes in the Désert du Carlit. It will add an extra day to your journey, but it will be a day to savour.

Should you have followed the GR10 on day 38 and not climbed the summit of Pic du Canigou (2784m), but gone around the mountain on a safe route, then it's worth considering climbing this famous mountain the next day from Cortalets (see day 38). The route described is not just the classic route to the summit but an exciting circuit via the Porteille de Valmanya and the Crete de Barbet. A superb walk!

MOUNTAIN SAFETY AND FIRST AID

Accidents can occur, even when you take every possible measure to prevent them. In order to reduce risks, you would be advised to take the following measures.
- Do not walk the Haute Route or parts of it on your own.
- Whenever possible tell someone (for example the guardian of a

The Haute Route crosses one of the most famous mountains of the Pyrenees: the Pic du Canigou (2784m, day 38)

*Pyrenean ramonda
(Ramonda myconti):
don't pick any flowers or plants*

RULES FOR WALKERS IN THE PYRENEES

- Don't leave any rubbish behind in the mountains, but take it out with you.
- Never make an open fire – it's strictly forbidden in the national parks and in the Spanish Pyrenees.
- Walk on tracks as much as you can.
- Don't pick any flowers or plants.
- Don't damage any trees or shrubs.
- Close fences that are meant to keep cattle within a certain area.
- Respect local habits and regulations.
- Respect local properties, such as *cabanes,* as basic or simple as they may sometimes seem.
- Don't make excessive noise.
- Try not to disturb any animals.

mountain hut or the owner of a campsite) your plans for the day or the days to come.

- Give your family, relatives or a friend as detailed an overview as possible of the route you are going to follow, with a time schedule. Inform them frequently of the progress you are making and of any change of plans.

- Carry a first aid-kit that contains not only the usual stuff but also sports tape, a blister treatment pack and sedatives

- Take a GSM with you, so that you can call a rescue service in case of emergency. A GSM doesn't always function in the mountains, unfortunately, but carrying one significantly improves your safety. Remember that the relevant telephone numbers of rescue services, local fire services (*bombers*) and police are always found on walking maps.

- There are still a few remote corners in the Pyrenees, where only very few walkers go and help may take a long time to arrive. Carry a mountain safety bag or blanket to prevent yourself or the victim from becoming hypothermic.

- If you go with a group, at least one of the participants should have a first-aid qualification, so that first medical assistance can be given immediately.

- Remember the emergency signals to rescue helicopters: hold both arms above your head in an Y-shape if you need help (never wave with both hands to a rescue helicopter when you don't need help!). A clear indication that you don't need help is to hold one arm up and the other down in such a way that they form more or less a straight line. Both signals are internationally accepted.

- Always carry a brightly coloured piece of clothing with you and wear it in case of an emergency. It will make it much more easier for rescue workers to locate you.

- Take a whistle with you in order to give the alpine emergency signal when necessary. Make the same signal (for example a blast on a whistle, a yell or flickering with a lamp) six times in a minute with similar intervals. Than wait for a minute and repeat the signal until you receive an answer. The alpine answer is three signals per minute, followed by a minute of silence.

Emergency signals to rescue helicopter

Help required:
raise both arms above head to form a 'Y'

Help not required:
raise one arm above head, extend other arm downward

NATIONAL PARKS

There are three national parks in the Pyrenees, two in Spain and one in France. The two Spanish national parks are the Parque Nacional de Ordesa i Monte Perdido (Aragon) and the Parc Nacional d'Aigüestortes i Estany de Sant Maurici (Catalunya). The only French national park is the Parc National des Pyrénées Occidentales ('the national park of the western Pyrenees').

The French national park was founded in 1967 and has an area of 45,700 ha. The park forms an area of land lying against the French–Spanish border, stretches from the Vallée d'Aspe in the west to the Vallée d'Aure in the east. The park has a length of about 100km. On the eastern edge of the national park lies the Néouvielle nature reserve, which is named after the Pic de Néouvielle (3091m). The Parc National offers visitors an immense variety of landscapes, more than 200 mountain lakes, a number of natural limestone amphitheatres – such as the Cirque de Gavarnie, Cirque de Troumouse and Cirque d'Estaubé, and some of the finest peaks of the entire mountain range – Vignemale (3298m), Balaïtous (3144m), Pic du Midi d'Ossau (2884m) and Pic Long (3192m).

The environment within the limits of the national park receives official protection. There are no permanent inhabitants in the park (shepherds are allowed to stay in *cabanes* in the park during the summer season). The national park is surrounded by what the French call the *zone periphérique*, an area of about 200,000 ha that encloses several villages. Economic activity is allowed in this area, but the natural environment is still protected to a certain extent.

Six valleys give access to the Parc National: Aspe, Ossau, Azun, Cauterets, Luz and Aure. Thanks to good infrastructure, the many marked footpaths (over 350km), a large number of mountain huts and, of course, its natural beauty, the Parc National attracts an enormous number of tourists each year.

The Spanish Parque Nacional de Ordesa i Monte Perdido is located south of the famous Cirque de Gavarnie. This national park has gained international fame because of a number of monumental, beautifully coloured and shaped limestone canyons. As early as the start of the twentieth century, the largest of the canyons, the Valle de Arazas (also called Valle de Ordesa), was regarded as a prodigy of nature that deserved to be protected. As a result, the Ordesa national park was founded in 1918, but it included only the Valle de Arazas and covered only 2175 ha. Finally, in 1982 the Añisclo canyon, the Garganta d'Escuain, a small part of the Valle de Pineta, the area north of the Valle de Arazas and the Monte Perdido massif (3355m – Monte Perdido, meaning 'lost mountain', is Europe's highest limestone mountain) were added to the national park, which now has an area of 15,600 ha. In 1997 the French– Spanish region Cirque de Gavarnie – Parque Nacional de Ordesa i Monte Perdido was added to UNESCO's world heritage list, which underlines the unique character of this region.

Not canyons but mountain lakes are the trademark of the second national park in the Spanish Pyrenees – the Parc

The remarkable canyon landscape of the Parque Nacional de Ordesa i Monte Perdido is internationally famous

Nacional d'Aigüestortes i Estany de Sant Maurici ('meandering waters'). In and around the national park, which is to be found in the western section of the Catalonian Pyrenees, there are over 300 lakes. The national park is surrounded by the Vall d'Aran in the north, the Rio Noguera Ribagorcana in the west, the Rio Noguera Pallaresa in the east and the Montsent in the south. The villages of Espot (western section) and Boi (eastern section) give access to the Aigües Tortes national park. The park was founded in 1955 and initially covered an area of 10,500 ha. Walkers could (and still can) easily cross the park from west to east in one day by the Porterra d'Espot, a pass in the centre of the park. The park was enlarged in 1995 and now covers an area of 14,119 ha.

The landscapes of the Aigües Tortes national park are a delicate combination of pine forests (some trees survive even at an altitude of 2500m), sharp granite peaks, meandering streams, tumbling cascades and countless lakes. As a result of the 1995 enlargement the national park now has a few summits that exceed the 'magic' 3000m, such as Punta Alta (3014m) and the Pico de Comaloforno (3033m, highest summit of the park). Many peaks in the park come close to 3000m, including Pic de Peguera (2982m, which used to be the park's highest summit), Pic de Subeniux (2949m) and Pic de Contraig (2957m). None of these high mountains is well known, and a mountain of rather modest height thus attracts practically all the attention of the park's visitors: the

Encantats, a twin mountain that consists of two granite summits of similar height (2747m and 2738m) and shape. This mountain forms a delightful combination with the extensive pine forests and the large, deep blue Estany de Sant Maurici. It offers a challenge for climbers and a magnificent view for walkers.

The Pyrenean Haute Route doesn't pass through all three national parks. However, the second section of the route gives an excellent impression of the various landscapes of the Parc National des Pyrénées Occidentales. The Parque Nacional de Ordesa i Monte Perdido is not visited at all by the Haute Route. In the third section of the route walkers pay only a brief visit to the Parc National d'Aigüestortes i Estany de Sant Maurici. So there are a few very good reasons to return to the Pyrenees for further exploration!

WILDLIFE AND FLOWERS
Mammals

The Pyrenees are still a last refuge for a few species, but for how long? The Pyrenean brown bear (*Ursus arctos*) will soon be extinct. In the Spanish Pyrenees there isn't one bear left, and in France, in the Vallée d'Aspe and the Vallée d'Ossau, there could be about two or three individuals. The French *Pyrénées Magazine* reported that a bear was born in the year 2000, so it could take some time until the very last bear finally has gone. In 1996 three Slovenian brown bears (two females, one male) were released in the mountains near the hamlet of Melles in the Haut-Comminges (France). Soon three baby bears were born. A fine start to the

experiment, but the mother was shot by a hunter and only two of the three bears survived. Due to protests by the local population the experiment has been cancelled. The bears are allowed to stay, but there will be no other bears released in the future. Despite many plans launched in recent years, there hasn't been a serious effort to save the bear from extinction.

Unfortunately the Pyrenean ibex (*Capra pyrenaica pyrenaica*) has recently vanished from the Pyrenean mountains. The last ibex, a 13-year-old female, was found dead in January 2000 under a fallen tree in the Ordesa National Park. In the 19th century the ibex was almost shot out of existence by hunters, but a small group of about 25 managed to survive in the 20th century in the Ordesa National Park. The official protection the ibex was granted in 1973 came too late. In 1996 there were only five individuals left, and the last ibex died six days after the millennium. The Pyrenean ibex was a sub-species of the Spanish ibex (*Capra pyrenaica hispanica*) that lives elsewhere in mountain ranges of central and southern Spain. There seems to be a plan to release some Spanish ibexes in the Catalonian mountains, but we will never see the Bucardo d'Arazas, as the Pyrenean ibex is called in Spain, again. Unless, that is, scientists succeed in cloning it in the future – the DNA of the Pyrenean ibex is being kept in a laboratory.

Other mammals that face the threat of extinction are the lynx and the Pyrenean desman (*Galemus pyrenaicus*). The desman is without doubt the most peculiar animal that lives in the

Pyrenees. The desman looks like a mole (and is about the same size), but has a rat's tail, webbed feet and a long snout which it uses as a snorkel. The desman lives in clean mountain streams, where it hunts for insects and sometimes little fish and frogs.

Fortunately there are a few mammals that survive easily in the Pyrenean mountains, such as the Pyrenean izard (*Rupicapra rupicapra pyrenaica*), the chamois of the Pyrenees. A few years ago it was estimated that about 50,000 izards live in the Pyrenees – an amazing number. The habitat of the izard stretches from the Pic d'Orhy in the Basque territory to the eastern slopes of the Canigou massif in the eastern Pyrenees. On your way to the Mediterranean Sea you'll see small herds of izard here and there.

Another animal that survives without any problem is the marmot (*Marmota marmota*). Marmots became extinct in the Pyrenees many years ago, not due to human activity but as a result of the last Ice Ages. In the course of the 20th century some marmots (caught in the Alps) were released in the Pyrenees. A large number of marmots are now to be found in the high mountains of the Pyrenees, on both sides of the watershed. Whilst walking the Haute Route you'll frequently hear the characteristic (alarm) whistle of the marmot. There are some areas with large concentrations of marmots, for example the Ossau valley and the Vignemale region.

A relatively new animal in the Pyrenees is the (Corsican) mouflon, which was introduced in the 20th cen-tury. The mouflon is found only in the eastern Pyrenees, especially in the Carlit region, the Nuria region and eastern mountains of Andorra. There is a slight chance of spotting mouflon on days 34 and 36 of the Haute Route.

Other mammals that live in the Pyrenees include deer, fox, squirrel, badger, wild boar, otter and ermine.

Reptiles and Amphibians

There are a number of reptiles and amphibians found in the Pyrenees. These include the Grass snake (*Natrix natrix*), Western whip snake (*Coluber viridiflavus*), Asp viper (*Vipera aspis*), Smooth snake (*Coronella austriaca*), Pyrenean brook newt (*Euproctus Asper*, the young often have a yellow stripe on their back and yellow spots on the flanks and tail – these marks often disappear when the animal reaches maturity), Fire salamander, Common toad (*Bufo bufo*), Common midwife toad (*Alytes obstetricans*), Common wall lizard (*Podarcis muralis*), Viviparous lizard (*Lacerta vivipara*), Green lizard (*Lacerta viridis*) and the Ocellated lizard (*Lacerta lepida*). In 1993 a new species of frog was discovered in the Spanish Pyrenees: the Pyrenean frog (*Rana pyrenaica*).

There is an excellent guide on reptiles and amphibians: *Reptiles and Amphibians of Europe* (2nd edition 2002, Princeton Field Guides), written by E. Nicolas Arnold. ISBN 0-691-11413-7. Internet: www.guides.princeton.edu

Birdlife

The Pyrenees are a paradise for ornithologists, especially in autumn, when large numbers of migratory birds cross the

Pyrenees. Particularly well known are the Pyrenean vultures and birds of prey. Vultures are represented by the Griffon vulture, the Bearded vulture (also called Lammergeier) and the Egytian vulture (that returns to Africa in winter). The Bearded vulture is quite rare, but there is a fair chance of spotting this impressive bird during your traverse of the Pyrenees, especially in Aragon. The Griffon vulture has become a common sight in the Pyrenees, especially in the Basque territory, the valleys of Aspe and Ossau, and Aragon. There are four species of eagles to admire in the Pyrenees: the Golden eagle, Booted eagle, Short-toed eagle and (very rare) Bonelli's eagle. Other birds of prey include the Common buzzard, Honey buzzard, Eurasian sparrowhawk, Northern Goshawk, Red kite, Black kite, Common kestrel and Peregrine falcon.

Don't give him (Griffon vulture) the wrong idea: keep walking!

Forests and shrubs are home to birds including the Long-eared owl, Eagle owl, Tawny owl, Eurasian scops owl, capercaillie, Black woodpecker, Green woodpecker, Great spotted woodpecker, White-backed woodpecker, Red-backed shrike, Golden oriole, chaffinch, European serin, Citril finch, goldfinch, bullfinch, linnet, Common crossbill, yellowhammer, Western rock nuthatch, Eurasian treecreeper, Crested tit, Blue tit, Great tit, Coal tit, Long-tailed tit, Spotted flycatcher, goldcrest, chiffchaff, Bonelli's warbler and Common stonechat. Yellow wagtail and dipper live along mountain streams. In the high mountains you'll notice Red-billed chough, Yellow-billed chough, Common raven, Snow finch, Black redstart, Northern wheatear, Rock thrush, Blue rock thrush, Ring Ouzel, wallcreeper, ptarmigan (brown and white in summer; all white except for some black on the tail in winter) and Alpine accentor. Maybe you should take the binoculars with you after all!

Flowers

The Pyrenean flora is quite spectacular. There is an enormous variety of flowers and more than 160 of them are endemic, for example the Pyrenean saxifrage (*Saxifraga longifolia*), a large pyramid saxifrage that decorates limestone boulders and rock-faces; the Pyrenean Ramonde (*Ramonda myconi*, named after the founder of the Pyreneism: Ramond de Carbonnières, 1755–1827), a beautiful purple flower that belongs to a large tropical family and is to be found only on shady limestone rocks in early summer; the Grémil

Pyrenean saxifrage
(Saxifraga longifolia)

de Gaston (*Buglossoides gastonii*, named after a Pyrenean shepherd: Pierrine Gastou Sacaze), which is only found on limestone in the western Pyrenees (especially in the limestone mountains near Lescun); and the Pyrenean thistle (*Carduus carlinoides* or *Carduus pyrenaicus*), a pink thistle that survives in clusters at high altitudes on scree slopes.

Common flowers that decorate the lower slopes and pastures in spring and early summer are narcissi (*Narcissus poeticus*), Asphodel (*Asphodelus albus Miller*) and gentians (*Gentiana verna*). In summer mountain slopes are often filled with Great yellow gentian (*Gentiana lutea*), Rosebay willowherb (*Epilobium angustifolium*), Alpenrose and Pyrenean iris.

Unusually, there are numerous species of orchids quite easily found in the Pyrenees: Black vanilla orchid (*Nigritella nigra*), Birdsnest orchis (*Neottia nidus-avis*), Fragrant orchid (*Gymnadenia conopsea*), Heath spotted orchid (*Dactylorzia maculata*), Early purple orchis (*Orchis mascula*), Burnt orchid (*Orchis ustulata*), Elder-flowered orchid (*Dactylorhiza sambucina*), Pyramidal orchid (*Anacamptis pyramidalis*) and Lesser-butterfly orchid (*Plathantera bifolia*).

Beside streams and in marshy areas there are globeflower (*Trollius europaeus*), Marsh marigold (*Caltha palustris*), Common monkshood (*Aconitum napellus*), Marsh Felwort (*Swertia perennis*), White false helleborine (*Veratrum album*) and Common butterwort (*Pinguicula vulgaris*). On rocks grow all sorts of saxifrage, Mountain houseleek (*Serpervivum montanum*) and Moss campion (*Silene acaulis*).

In forests and open spots on lower slopes are found Martagon lily (*Lilium martagon*), Alpine sow-thistle (*Cicerbita plumieri*), Great masterwort or

Iris (Iris Xyphoides)

Mountain sanicle (*Astrantia major*), Wood cranesbill (*Geranium sylvaticum*), Common columbine (*Aquilegia vulgaris*), Betony-leaved rampion (*Phyteuma betonicifolium*), Spiked rampion (*Phyteuma spicatum*), Fringed pink (*Dianthus monspessulanus*), St Bruno's lily (*Paradisea liliastrum*) and the beautiful endemic Pyrenean lily (*Lilium pyrenaicum*).

In open fields at the sub-alpine level grow Alpine aster (*Aster alpinus*), Pyrenean Eryngo (*Eryngium bourgatti*), Merendera (*Merendera bulbocodium*; appears in large numbers in August), Trumpet gentian (*Gentiana acaulis*), Pyrenean gentian (*Gentiana pyrenaica*), Sweet William (*Dianthus barbatus*) and Spotted gentian (*Gentiana burseri*; endemic). Where snow has just melted in summer Alpine snowbell (*Soldanella alpina*) and Pyrenean buttercup (*Ranunculus pyrenaeus*) make their appearance.

Some flowers try to survive at high altitudes on rocks and scree: Alpine

Pyrenean lily (Lilium pyrenaicum)

toadflax (*Linaria alpina*), Purple saxifrage (*Saxifraga oppositifolia*), Pyrenean thistle (*Carduus carlinoides*), Alpine hawksbeard (*Crepis pygmea*) and Glacier wormwood (*Artemisia glacialis*; eastern Pyrenees).

Only a few of the region's flowers can be included here, but hopefully will illustrate that Pyrenean flora is well worth studying. During your walk through the Pyrenees allow yourself some time here and there to admire the secret life of Pyrenean plants. A very good book in English is Christopher Grey-Wilson and Marjorie Blamey's guide *The alpine flowers of Britain and Europe*, which contains a number of Pyrenean flowers (HarperCollins).

Alpine aster (Aster alpinus)

Ancient cabane and Punta Suelza (Walk 18)

THE PYRENEAN HAUTE ROUTE

SECTION 1: HENDAYE TO LESCUN
Through the Basque Territory

At first sight the Basque Country (known in French as the Pays Basque and in Spanish as the Pais Vasco) seems to be the ideal area to start for Haute Route walkers who have set their mind on the long walk from the Atlantic Ocean to the Mediterranean Sea. There are no high mountains, snowfields or dangerous-looking steep rocky slopes, but instead emerald-green grassy hills, extensive forests, herds of sheep grazing on pastures and charming half-timbered farmhouses. It does not appear to be a mountain wilderness, this Basque country, in which the civilised world – in the form of numerous charming villages – is always within reach. It will be easy walking to Lescun, you might think, but you would be wrong.

The Basque country is a treacherous area with different faces. In good weather conditions experienced mountain walkers won't encounter any major problems on their way to Lescun, but the weather can change rapidly and dramatically, especially in this part of the Pyrenees. The influence of the Atlantic Ocean means that there is always a fair chance of rainfall and mist developing in this area when temperatures drop. Mist is the worst enemy of every walker who traverses the Basque territory or the French Pyrenees, as it often reduces visibility to not more than a few metres. Even experienced walkers who are able to work with map and compass can get lost temporarily in the Basque territory due to mist. The Haute Route to Lescun has several sections without path and marks, where problems with orientation are inevitable in mist! And beware: the mist can easily last a day, sometimes even two.

The route to Lescun leads gradually into the high mountains of the Pyrenees. It will take some time until you see a 'real mountain'. You'll encounter some high hills in the beginning, like La Rhune (900m, on the first day), followed by lots of lesser known mountains (Mendi-Chipi, 1506m, and the Occabé, 1456m). At last, on the seventh day you'll encounter the first summit higher than 2000m: Pic d'Orhy (2017m). This is also the first mountain likely to make an impression on walkers, due to its steep, rocky north face. The Haute Route crosses the summit of Pic d'Orhy. On the final day of the first section you'll enter the high mountains of the Pyrenees at last. On that day you'll have to find your way through the limestone plateau region east of the Pic d'Anie (2504m, the first summit higher than 2500m). A natural labyrinth of pine trees and, in the higher regions, of bare rock, it's a tremendous adventure to walk through this bizarre plateau, where only few people dare to come. Here you won't find any water, and highly weathered grey rocks have created an almost unrealistic mountain scenery.

The final part of the walk, from Belagua to Lescun, has everything to make a classic walk in the Pyrenees. Most striking, perhaps, are the Arres d'Anies that form a moon-like landscape, the complete silence, the surprising presence of isards and marmots, the pastoralism in the Vallon d'Anaye, where bare summits like the Pic d'Anie (2504m), the Pic de Countendé (2338m) and the Billare (only 2309m but what a giant!) dominate the scenery, and the romance of the Plateau de Sanchèse. Afterwards you'll be happy to be one of the few to have ventured into this still secretive part of the Pyrenees. What a way to end the first section, and what a way to enter the high mountains of the Pyrenees!

Practical information
Public Transport to Hendaye
Hendaye is situated at the Atlantic Ocean, near the French–Spanish border. The village is accessible by train. Take the Eurostar to Paris and arrive at Gare du Nord. Take the subway to Gare d'Auterlitz and catch the train (preferably the night-train that arrives early in the morning at Hendaye) to Hendaye.

Facilities in Hendaye
These include banks, cash dispensers, post office, supermarkets, bars, restaurants and all sorts of shops. Hendaye has numerous, often quite expensive, hotels. Suitable for walkers are Hotel La Palombe Bleu (near the station, tel. 05 59 20 43 80; rooms start at 32 Euros), Hotel de la Gare (also close to the station, tel. 05 59 20 81 90, fax 05 59 48 18 28; rooms start at 38 Euros), Hotel Subernoa (on the GR 10 trail in the Rue Subernoa, tel. 05 59 20 08 33; rooms start at 32 Euros) and Hotel de Paris (in Hendaye-Plage, tel. 05 59 48 02 82). Camping is possible at camping Alturan (Hendaye-Plage, close to the beach, tel. 05 59 20 04 55).
Hendaye on the internet: www.hendaye.com

Start Point
The walk from Hendaye railway station to Residence Croisière in Hendaye-Plage, where the Haute Route begins.

Turn left after leaving the station and walk NE along the road that follows the railway. Turn left at the first junction, cross the railway by a bridge and walk N. Notice a small park on your left (nice view of Hendaye's port) and, a little further, a sports ground (also on your left). Leave the road that follows the coast and take the Boulevard du Maréchal Leclerc, which goes in a straight line to Residence Croisière at Hendaye-Plage (Résidence Croisière is a large building with shops, bars and restaurants). The Haute Route and GR10 begin here. The walk from Hendaye station to Résidence Croisière takes about half an hour. It's also possible to take the bus opposite the railway station. This bus to St-Jean-de-Luz also stops at Résidence Croisière.

Food

Food can be bought only in Arizkun (where you'll arrive on the second day), Les Aldudes (day 3) and on the Col Bagargui (day 6). It's possible to have a meal at the Col d'Ibardin (day 1) and at Chalet Pedro (day 6).

Morning magic near the Col de Mizpira (day 4)

Note on Day 7

This is an extremely long walk, and it might be a good idea to split this day in two (see 'Two-day alternative route' at the end of the day 7 route description). There is also a useful bad-weather variant provided for this day at the end of the route description.

Maps

- IGN Carte de Randonnées, 1:50,000, no 1: Pays Basque Ouest
- Editorial Alpina, 1:40,000, Alduides Baztan
- IGN Carte, 1:25,000, 1346 OT: St.Jean-Pied-de-Port
- IGN Carte de Randonnées, 1:50,000, no 2: Pays Basque Est
- IGN Carte de Randonnées, 1:50,000, no 3: Béarn

Note: The Haute Route is not marked on the Editorial Alpina, 1:40,000, Alduides Baztan map.

Accommodation: Contact Details

All numbers and other information on accommodation along the Haute Route is also found in the route description.

Day 1: Lizuniaga – 948 631 031

Day 2: Arizkun (Fonda Etxeberria) – 948 453 013 or 948 453 342

Day 3: Les Aldudes (Hotel Baïllea) – 05 59 37 57 02

Day 4: Roncevalles: La Posada (948 760 225), Casa Sabina (948 760 012), the monastery (948 760 015 or 948 760 302)

Day 5: no accommodation

Day 6: Col Bagargui – 05 59 28 51 29 (fax 05 59 28 72 38)

Day 7: Refugio de Belagua – 948 394 002 or 948 224 324

Day 8: Lescun: Hotel du Pic d'Anie (05 59 34 71 54, fax 05 59 34 53 22), *gite d'étape* next to the hotel (16 places, 05 59 34 71 54, fax 05 59 34 53 22), *refuge* in the village (Maison de la Montagne, 22 places, 05 59 34 79 14 or 06 86 86 43 99, email: lescundom@aol.com)

DAY 1
Hendaye to Col de Lizuniaga

Route:	via the Col d'Ibardin (317m) and la Rhune (900m)
Grade:	2
Time:	8hrs 15mins
Height gain:	1300m
Height loss:	1070m
Map:	IGN Carte de Randonnées, 1:50,000, no 1: Pays Basque Ouest

A long, strenuous walk on footpaths, forest tracks and dirt roads. Navigation should be easy under normal conditions. The Haute Route follows the GR10 from Hendaye-Plage to the Col d'Ibardin. After that pass you're on your own!

0.00 Residence Croisière at Hendaye-Plage (*for access to the start point see above*). Opposite the Residence Croisière there is a roundabout and the first signpost for the GR10. Turn your back on the Residence and the Atlantic and follow

The port at Hendaye

43

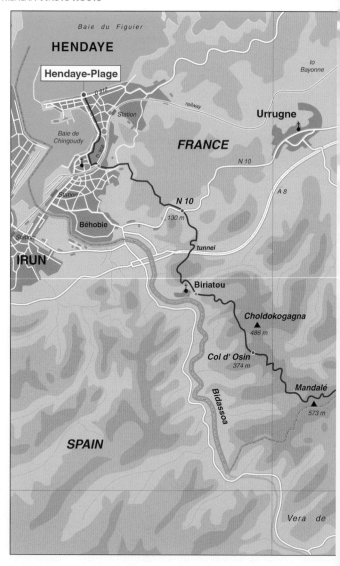

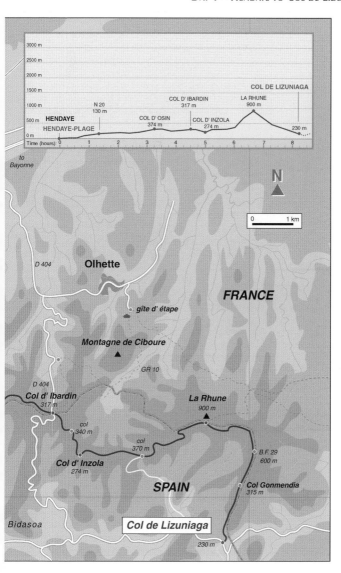

45

the Boulevard du Maréchal Leclerc to a roundabout. Turn right and take the third road, the Rue des Citronniers. Follow the road until the Boulevard de la Baie de Chingudy (the road that follows the coastline) is reached. Turn left and walk along the shore. The boulevard soon joins the Boulevard du Maréchal Leclerc, that comes in a straight line from Residence Croisière. Pass a sports ground (to the right, below), turn left and follow a road towards the *complexe sportif*. Pass a small park and go down the road to a roundabout. Keep walking in the same direction and turn left at the next square, in the direction of Hotel Subernoa. Follow this small Rue de Subernoa until you reach a tunnel under the railway. Go through the tunnel (not for cars) and climb E on the rue de Biantenia until you reach the D 358. Climb this road and after 150m, at a junction where the D 358 turns left, climb further on the rue de Errondenia. At a T-junction turn right and follow a track for 250m. Turn left and follow a track that goes down slightly, then goes up and goes down again. Pass a house (left of the track) and go down to the:

1.20 N 10. Cross the road and turn left. Follow the road for some 50m. Turn right and follow a track that goes down between trees. The path soon forks. Turn right and follow a large track that arrives near a few houses at a tarmac road. Go down on this road until a junction and turn left (Route de Garlatz). Follow the small road and turn right on a sort of a pass (high-tension poles). Keep following the so-called Route de Garlatz, ignore a minor road that branches of to the left and turn left a little further on to go down to the floor of the valley. Turn left, follow the road for 100m and turn right on a junction to climb S to a tunnel under the motorway (A 63). Notice a magnificent Basque house on your right just before the tunnel (Xori Kanta). Go through the tunnel and climb on a small road. Cross a stream and climb steeply. Don't turn left to go down at a junction, but follow the road that becomes level. Above the hamlet of Biriatou, near the Maison Mouniort, the road turns into a dirt road. Follow this dirt road SE and take the path that branches off to the right after the last house. Climb on a crest towards the Choldokogagna (486m), but turn right at a junction when you are between two high-tension poles. Walk SE on the west slope of the mountain and climb towards the:

3.15 Col d'Osin (374m). Go down SE on an obvious path to the Col des Poiriers (316m) and climb SSE left of a forest (on your left-hand side, in a distance, is an artificial lake) towards the Col des Joncs (419m). Keep the pass on your right-hand side and continue climbing, now E, and just before a small stream the path makes a sharp turn left. After a short climb N you reach a small plateau where the path turns to the right. Pass the Mandalé (573m), walking E on a sort of a balcony and staying north of the mountain. Past the Mandalé you follow a forest track, right of a pine forest. Go down to a tarmac road and go down steeply on this road past numerous bars, restaurants and souvenir shops to the:

4.30 Col d'Ibardin (317m, but 347m according to a sign on the col) on the French–Spanish border. Leave the GR10 here. Turn right and go down into Spain for 50m. Turn left and follow a small tarmac road NE that climbs gently. After around 700m the road reaches a pass and turns into a concrete road. On your right you'll notice the large building of Restaurant Okalarre (the name is written in large letters above the building). Leave the road, turn right and walk towards the building. Keep the building on your right and you'll find a path. Follow this path, which climbs a little initially, then descends SE to a dirt road. Turn left and walk along a picnic area to the:

5.00 Col d'Inzola (274m), where a number of dirt roads meet. La Rhune (Larrun) is indicated. Follow the track that climbs gently E and reach a dirt road that gives access to the summit of La Rhune (900m). Climb this road, which passes La Rhune on its south side. Pass below the Col Zizkouitz (665m, border stone no 22), and at the end of the climb the road makes a turn to the left. Walking all the way to the buildings on the top is optional (souvenir shops, bar, restaurant, *table d'orientation*, excellent views). When you have the buildings in front of you, past a *cabane* on the right, leave the road, turn right and find border stone no 25. Walk through the grass E towards border stone no 26 and go down on a path marked with cairns to border stone no 27. Continue to go down SE on an obvious path until the path forks. Take the right path, which is not marked, and walk S to borderstone no 29 (on a small, grassy plateau with bracken). Pay attention, because the junction can easily be missed (the left path is marked with blue-and-red paint flashes). Go down steeply on the frontier ridge SSW to reach the Col Gonmendia (315m, border stone no 32 and a wooden barn), where several tracks meet. There are two parallel tracks that climb SSW. Take the right track. Past the place where both tracks meet again take the right track at a junction and go down finally to:

8.15 Col de Lizuniaga (230m, in Spain, close to the border), which is crossed by a tarmac road. Hostal-Restaurante Linuziaga used to be a bar-restaurant, but since 2002 it also has a few rooms available (rooms for two start at 45 Euros), tel. 948 631 031. Haute Route walkers are usually allowed to camp on the grass in front of the building. Ask for permission in the bar/restaurant and order a few drinks or a good meal in return. Campers are not supposed to use the sanitary facilities in the building!!

DAY 2
Col de Lizuniaga to Arizkun

An easy walk in normal conditions. The Haute Route follows mainly the GR11 (red–white marks), so navigation is not difficult. A lot of walking on dirt roads. Some improvisation needed on the descent to Arizkun.

Route:	via the Col de Lizarrieta (441m), Col de Esquisaroy (515m) and the Col Bagacheta (793m)
Grade:	2
Time:	7hrs 15mins
Height gain:	800m
Height loss:	650m
Map:	IGN Carte de Randonnées, 1:50,000, no 1: Pays Basque Ouest; Editorial Alpina, 1:40,000, Alduides Baztan (Haute Route is not shown on this map)

0.00 Col de Lizuniaga. Cross the road and follow a concrete road that soon turns into a dirt road. The road climbs gently between pastures. After 2km you meet the GR11 coming in from the right. Don't turn right, but keep following the dirt road that bends to the left and climbs gently to the:

1.25 Col de Lizarrieta (441m). Border stone no 44. On the left there is a house, and on the right a bar/souvenir shop (probably closed). Cross a small road and climb steeply SE on a dirt road and then go down to the Col de Usategi (475m, border stone no 46), ignoring a path to the bar/restaurant Usategi. Notice a large tower (for hunters) made of stone left of the road and keep following the road, on the French side of the border, until:

2.00 Col de Nabarlatz (477m), where several paths meet near border stone no 50. Turn right, go down S between bracken and turn left on a junction. Go down in a forest until the Basate stream. Cross the stream and climb on a muddy track W to a farm. In front of the farmhouse the dirt road bends sharply to the left. Keep following the road until a junction. Turn right and walk a few minutes on a practically level dirt road. Turn left at the next junction (possibly water available left of the road) and climb on a dirt road SE. Past the highest point (building on the left, barn on the right) and continue down on the dirt road. Ignore a dirt road that comes in from the right and take a path (between bracken) on the left that soon brings you to:

3.20 Col de Irazako (540m, large trees), where a number of dirt roads meet. Climb the dirt road E left of a fence. Notice a farm/barn on the right and walk underneath a high-tension

Mist developing near the Col de Lizuniaga

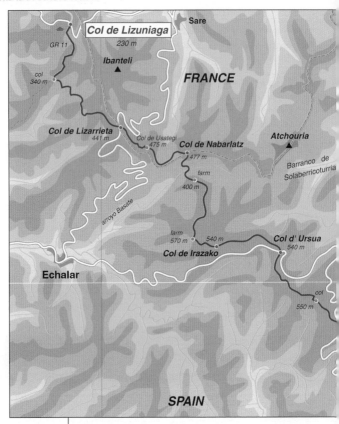

cable near the highest point. Go down SE on the right side of a ridge to:

3.40 Col d'Ursua (540m). Cross a small road and climb S on a dirt road. Past a kind of pass the dirt road bends to the left and you climb SE in a pine forest to the Col de Palomeras (610m, large building for hunters). Ignore a dirt road on the left and one on the right side soon after the pass. Soon you leave the forest. Go down SE to a pass (550m, old oak tree, several roads meet here). Continue to go down SE, pass a farmhouse to the left and follow the dirt road that bends to

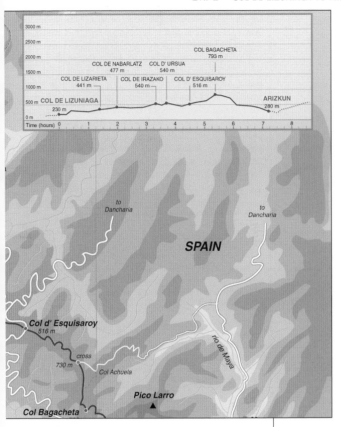

the right. Walk under a few beech trees and take a path on the right side of the dirt road. Walk on almost level terrain towards a dirt road. Turn left and soon you reach the:

4.30 Col d'Esquisaroy (516m). Cross a small tarmac road and climb steeply SE between pastures on an eroded dirt road. Gradually the climb eases. Leave the dirt road and turn right near a small iron cross (730m, standing or lying in the grass). Climb S to the:

5.25 Col Bagacheta (793m). Leave the GR11, which goes S, and follow a path NE.

Initially level, the path goes down SE to a col (670m). Go down SE to a farm that is surrounded by large trees. Go down SE on the dirt road that gives access to the farm. The dirt road meets a concrete road near a farm. Follow this road, ignore a road coming from the left and go down gently. After a short climb you reach a junction east of the small hamlet of Azpilkueta (370m). Turn left and walk on a road (Na 4457) to the N 121b (250m, near the village of Arizkun). Cross the road and turn right past a few buildings after about 150m. Walk towards an old stone bridge (signpost Arizkun, yellow marks). Cross the bridge and climb finally to the centre of the village of:

7.15 Arizkun (280m), a small attractive Basque village where you can stay for the night in the charming Fonda Etxeberria (a tavern with a small shop, tel. 948 453 013 or 948 453 342). It's the only place to stay in Arizkun!

If visibility is poor it makes sense to follow the GR11 all the way to the village of Elizondo (shops, several hotels and restaurants), 4.5km south of Arizkun. Follow the N 121b from there to Arizkun to join the Haute Route.

DAY 3
Arizkun to Les Aldudes

Route:	via Burga (872m) and the Col de Berdaritz (685m)
Grade:	2
Time:	5hrs
Height gain:	800m
Height loss:	500m
Map:	IGN Carte, 1:25,000, 1346 OT, St. Jean-Pied-de-Port (this map does not cover today's entire route); Editorial Alpina, 1:40,000, Alduides Baztan

An easy walk on paths and dirt roads. Navigation is not difficult in good weather.

0.00 Arizkun. Take the road at the back of the *fonda* and walk to the NE part of the village. Past the church, in the highest part of Arizkun, turn right and follow a small concrete road (white–yellow marks). After a few minutes notice a house on your left. Ignore a dirt road coming from the right and turn right a few steps further on. Climb on a path alongside stone walls and a fence through a forest. Soon the path reaches its highest point and bends to the left. The level path arrives soon at the concrete road you have just left (*it is possible to follow the concrete road all the way – it takes about 20mins but is a less attractive option*). Turn right and follow the concrete road that climbs gently and ends (in 2003) at a cattle grid. Ignore a dirt road to a farm on your right and follow the dirt road, ignoring all possible turns until a pass. The dirt road makes a sharp turn to the left on the pass. Notice a small white building (with a blue door) on your left, about 100m away, as you climb gradually. Now the dirt road makes a sharp turn to the right. For 45mins you climb gradually S on the dirt road. Finally you reach a:

1:50 pass (695m, pasture on the right). Take the right-hand dirt road at a junction and climb further until the dirt road ends. Cross a fence and walk S through a pasture towards a crest, which is reached near a forest. Cross another fence

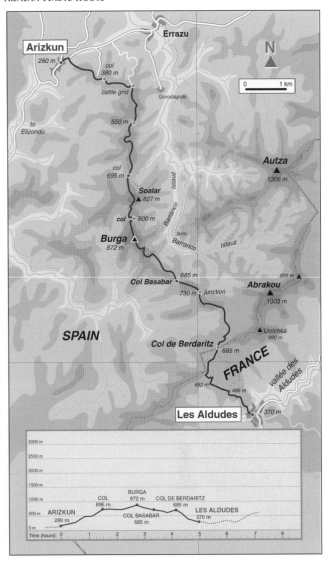

A Basque village: Les Aldudes

and try (no path, no marks) to follow the crest. Avoid some rocks, keeping right of them, and climb S through the wood to:

2.50 Burga (872m), the highest point of the crest. The forest ends here and Burga offers fine views south. Turn left and go down on a path marked with some cairns alongside the forest, with a steep slope full of bracken on your right. Continue to a farm. Walk between the farm and a stone wall and continue in the same direction. Pass underneath a high-tension cable and reach the:

3.20 Col Basabar (685m). Cross a small road and climb on a dirt road SE for a few minutes. Keep following the dirt road until a place where several dirt roads meet in the forest (730m). Turn right and walk SSE on an almost level dirt road that turns into a track. After a few minutes you'll see today's last pass in front of you: the Col de Berdaritz. The path bends to the left and soon enters a forest in which three streams (possibly dry in summer) are crossed. Notice farm/*fonda* Urrasca on your right side (below) and walk to the:

4.10 Col de Berdaritz (685m), border stone no 117. Several dirt roads meet here. Les Aldudes is indicated. Take the track that goes down SSW a few metres, then climbs and goes down again until you can see Les Aldudes deep down below in the Vallée des Aldudes. Turn left and go down SE on a dirt road that turns into a small tarmac road as you approach the village of Les Aldudes. Go all the way down to:

5.00 Les Aldudes (370m). Nice Basque village with a simple hotel (Hotel Baïllea, tel. 05 59 37 57 02, rooms start at 25 Euros) near the church. Should there be no rooms available, you might try your luck at Mano and Michel Hegny, Gites de France (single rooms start at 30 Euros, tel. 05 59 37 57 68), a charming old house in the village, about 50m from the hotel. Les Aldudes has a post office, bar/restaurant and a small food store (at the petrol station). No campsite.

DAY 4
Les Aldudes to Roncevalles

Route:	via the Redoute de Lindux (1220m) and the Col de Roncevaux (1057m)
Grade:	2
Height gain	1000m
Height loss:	400m
Maps:	IGN Carte de Randonnées, 1:50,000, no 2: Pays Basque Est; IGN Carte 1:25,000, 1346 OT: St. Jean-Pied-de-Port (however, today's route is not marked on this map)

Under normal conditions this is a pleasant walk on paths and dirt roads, through forest and pastureland. There are no difficulties under normal conditions, but mist will make navigation very difficult, especially in the first part of the walk (until Col de Méharroztéguy), where path and waymarks are not always present. For the first time you'll be walking above 1000m!

0.00 Les Aldudes. Walk from the hotel to the river Nive. Cross the bridge, turn right and walk S on the road towards the petrol station. Turn left just before the petrol station and climb a staircase made of concrete (yellow marks). Climb in zigzags on a well-worn path E and then in a straight line to the Col Lepeder (495m, a few trees and cabins for hunters). Past the col the path bends to the right. Leave a wooden watch-tower for hunters to the left and walk SE on the left side of a ridge on a slope full of bracken. Arrive at a large track (signpost 'Otsamunho'). Turn left and follow the path, which arrives at a dirt road. Turn right and climb a few metres to a small tarmac road (notice a barn and a fence to gather sheep on your right). Turn left and walk on this more or less level road until a junction. Turn right and climb the road S until a kind of pass (shepherds' hut on your right). A signpost indicates the route to the mountain Otsamunho.

Follow the track (yellow marks) to the Otsamunho. Climb E on a large track and you soon arrive at a large grassy pass. Leave the track to the Otsamunho here and turn right. Follow a large track that goes down gently. Cross a stream, climb a few metres along trees and walk to a kind of pass, which offers fine views. The path makes a sharp turn left and climbs E towards a few trees. Keep the trees on your left-hand side and make a turn right. Climb on an obvious

57

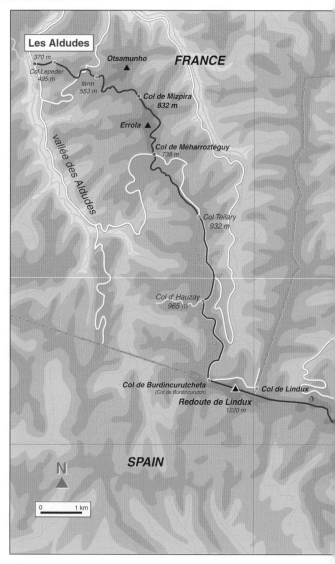

Les Aldudes

370 m
Col Lepeder
495 m
Otsamunho ▲
FRANCE
farm
553 m
Col de Mizpira
832 m
Errola ▲
Col de Méharroztéguy
738 m
vallée des Aldudes
Col Teilary
932 m
Col d' Hauzay
965 m
Col de Burdincurutcheta
(Col de Burdincurutch)
Col de Lindux
Redoute de Lindux
1220 m
SPAIN
N
0   1 km

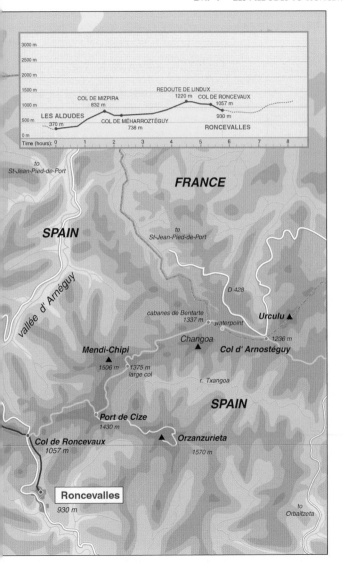

In poor visibility it may be advisable to follow the route (yellow marks) to the Otsamunho. From the junction on the grassy pass follow a small but obvious track that climbs gently on slopes filled with bracken. Soon the path becomes more or less level and goes round the west slopes of the Otsamunho. Arrive finally at a larger track, turn right and climb a few metres to a pass north of the Otsamunho. Don't go down on the other side of the pass but follow a dirt road and walk S, keeping the bare summit of the mountain on your right. Go down to the Col de Mizpira. This diversion adds about 20mins to today's walk.

One of the many constructions for hunters

path to a few rocks, where the path turns to the left and climbs gently to the large:

1.40 Col de Mizpira (832m), near a drinking trough for cattle. Don't go down on the east side of the pass, but follow a track SE that stays close to the ridge and soon arrives at a small pass. Keep climbing the crest SE on a vague dirt road

until the Errola summit. Go down steeply S on the ridge on an obvious track which turns into a dirt road (it's also possible to take a dirt road just before the summit of the Errola which goes round the east side of the mountain). Notice a farm and a pasture on your left and arrive at the:

2.15 Col de Méharroztéguy (738m, on your left there is a construction that farmers use to gather and disinfect sheep). Cross a small road and climb on a broad track SE (there are numerous primitive constructions for hunters beside the track). In a forest the climb eases somewhat and you arrive at a ridge (900m). Follow this ridge on the left, staying very close to it, and go down a little to arrive on a small road on the Col de Teilary (932m, perhaps a water point). Follow the road SSE to the place where it forks. Turn right and climb gradually S on road until the:

3.30 Col d'Hauzay (965m, water available), where four small tarmac roads meet (just a few years ago all of these roads were dirt roads). Lindux is indicated. Turn left and climb gradually, mainly SE, on a road to arrive at the Col de Burdincurutch (1092m, border stone no 152; there is a shepherds' hut a few metres below the pass). Leave the road (that makes a sharp turn to the left to go E) and climb SSE the ridge that marks the border, staying to the right of a forest.

In poor visibility it makes no sense to climb to the Redoute de Lindux. Just follow the road.

The climb ends at the:
4.30 Redoute de Lindux (1220m, border stone no 153). There is a fence on the French–Spanish border. Follow the fence, staying on the left of it, and go down to the Col de Lindux (1166m, border stone no 154). You'll arrive on the road you've just left. Cross a cattle grid near border stone no 155 and go down SSE through a forest on Spanish territory on the road. Go down the road until the:

5.20u Col de Roncevaux (1057m, chapel and a monument to Roland), also called Puerto de Ibañeta. The pass is crossed by a road. Cross the road, turn right and go down S on a track (red–white marks of the GR11; yellow marks of the

GR65 to Santiago de Compostella) that soon enters a beech forest. Go down until the forest ends and arrive at a junction. Turn right (there are nice places to camp here near a stream) and walk finally on a broad track to the buildings of Roncevalles, which you can see from afar.

5.45 Roncevalles (930m). No shops, but two hotels (Casa Sabina, tel. 948 760 012 and La Posada, tel. 948 760 225) and a visitor centre (information about Roncevalles, the route to Santiago de Compostella, souvenirs). The best thing to do is to try to get a bed in the monastery, where pilgrims stay for the night. 'Normal' walkers, however, are not always accepted; tel. 948 760 015 or 948 760 302.

DAY 5
Roncevalles to Egurgui

Route:	via the Col d'Arnostéguy (1236m), the Col d'Orgambidé (988m) and the Col d'Errozaté (1076m)
Grade:	2
Time:	6hrs 45mins
Height gain:	900m
Height loss:	850m
Map:	IGN Carte de Randonnées, 1:50,000, no 2: Pays Basque Est

A pleasant walk on roads, paths and dirt roads through forest and along grassy ridges that offer superb views in good conditions. There will be no problems under normal conditions. The route is almost all along the GR11 during the first four hours.

0.00 Roncevalles. Return to the Col de Roncevaux. Turn right near the chapel and climb E on a small road (*it's possible to cut the road several times, but this makes the climb harder*) that winds in numerous curves. After about 4km you arrive at a pass called Port de Cize (1430m, also called the Col Lepoeder). Leave the road, turn left and follow a dirt road (notice the Mendi Chipi (1506m) on your left). The dirt road descends gently. Ignore a dirt road coming from the right and arrive, past the Mendi Chipi, at a:

1.30 large pass (Col d'Intzondorre, 1375m). Don't turn left but keep walking NE on the dirt road that enters a forest. Notice a ruined chapel on your right and a shepherds' hut (with a fence to collect the sheep) on your left. Soon after leaving the forest you arrive at the remains (only a small part of the walls are left) of the cabanes de Bentarte, on the right of the *pista*. Here the dirt road makes a large curve to the left to go N to St.Jean-Pied-de-Port *(follow this road for about 150m to find the fontaine de Roland, where water bottles can be filled)*. Leave the dirt road, turn right and follow the GR11 markers. Climb through the grass to a kind of pass (1337m) and arrive at a fence that marks the border (there are three fences that come together here). Leave the GR11, cross the fence using a ladder, and follow the border fence and border stones nos 200–204, staying on the French side of the border with the fence on your right. Near border stone no 201, at the Spanish side, there is a water point, but it's better to fill water bottles at the fontaine de Roland. Walk along the border until the:

2.45 Col d'Arnostéguy (1236m), near border stone no 205. Small parking area beside the D 428, the road that's coming from St.Jean-Pied-de-Port. From the pass you can clearly see

Roncevalles: the Battle of Roncevalles (AD778), when the rearguard of Charlemagne's army – on its withdrawal to France – was attacked by the Basques

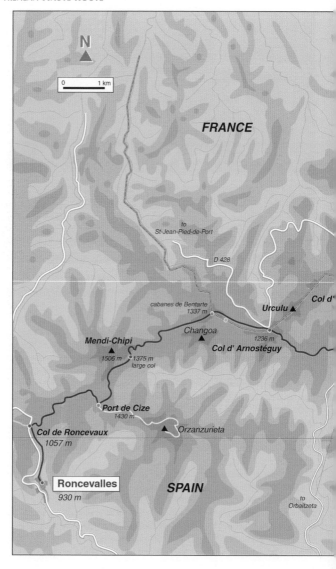

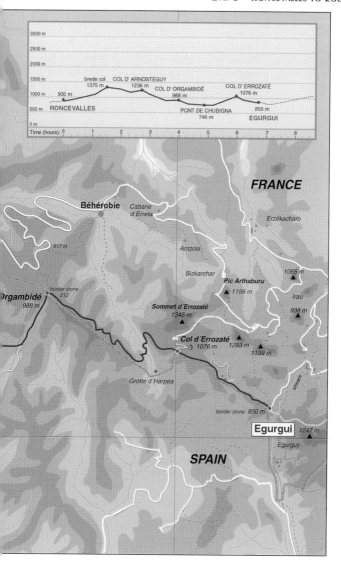

the Urculu summit, with its remains of what was perhaps a roman tower. The Col d'Orgambidé is indicated on the col. Follow a broad track (red–white marks of the GR11 again; also yellow and blue marks) SE, which climbs very gently to a pass. Still on a broad track, go down gradually, ignoring all other paths. Just follow this broad track, leaving a forest and a stream to the right. Notice a few farms on your left. Cross a few streams and walk to a dirt road (975m). Leave the GR11, turn left and climb the dirt road NE until you arrive at the:

4.00 Col d'Orgambidé (988m), border stone no 212. There is a small cabin for hunters a few metres below the col. Here you meet a small road. Turn right and walk SE on the road that initially climbs a little, then descends to a kind of col (910m; on your left hand you'll see a few shepherds' huts). Follow the gently descending road for about 300m until the lowest point is reached and turn left. Pass a *cabane* and a fence to gather sheep and go down (improvisation is needed because there's not a clear path) to the:

4.55 Pont de Chubigna (746m). Cross the bridge and follow the stream N until a junction (easily missed, so pay attention) just before a small ravine (gully). Turn right and climb on a vague track (somewhat overgrown by grass, but there are a few ancient marks) that zigzags E to the:

6.00 Col d'Errozaté (1076m). Don't go down on the road below the pass, but go down directly ESE through a small valley in which there is no mountain stream in the highest section. Pass a *cabane* and go down to the lower part of the valley. You'll find a small stream, which is followed on its right side to border stone no 223. Cross the stream and follow it until the farmhouses of Uhartégain (915m). Go to the road and continue down to the bottom of a valley, where you'll find:

6.45 Border stone no 224, near a confluence of streams (850m). There are some places to camp along the stream, which comes from the Col d'Errozaté. Unfortunately the unstaffed Point d'Accueil Jeunes of Egurgui has always been closed in recent years. You'll find the building east of the stream.

DAY 6
Egurgui to Col Bargargui

Route:	via the Col Curutche (1285m), the Col d'Oraaté (1303m) and the plateau d'Occabé (1446m)
Grade:	2
Time:	5hrs 15mins
Height gain:	900m
Height loss:	400m
Map:	IGN Carte de Randonnées, 1:50,000, no 2: Pays Basque Est

There are practically no paths or marks until the Col d'Oraaté. In mist it would be very difficult to stay on course, and even under normal conditions route finding is not easy. On the plateau d'Occabé you'll find the red–white marks of the GR10. Just follow the GR10 from the plateau to Col Bargargui. A nice route with a fine mixture of grassy hills that offer excellent views and dense forests.

0.00 Egurgui. Cross the bridge and climb SE on a steep, grassy slope. As both path and marks are missing you'll have to find your own way. Soon the route bends towards the east and climbs in the direction of a pass (1190m) situated between the south-west summit and the central summit of the Urculu ridge. Don't go all the way to this pass, but leave it to the right and climb to the pass between the central summit and the north-east summit. Pass the north-east summit (1333m) to the left, after which the route makes a

Morning magic near Egurgui

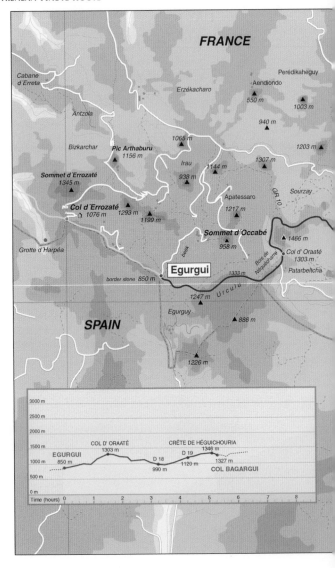

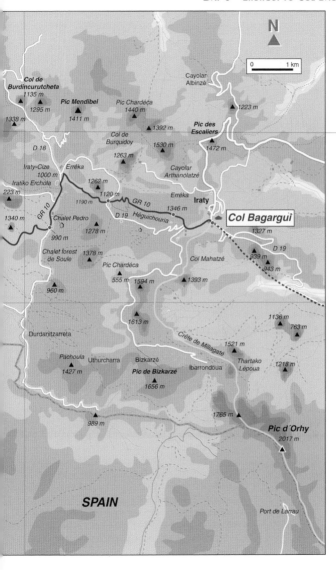

Cromlechs on the Occabé plateau

sharp turn to the right to go SE to the Col Curutche (1285m). Walk NE in the upper section of a small forest (Bois de Néquécharre), where you'll find a track. Follow the almost level track until, once out of the forest, you reach the:

1.50 Col d'Oraaté (1303m, there is a sign indicating the pass), where a small road ends. Ignore the road and follow a dirt road N, climbing very gradually and passing the Occabé summit on its west side. Past the Occabé you'll arrive at a extensive grassy plateau, the plateau d'Occabé. It is here that you'll meet the GR10 (*walk N for a few moments along the GR10 to find a few cromlechs*). From now on the Haute Route follows the GR10 until the Col Bagargui. Turn right and follow an obvious broad track that climbs a little E and then goes down NE to a plain filled with bracken. Don't turn left at a junction, but take the track that goes down into a beech forest as far as the bottom of the valley at the:

3.15 D 18 (990m). Turn left, notice bar/restaurant Chalet Pedro on your right (not really a place to spend the night for walkers but there seems to be a *gite* with place for four persons, tel. 05 59 37 02 52), a fine place to have lunch or just a cool drink, and climb a little N on the road. Notice also an unstaffed hut on your left (a useful emergency shelter). Cross a large flat area (lots of campers, bar/restaurant left of the road). After 1.5 km the road forks at an artificial lake (1000m, on the left side of the road). Turn right, taking the road that leads to Larrau, and turn right after about 100m. Climb SE in a forest on a dirt road until a pass (1190m) and go down to the:

4.15 the same road (D 19) you've just left. Cross the road, walk over the dam of an artificial lake (1120m) and climb SE in zigzags on a dirt road to the:

5.05 *crête* (= *ridge*) de Héguichouria (1346m). Pass a few chalets and go down to the Col Héguichouria (1319m), where you'll meet the D 19 again. Follow the almost level road E until the:

5.15 Col Bagargui (1327m, also called Col Bagargiak), in the Iraty tourist complex. It isn't the most attractive place to stay for the night, but there is a bar/restaurant, a small shop next to the restaurant (should be open in July and August; ask at the restaurant for the shop to be opened if it is closed) and a *refuge* (tel. 05 59 28 51 29, fax 05 59 28 72 38, email: chalets.diraty@wanadoo.fr). You have to announce yourself at the office (the Bureau d'Accueil), where information about the Iraty forest can be obtained and where a weather forecast will be available).

Note: if you go down on the road to Larrau for about 300m you'll find the so-called Col d'Orgambideska (Orgambidexka), a grassy bluff next to the road. Especially in autumn, when migratory birds cross the Pyrenees, lots of ornithologists gather on this pass, where hunting is not allowed, to watch the birds. Bird lovers also come to the pass in summer, especially to watch vultures and birds of prey. Sometimes there is some information available about the Col d'Orgambideska and the birds that have been seen. There are also several internet sites that contain information about this famous pass. Worth a visit!

DAY 7
Col Bagargui to Refugio de Belagua

A very long walk, which can, however, be divided into two days (see the alternative route at the end of the main route description). Even under normal conditions route finding can be difficult as there is often no path. Severe problems with navigation are inevitable in bad weather, especially in mist. There is often a fierce wind that makes the crossing of pic d'Orhy difficult and even risky. Care is needed on the Zazpigagn ridge. For the first time you'll be above 2000m! In good conditions this is a superb walk during which you stay very close to the frontier ridge. There is a useful escape route to the Cabane d'Ardanne (see 'Two-day alternative route' at the end of the main route description) and a useful →

Route:	via the Pic d'Orhy (2017m), the Port de Larrau (1585m) and the Col Uthu (1664m)
Grade:	1
Time:	9hrs 50mins
Height gain:	1200m
Height loss:	1100m
Map:	IGN Carte de Randonnées, 1:50,000, no 2: Pays Basque Est

0.00 Col Bagargui. Cross the D 19 at the Bureau d'Accueil and climb a small tarmac road, passing several chalets. Near the highest chalet you'll notice a dirt road on your right. Leave the road, ignore the dirt road and climb in a straight line on a very steep path (indicated by a small signpost, 'Crete de Millagaraté') S to the crête d'Orgambidesca (1400m). (*The Crète d'Orgambidesca is an excellent place to admire the sunrise. It's worth making a very early start!*) Turn right and follow the ridge SW with the forest on your right-hand side. Walk towards a few antennas. Past the antennas go down a few metres to a high-tension pole. Turn left and follow the high-tension cable on your way down to the:
0.30 Col Méhatzé (1383m, a few beeches and a hut for hunters), where the Haute Route nearly touches a road on your right. Follow an almost level track S a few metres above the road. Past a drinking trough for cattle, climb SW. Cross a dirt road (1420m) and climb on another dirt road to the:
0.50 Col Lapatignégagne (1453m). Go down SW on a dirt road that goes to a hut for hunters. Don't go all the way to the hut, but leave the dirt road to your left about 50m before you reach the hut. Follow an almost level path S. Cross a few streams (possibly dry in summer) and reach the Millagaté ridge (1460m) after a short ascent. Walk to a hut for hunters beside a dirt road and follow this dirt road SE until you arrive at a large hut for hunters on the:

1.55 Col de Tharta (1431m), where the ascent of Pic d'Orhy actually begins. Climb S on a grassy ridge, following a line of shelters for hunters (each with a different number), until the crête de Zazpigagn (1765m). Follow this limestone ridge SE for a short while and go down steeply to reach a small gap. Leave the ridge on your left (north-east side), go down a few metres through loose scree and climb to reach the ridge that leads to the Pic d'Orhy. Climb SE, staying close to the frontier ridge, to the summit of:

3.55 Pic d'Orhy (2017m; *your first 2000m summit!*). Follow the ridge east of the summit or, better, go down to find an obvious path on the Spanish side of the ridge that goes down SE to the:

4.50 Port de Larrau (1585m, parking area on both sides of the pass, border stone no 237).

> ← variant (via Larrau) in case weather conditions are not in your favour.

> In case of bad weather, you have the option to leave the border ridge at the Port de Larrau. Go down N on the road for 1km until a junction. Turn right and follow a dirt road E that leads to the shepherds' hut of Ardanne. This route is not interesting, but it is safe.

Cross the road, pass border stone no 237bis and follow the frontier ridge SE. Arrive at the Pic de l'Achourterrigagna (1660m, border stone no 238). Stay on the ridge and go down to the Port de Betzula (1540m, border stone no 239). Climb to the Betzulagagna (1590m), go down to the Col de Bildocharréko (1565m, border stone 240) and climb E to the:

6.10 Pic de Gastarrigagna (1732m, border stone no 241). Pass the top on its south side and go down on the ridge to the Col Elhurrosoko (1650m, border stone no 242). Keep staying on the ridge and climb SE to about 1750m. Leave the ridge and follow on the French side of the ridge a vague track against the slope of the Otchogorrigagna. Walk ENE towards the border north of this mountain. Arrive at the border at:

7.25 Col Uthu (1664m, border stone no 247). Go down E in Spain (sometimes a vague track or tracks made by cattle) along the southern slopes of the Chardékagagna (1893m).

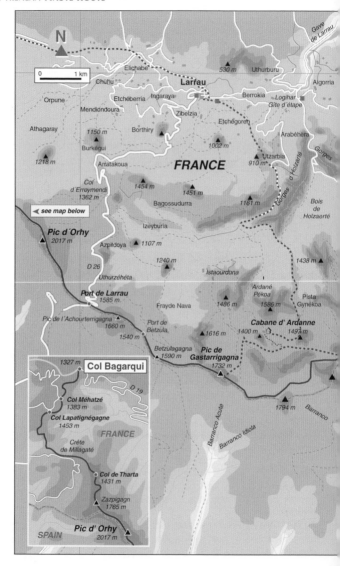

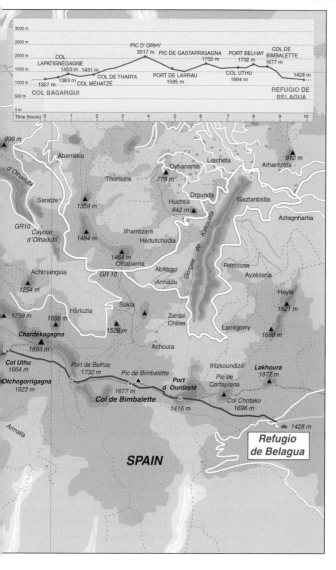

Ignore the Col de Chotako (1696m, situated directly east of the Chardékagagna) and climb when you are under this pass SE to find the:

8.00 Port de Belhay (1732m, border stone no 250). Go down on the French side to a fence. Cross the fence, go down a few metres and turn right. Climb gradually E on a vague track (a few ancient red–white marks, some cairns) through scree against the slope of the mountain to your right. Past this mountain you walk through grass mainly E (*improvisation needed because path and marks are missing*). Eventually you reach border stone no 253 (*here the border doesn't follow the ridge*). Your route bends a little to the right. Go down SE until the:

8.30 Col de Bimbalette (1677m, border stone no 254). Go down on the Spanish side and pass the Pic de Bimbalette on its south side, using several cattle tracks. Once past the mountain, go down to a very large pass on the frontier: the Col d'Ourdayté (1416m, border stone no 255). Stay in Spain and walk through grass ESE. The almost level path (unmarked) passes a drinking trough for cattle. Notice a former customs house on the right and arrive at a road (that goes to the Col de la Pierre-Saint-Martin). Turn left and climb the road to:

9.50 Refugio de Belagua (1428m, also called Refugio Angel Oloron), on the right side of the road at the end of a large parking area. The *refugio* is open all year. A reservation is not usually necessary in summer, tel. 948 394 002 or 948 224 324. Meals service, 106 places.

Two-day Alternative Route

Considering the length of today's walk, it might be a good idea to spend the night near Cabane d'Ardanne (Ardané, a shepherds' hut). In that case go down N from the Col Elhurrosoko (border stone no 242) to a dirt road on the French side of the border. Turn right and follow the dirt road until it makes a sharp turn left. Leave the dirt road at this curve, turn left and pass the Cabane d'Ardanne (1330m). Continue to a solid *cabane* (1310m) ahead of you on the other side of a stream. There is water available behind the *cabane*. Unfortunately there can be mice and rats in the *cabane*. It is possible to pitch the tent for the night. Take seven hours for the walk to Ardanne. The next day to

Belagua will take about three hours. Return to the dirt road, cross it and climb ESE staying left of a stream until a small plateau. Keep climbing in the same direction to the Col Uthu and follow the Haute Route from there.

Variant
Col Bagargui – Ardanne
via Larrau and the Col de Jauregeberri

Grade:	2
Time:	8hrs 10mins
Height gain:	1100m
Height loss:	1100m
Map:	IGN Carte de Randonnées, 1:50,000, no 2: Pays Basque Est

0.00 Col Bagargui. Go down on the D 19 to Larrau for 300m and arrive at the Col d'Orgambideska (1284m), where the road makes a sharp turn to the right. Take a short-cut, cross the road and go down on a large track, passing a black hut for hunters (on your left) and another building (on your right). Go down ESE on an obvious stony path. Eventually the path becomes level, passes several trees and arrives on the road again (notice a drinking trough and a post indicating Chalet Pedro). Follow the road E for about 700m and take a broad, grassy track on the left side of the road. The track climbs a few metres and arrives very soon at the:

0.55 Col de Curutcheta (921m). Go down NE along slopes filled with bracken and pass several pastures. A somewhat eroded path brings you to Inchauspe farm, where a tarmac road ends. Turn left, and past the farm you'll find a path that goes down generally E in zigzags and arrives finally on a small tarmac road. Turn right, cross a bridge and arrive once again on the:

2.00 D 19. Turn left and follow the D 19 for about 500m. Arrive at a junction and turn left. Follow a small level road SE for about 10 minutes, keeping the Gave de Larrau on

Georges Veron, inventor of the Haute Route, suggests in his French HRP guide that in the case of bad weather or poor visibility walkers can go down on the D 19 to Larrau and walk from there via the Pont d'Amubi to Cabane d'Ardanne. That's 13km on tarmac road! The alternative route in this guide is just as quick, just as safe, but much more elegant.

Bird watching on the Col d'Orgambideska

your left-hand side. Don't cross the river, but leave the road and walk towards a barn. Keep the barn on your right, follow a level dirt road, cross a minor stream and arrive at another barn, where the dirt road makes a sharp turn to the right. Leave the dirt road, turn left and enter a forest. Go through a gate in a fence, cross another stream and gain height in the forest to arrive at a tiny open field, where the path becomes faint. Continue in the same direction. The track continues among trees, bends to the right, then to the left, crosses a stream and follows a fence along a pasture. Go through a gate and climb finally on a stony path to:

3.00 Larrau. Small Basque village with a baker's shop, two hotels (Etchemaite, tel. 05 59 28 61 45, fax 05 59 28 72 71, on your left when you enter Larrau and Despouey, tel. 05 59 28 60 82; Hotel Despouey has also a tiny food shop). There is a small, basic but shady campsite on the east side of the village. On entering the village by the main road, turn left and walk to Hotel Despouey. Just past the hotel, follow the small road E that climbs a few metres and arrive at a signpost indicating the Col de Jauregeberri (yellow marks). The road turns into a track. Follow this track E, keeping the campsite on your left. Go through a gate in a fence and follow the obvious path, soon with a forest on your left and a steep slope with bracken on your right. Continue along a fence, and the landscape opens and the path forks. Take the track that goes down a few metres and arrive at a dirt road near a sharp curve. Climb the dirt road, cross a stream and arrive soon at a pass with a farmhouse (Hardoya) on your right. Go through a gate and follow the dirt road that descends a little before arriving at a junction. Leave the dirt road and turn left. Cross a stream by a footbridge and climb on an obvious path through a lovely beech forest. Cross a tiny stream before you emerge from the forest and climb on a vague track through an open field with bracken. Continue to climb on a track (could be muddy in places), pass an old drinking trough and arrive at the:

4.20 Col de Jauregeberry (Jaureguiber), 855m, slightly hidden between pastures. The path turns right, crosses a muddy section, passes a drinking trough and goes down between trees to a dirt road. Arrive at the buildings of Uztarbia (742m) on the dirt road. Turn right and follow this road S for about 45mins. The road descends gently below the rocky slopes of Odihandia and above the west side of the Gorges d'Holzarté and arrives at the:

5.15 Pont d'Amubi (670m). Cross the bridge, ignore a dirt road coming from the right after 50m and keep following the dirt road that climbs gently E and then SE. Arrive finally at the Pont de Pichta (730m). Cross the Ruisseau d'Ardané by this bridge and follow the road for around 50m until a junction indicated with a cairn. Leave the road, turn right, enter a forest and climb steeply SSE. The path is obvious; it crosses a few large forest tracks and arrives at an open place with bracken at 970m. A large cascade, the Cascade de Pichta, can clearly be seen ahead of you. Climb towards the cascade, always staying on the right of the stream. There is a vague track that leads to the cascade (1130m). Keep the cascade about 100m to your left and climb on a clear path generally S until you arrive on a grassy bowl at:

7.45 Cabane de Pista Ganekoa (1433m, a shepherds' hut). Pass this *cabane* and another, and climb S on a dirt road to a pass (1497m). From here follow the dirt road that makes a long zigzag before arriving at Ardanne, or take a short-cut by following a path that goes down SW and arrives on the dirt road again near:

8.10 Cabane d'Ardané (1330m).

DAY 8
Refugio de Belagua to Lescun

A pleasant walk through a beech forest followed by an exciting climb through a grotesque limestone landscape, a natural labyrinth in which the waymarks have to be followed very carefully to stay on course. Route-finding problems are inevitable in mist. Today you'll enter the high mountains of the Pyrenees.

Route:	via the Col d'Anaye (2011m)
Grade:	2
Time:	7hrs
Height gain:	700m
Height loss:	1200m
Map:	IGN Carte de Randonnées, 1:50,000, no 3: Béarn

0.00 Refugio de Belagua. Behind the *refugio* you'll find red marks. Follow a cattle track E on an almost level pasture towards a small rocky face. Cross a tiny stream (possibly dry in summer) before you reach the rocky face and pass it to the right. The red marks stop as soon as you have crossed the stream, but on the other side of the stream you'll find ancient yellow marks. These marks are followed all the way to the Col d'Anaye. After a small pass the route enters a beech forest, in which you go down E gently. At an open spot the route turns sharply to the right, then makes a curve to the left and climbs E through the dense forest. Here and there the route is blocked by fallen trees, but the route is generally easy to follow. After a pass, a short descent and a short climb, you reach:

2.20 a pass (1800m), which offers a fine view on the Arres d'Anies, where only some pine trees (and a few beeches initially) can survive. After a short descent the path swings E inimitably (pay attention to the yellow marks) between deeply carved limestone rocks. As you climb towards the Col d'Anaye the number of trees decreases dramatically and finally you find yourself walking in a completely bare landscape. The route reaches a pass (2040m), descends a few metres, passes a pool (dry in summer) to the left and goes to the:

4.00 Col d'Anaye (2011m, a pass on the border that gives access to the Vallon d'Anaye in France). Go down E on a path (a few ancient red marks, some cairns) to the floor of the Vallon d'Anaye. Pass a few rocks and cross a clear stream that has its origin here and provides water of good quality. Go down on the right side of the stream, which soon flows underground but reappears near the shepherds' huts of Anaye. Cross the stream, the Ruisseau d'Anaye, by a foot-bridge near the lowest of the two huts. Turn right and go down on a well-worn path (yellow marks) through forest and pasture on the left side of the stream, which could be dry in summer. Finally go down steeply in zigzags close to the impressive limestone walls of the Pic de la Brèque to the: **5.45 Plateau de Sanchèse** (1090m). Cross a stream immediately by a solid bridge. Turn right and walk to a dirt road. Turn left and climb a little on this dirt road until a small

The bizarre limestone landscape near the Pic d'Anie

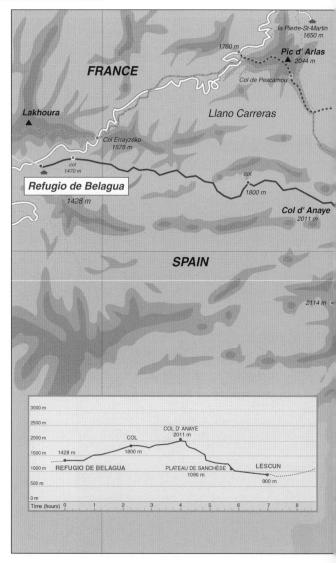

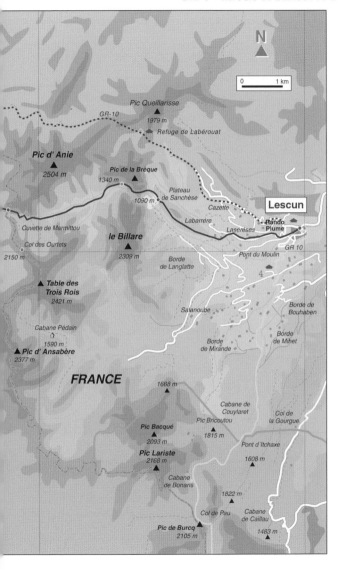

parking place, where the dirt road turns into a road. Go down SE gently on this road to the village of:

7.00 Lescun (900m). Near the village you'll reach the junction 'Sanchèse – Labérouat'. Turn right, ignore the road signed 'Anapia – Lac de Lhurs' and walk to the centre of Lescun. For practical information about Lescun see the introduction of the next section of the Haute Route.

Alternative Routes

In case of poor visibility a safer alternative is to follow the tarmac road from Belagua to the Port de la Pierre-Saint-Martin (2hrs 30mins from Belagua) and to go down, still on the road, from there to the village of Arette-La Pierre-Saint-Martin (3hrs 15mins from Belagua, all on road). From the village you can follow the GR10 through an unattractive ski area to the Pas de l'Osque. From there the GR10 goes to the Pas d'Azuns and continues down towards Lescun, passing Cabane du Cap de la Baitch and Refuge de Labérouat.

Another option, which is less safe and very demanding, is to follow the road from Belagua to the Col de la Pierre-Saint-Martin and then to walk as follows:

2.30 Col de la Pierre-Saint-Martin (1760m), a pass on the frontier where you'll find the magnificent border stone 262 (date: 1858). Go down on the French side of the pass for about 150m. Leave the road, turn right and follow a path (yellow marks) that climbs a little SE and approaches the Pic d'Arlas (2044m). Follow the path that goes round this mountain, keeping it on your left-hand side. East of the Pic d'Arlas you arrive at the:

3.15 Col de Pescamou (1918m, border stone 265 a few metres left of the pass). Follow the marks (there are red and yellow marks; concentrate on the red marks) as you walk SE. Notice a *cabane* (metal) a little further on, on your left. The path climbs, then goes down, and the route (in good visibility) becomes clear. Keep following the red marks and cairns as they lead through narrow gullies between the rocks. The path goes up and down and finally, after a short climb, reaches the:

4.45 Col des Anies (2080m), which is hard to distinguish in the chaotic limestone landscape. The 'real pass' is in fact

One of the best known border stones of the Pyrenees – no.262 on the Port de la Pierre-Saint-Martin

50m below on your right. Notice the Pic de Soum Couy on your left and the Pic d'Anie (2504m) in the south. The route forks. Ignore the red paint flashes that branch of to the right, towards the Pic d'Anie, and follow the marks (also red) that go east. Soon you are walking on grass instead of rocks. Notice a small pool (possibly dry in summer) on your right, cross a small stream on a small grassy plateau and follow an obvious path to Cabana de Cap de la Baitch, which you can see now deep down below NE of you.

5.30 Cabane de Cap de la Baitch (1689m, in summer a shepherds' hut), where you'll find the GR10. Turn right and walk E on a path that descends. Notice Cabane d'Ardinet (1570m) above the path on your left and enter a forest. Soon after emerging from the forest you arrive at the:

6.50 Refuge de Labérouat (1442m), a staffed mountain hut. Open in July and August, tel. 05 59 34 50 43. Not really a place for walkers to stay because of the many youngsters

Winter in Lescun

that fill the hut. It's more a *colonie des vacances*. There is a tarmac road from the *refuge* to Lescun. In bad weather it's a good idea to follow this road, because now and then the GR10 follows a track that becomes extremely muddy. Follow the road on your way down, ignore the GR10 that branches off to the right (very muddy section that should be avoided) and go down on the road until about 1200m. The GR10 reaches the road again and branches off to the left. Follow the markers SE until you arrive in the village centre of:

8.20 Lescun (900m).

SECTION 2: LESCUN TO GAVARNIE
Highlights of the Parc National des Pyrénées Occidentales

During the second section of the Pyrenean Haute Route walkers spend most of their time in French territory. Spain is visited a few times, but these visits are very brief. On the first day, as you climb from Lescun to the Col de Pau on the French–Spanish border, you enter the Parc National des Pyrénées Occidentales. This is the only national park in the French Pyrenees, a thin ribbon that stretches from the Aspe valley in the west to the Vallée d'Aure in the east. The Parc National has a length of about 100km and an area of 45,700 hectares. The environment within the boundaries of the national park merits official protection.

This second section of the Haute Route gives a good impression of the Parc National, as almost the whole route falls within the park. It is not hard to under-stand why this section has gained enormous popularity among walkers through the years: some of the most remarkable and beautiful mountain peaks of the entire Pyrenees are to be found within the national park (Pic du Midi d'Ossau, Balaitous, Vignemale), at the end of each day walkers can spend the night in a staffed mountain hut, and the route is generally not difficult to follow (the tracks are clear and there are signposts everywhere).

In my opinion the real strength of the Parc National is the enormous variety of landscapes: the soft green Vallée d'Aspe with its herds of sheep and small *cabanes*, the beautifully shaped Pic du Midi d'Ossau (2884m) that dominates an entire valley, the granite wilderness of Balaitous and Larribet that hides numerous icy tarns and pools, the enchanting Vallée du Marcadau with it's blistering streams and old pine-trees, the impressive north face of the Vignemale (3298m) and of course the monumental Cirque de Gavarnie. Every day is full of surprises, each pass hiding another landscape. The walk from Lescun to Gavarnie is not only a walk from hut to hut, but also a walk from one highlight to another.

The walk through the Parc National to Gavarnie is certainly not the most dif-ficult section of the Haute Route. It is easy walking on the first three days: clear paths and enough marks to stay on course. On the fourth day, however, you have to face the first serious obstacles of the Haute Route: the Passage d'Orteig and the Port du Lavedan are a serious test of your abilities as a mountain walker. Exposed ridges, steep sections, rough terrain and snowfields guarantee an exciting finale to this stage. Serious obstacles on the three remaining days are the Col de Cambalès (steep climb and steep descent on a slope full of rocks and scree; possible snow-fields on both sides of the pass; problematic navigation in case of poor visibility) and the Col des Mulets. The guide offers a **variant** (described at the end of day 13) which allows you to avoid the difficulties of the fourth day: the route from

Arrémoulit to Refuge Wallon. But whatever route you choose, it will still be a tough backpacking expedition to Gavarnie.

Walkers may wish to take a day off to climb one or more of the **classic summits** described in this section: Grande Fache (day 13), the Vignemale (day 14) and Le Taillon (day 15).

Lescun

Lescun (900m) is a tiny village situated in a remote valley west of the Vallée d'Aspe. It is considered to be one of the most beautiful villages of the entire mountain range. The authentic, simple, grey stone-built houses of Lescun are built on a steep grassy slope and overlook an enormous, lush green valley divided in small pastures. Isolated farmhouses, stone walls, small forests and hay barns decorate this enchanting valley. But it is more than just a romantic valley. South of the village rise many sharp grey limestone peaks that together form a giant amphitheatre: the Cirque de Lescun. What a remarkable contrast with the valley! Peaks like the Pic d'Anie (2504m), the Billare (2309m) and the Pic d'Ansabère (2377m) are not particularly high by Pyrenean standards, but due to the contrast with the Lescun valley they offer an impressive mountain landscape – one of the most admired in the Pyrenees. Lescun, as simple as it is, fits perfectly in this landscape, thanks to the fact that the village is still as authentic as it can be. It's worth staying a day in Lescun to admire the landscape. There is only one thing – the sun doesn't always shine in Lescun!

Refuge de Pombie is one of many staffed huts in the Parc National (day 11)

Autumn at Lescun (end of October)

Lescun

Practical Information

Facilities in Lescun
Facilities in the village include post office (no cash dispenser), hotel/bar/restaurant (Hotel du Pic d'Anie in the village centre, tel. 05 59 34 71 54, fax 05 59 34 53 22), *gite d'étape* next to the hotel (16 places, tel. 05 59 34 71 54, fax 05 59 34 53 22), *refuge* in the village (Maison de la Montagne, 22 places, tel. 05 59 34 79 14 or 06 86 86 43 99, email: lescundom@aol.com) and tiny food shop beside the-hotel. SE of the village along the GR10 trail you'll find the nice small camping municipal, Camping du Lauzart: good sanitary facilities, tiny shop, bread on delivery each morning. There's also a *gite* on the campsite (tel. 05 59 34 51 77). ***Vallée d'Aspe and Lescun on the internet:*** www.vallee-aspe.com/lescun/lescun.htm

Gavarnie
For further information on Gavarnie (facilities, public transport) see the introduction of the third section of the Haute Route.

Public Transport to Lescun

It's possible to get close to Lescun by public transport, but unfortunately there are no busses that go all the way to the village. Take the Eurostar to Paris Gare du Nord, take the subway to Gare d'Austerlitz and from there take a (night-) train to Pau. There is a train service from Pau to Oloron-Sainte-Marie (just a few trains a day, but if you take the night-train to Pau, you won't have to wait too long). In Oloron take the bus to that goes through the Aspe valley to the Valle de Canfranc in Spain. Leave the bus at the Pont de Lescun (bridge on the Gave d'Aspe, where the road to Lescun starts). What's left is a 5km walk on road (that climbs all the way!), but you could hitch – it's not difficult to get a ride to Lescun from here.

Pitching a Tent in the Parc National

Bivouacking (meaning in the Parc National pitching a small tent for one night, between 19.00hrs and 09.00hrs) is allowed to a certain extent within the borders of the national park: the location must be at least an hour's walk from any paved road. A bivouac near all the *refuges* in this section (except the Spanish hut Refugio de Respomuso, variant day 13) is allowed. There's often a designated area near the hut where walkers can pitch a tent.

Mountain Huts

This second section provides information on spending each night in a *refuge*. But beware: walking from one hut to another is becoming increasingly popular, and as a consequence you will have to make a reservation at each hut in order to ensure a place.

Note: *Refuge d'Arrémoulit (day 12) may be closed in 2004 because of modernisation. Information: CAF Pau, tel: 05 59 27 71 81, email: clubalpin-pau@wanadoo.fr*

Food

Food supplies for several days have to be carried because food can be bought only in the village of Candanchu (on the second day). Should this shop be closed, then going to

Canfranc-Estacion, 4km south of Candanchu, is an option. There is a bus service to Canfranc.

An easy but rather expensive solution is to have dinner in a hut each evening. Pitching the tent near the *refuge* and having dinner in the hut is also possible. Ask the gardian in advance if you can join the table!

Maps
- IGN Carte de Randonnées, 1:50,000, no 3: Béarn
- Mapa Excursionista/Carte de Randonnées, 1:50,000, no 24: Gavarnie–Ordesa

---

Accommodation: Contact Details

All numbers and other information on accommodation on the Haute Route are also given in the route description.

Day 9: Refuge d'Arlet – 05 59 36 00 99 (hut) or 05 59 34 76 88 (guardian)

Day 10: Candanchu: Refugio El Aguila (tel. and fax 974 373 291, email: elaguila@infobide.com) and Refugio Valle del Aragon (974 373 222)

Day 11: Refuge de Pombie – 05 59 05 31 78

Day 12: Refuge d'Arremoulit – 05 59 05 31 79 (possibly closed in 2004; contact the CAF Pau – tel. 05 59 27 71 81, email: clubalpin-pau@wanadoo.fr); Refuge de Larribet: 05 62 97 25 39 (hut) or 05 62 95 89 96 (guardian)

Day 13: Refuge Wallon – 05 61 85 93 43 or 05 62 92 64 28

Variant day 13: Refugio de Respomuso – 974 490 203

Day 14: Refuge des Oulettes de Gaube – 05 62 92 62 97 (hut) or 05 61 85 85 58 (guardian); Refuge de Bayssellance – 05 62 92 40 25 or 05 59 27 76 17 (guardian); internet: http://refuge.bayssellance.free.fr

Day 15: Refuge Grange de Holle – 05 62 92 48 77, fax 05 62 92 41 58 – Gavarnie. *Gite d'étape* Le Gypaete, 05 62 92 40 61 and Maison-refuge Jan Da Lo, 05 62 92 40 66 and fax 05 62 92 40 27

DAY 9
Lescun to Refuge d'Arlet

Route:	via the Col de Pau (1942m) and the Col de Saoubathou (1949m)
Grade:	2
Time:	6hrs 45mins
Height gain:	1300m
Height loss:	200m
Map:	IGN Carte de Randonnées, 1:50,000, no 3: Béarn

A very nice walk that will cause no problems on a beautiful day. There are top-class views over the Aspe region during this long walk close to the French–Spanish border. Today you'll encounter a Pyrenean lake for the first time. In summer it can sometimes be hard to find water between Cabane de Bonaris and Refuge d'Arlet.

0.00 Lescun. Leave the village (900m) on its south side and go down to the Pont du Moulin, where the road makes a sharp curve to the left. Cross the bridge, leave the road and follow the path that climbs steeply to Camping du Lauzart, where you'll meet the road again. Leave the campsite to the right and follow the road to a junction. Take the road that leads to 'Labrénère – Col de Pau' (indicated at the junction) and climbs initially with the GR10. Take a short-cut left of the road, cross a stream and reach the road again near a house. Take another, longer short-cut and return once again to the road. Leave the GR10 (which takes another short-cut and goes then NE towards the Lestrémau farm), turn right, climb in zigzags and then continue S, always on the road. Pass several farms and barns before reaching a hairpin bend, 3.5km from the campsite of Lescun. Leave the road, turn left and walk on a level dirt road that soon enters a valley in which the Labrenère stream flows. Walk S with the stream on your left-hand side, cross a cattle grid (a signpost indicates that Refuge d'Arlet is only 5 hours away and the Col de Pau 2hrs 45mins) and continue to a bridge. Cross the bridge, leave the dirt road and turn right immediately. Follow a small path (white– red–white marks) that soon meets a broad track. Climb the track that diverts a little from the stream, but bends again towards it to reach the:

1.45 Pont d'Itchaxe (1360m, a small bridge on the Labrénère stream). Cross the bridge, enter the Parc National

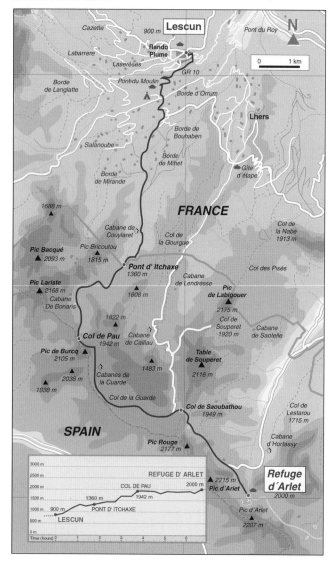

and climb SW, initially through a forest and later through open fields. Notice a few old *cabanes* on your right and climb to the Cabane de Bonaris, a hut that could be occupied in summer by a shepherd. The *cabane* is situated on the north side of a small plateau. Cross the plateau and climb S along rocky slopes on an obvious path to the:

3.45 Col de Pau (1942m), situated on the French–Spanish border and offering fine views over extensive Spanish sierras. Don't cross the pass, but stay in France, turn left and follow a well-worn path E to a pass. Climb a little on the northern slopes of the Pic de Burcq, go down a few metres and follow a more or less level path (a few metres below the border ridge) that stays very close to the border ridge. The path then bends a little away from the border and climbs a little E to the Col de Saoubathou. Ignore the path that descends to Cabane de Caillau and climb to the pass (1949m). On the east side of the pass the path goes up and down SE. Make a short descent, a short climb north of the Pic Rouge (which is indeed purplish red!) and a descend to the grassy Lapassa plateau. Notice Cabane de Lapassa on

Pastures, isolated barns and limestone peaks in the Lescun region

95

your left, ignore the path that goes down NE towards
Cabane d'Hortassy, and finally climb in a number of short
zigzags to:
6.45 Refuge d'Arlet (2000m), overlooking the Lac d'Arlet.
This staffed mountain hut is owned by the Parc National des
Pyrénées Occidentales. Open from mid-June until mid-
September, it offers accommodation for 36 persons and
meals service, tel. 05 59 36 00 99. Bivouac possible near
the lake.

DAY 10
Refuge d'Arlet to Candanchu

A pleasant walk
mainly through
pastureland and
sometimes forest.
The route follows the
GR11 from Ibon de
Astanes to
Candanchu. There
are no route-finding
problems under
normal conditions.

Route:	via the Col de Lapachouaou (1891m), the Pla d'Espélunguère (1400m) and the Pas de l'Échelle (1775m)
Grade:	2
Time:	6hrs 30mins
Height gain:	550m
Height loss:	1000m
Map:	IGN Carte de Randonnées, 1:50,000, no 3: Béarn. The last part of today's walk is not marked on old editions of the map. Route finding is easy, however, as you are following the GR11.

0.00 Refuge d'Arlet. Follow the path along the northern
shore of Lac d'Arlet. After the lake the path makes a sharp
turn to the left and climbs gently to a kind of pass NE of Pic
d'Arlet. Turn right and go down SE into the so-called Cirque
de Banasse. Pass Cabane des Caillaous (1890m), ignore at a
junction the path that goes down towards Cabane de
Gourgue Sec (a shepherds' hut on the left, below, near a tiny
lake) and climb a few metres to the:
1.00 Col de Lapachouaou (1891m). Again the path bends to
the right and you walk SE, practically on the borderline of
the national park, to the next col (1900m), where the

descent to the Pla d'Espélunguère starts. Go down S in zigzags. Pass Cabane Grosse (a shepherds' hut, 1560m), cross two streams and climb a few metres to the Col Platrière (not identified on the map). Go down through the Espélunguère forest. In this forest you'll find a dirt road, which you follow all the way down to the:

2.45 Pla d'Espélunguère (1400m). Turn left on the plateau and follow the dirt road to a junction. Turn right, go down to a stream and cross the stream by a footbridge. Climb a few metres through grass until the junction 'Sansanet–Estaëns' (indicated with a signpost). Turn right and take the path that goes generally S to the Lac Estaëns (or Ibon de Astanes, as the lake is situated in Spain). The path enters a beech forest and climbs steeply in zigzags to the lake, directly south of the French–Spanish border. Near the end of the climb, the path makes a sharp curve to the right and reaches the:

4.00 Pas de l'Échelle (1775m, on the border). Pass Ibon de Astanes (1754m) along its eastern shore and find, SE of the lake, the red–white marks of the GR11, which you'll follow from now on. Walk E and continue down after a grassy pass until the path forks (around 1680m). Turn right, walk S

Lac and Refuge d'Arlet (2000m)

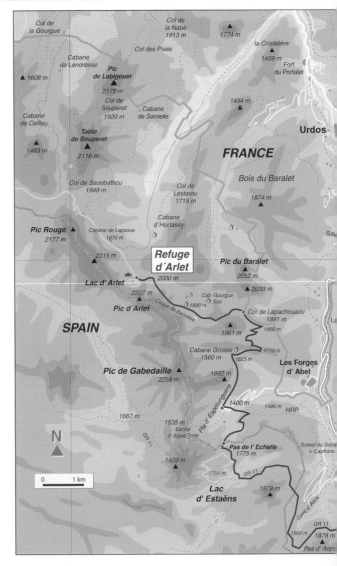

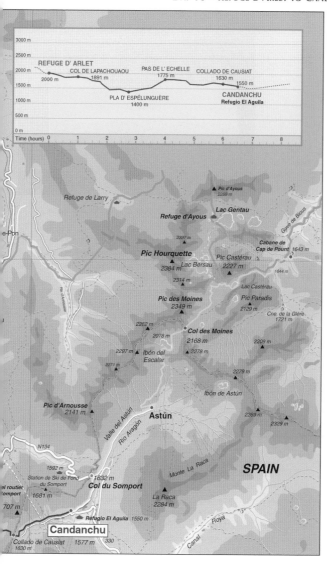

Cabane de Gourgue Sec in the Vallée d'Aspe

through grass and leave Spain for a while near border stone no 293 (easily overlooked, as it's some 30m left of the path). The path enters a forest and reaches the Gave d'Aspe. Cross the stream carefully and take great care on the other side of the stream, where a steep eroded scree slope has to be crossed. Follow the path NE, and after a small section with bracken and beech trees the route bends towards the east. Pass a small *cabana* and walk in open fields to the:

6.00 Collado de Causiat (1630m, on the border). Cross the border and once in Spain follow the marks of the GR11 through the ski resort of Candanchu. You'll reach a road which you follow until Candanchu. Notice a military school on your left, Refugio Santa Christina on your right and enter the village where the main road makes a hairpin bend. Turn right and walk along the *galleria commercial* (cafeterias, shops). (No one seems to notice that Supermercado El Bozo is open in summer, but it is! If you walk to the Col du Somport you'll find a bar/restaurant after 300m that has also a tiny shop.) Go down the road until a junction, where Refugio El Aguila is indicated. Turn right and walk a few metres to:

6.30 Refugio El Aguila (1550m, on the left side of the road), tel. 974 373 291. Excellent *refugio*, where meals are provided. The *refugio* may be closed during the day, but it should be open in the evening. Another possibility is the nearby Refugio Valle de Aragon (open July and August, 98 places, tel. 974 373 222).

DAY 11
Candanchu to Refuge de Pombie

Route:	via the Col des Moines (2168m) and the Col de Peyreget (2300m)
Grade:	2
Time:	6hrs 20mins
Height gain:	1300m
Height loss:	820m
Map:	IGN Carte de Randonnées, 1:50,000, no 3: Béarn

Not a difficult walk, but a tough one, mainly on well-worn paths. This is a splendid route along the symbol of the Pyrenees: the Pic du Midi d'Ossau (2884m). Rough terrain near the Col de Peyreget. First few kilometres on road.

0.00 Candanchu. Return to the main road and climb this until you arrive at the Col du Somport (1632m; the road that crosses the Col du Somport has become very quiet since the tunnel underneath the col, 8km in length, opened in 2003). Don't cross the border, but turn right and walk ENE on a road towards the ski resort of Astun. Keep left where the road forks and walk to the buildings of:

1.00 Astun (1710m). Astun consists of a number of large, ugly buildings. However, in summer some of the bar/ restaurants are open, and there might even be the possibility of replenishing food supplies in a tiny shop – but don't count on it and don't expect too much! Pass all the buildings and find a dirt road (*pista forestal*, indicated, closed for traffic). Climb on this road, go underneath a cable lift, make a turn left and go underneath the lift once again. The road keeps climbing N and approaches the stream coming from Ibon de Escalar. Cross the stream and follow a path on the west side of the stream. Cross the stream once more and climb N on an obvious path situated well above the stream that runs through a deep gully. You'll reach Ibon de Escalar (2078m), a lovely spot situated in a grassy bowl and an excellent place for a bivouac. Pass the lake to the right and climb E to the:

2.15 Col des Moines (2168m), on the French–Spanish border, border stone 309, offering excellent views on the Pic du Midi d'Ossau. Go down gently NE on a path that's not

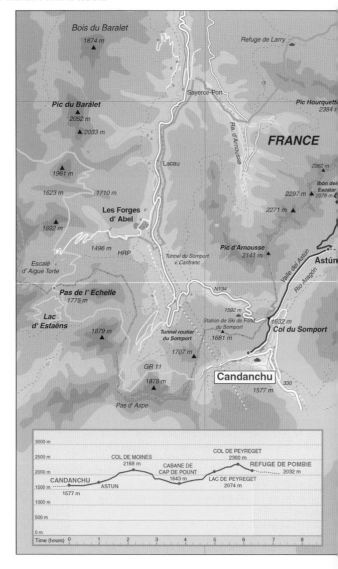

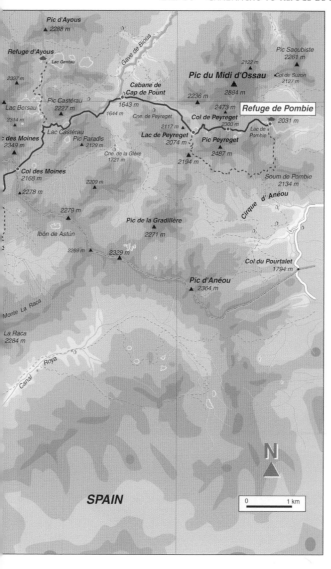

Pic d'Ayous
▲ 2288 m

Refuge d'Ayous
Lac Gentau

2337 m

Pic Castérau
2227 m

Lac Bersau

2314 m

Lac Castérau

: des Moines
2349 m

Pic Paradis
▲ 2129 m

Col des Moines
2168 m

▲2278 m

2209 m

2279 m

Ibón de Astún

2269 m ▲   2329 m

Gave de Bious

Cabane de
Cap de Pount
1643 m

1644 m

Cne. de Peyreget

Cne. de la Glère
1721 m

Pic de la Gradillère
2271 m

Pic d'Anéou
▲ 2364 m

Pic du Midi d'Ossau
▲ 2884 m

Pic Saoubiste
2261 m ▲

2122 m
▲

Col de Suzon
2127 m ▲

2236 m
▲

2473 m
▲

Refuge de Pombie
2031 m

2117 m ▲

Col de Peyreget
2300 m

Lac de Peyreget
2074 m ▲

Pic Peyreget
2487 m ▲

2194 m ▲

Lac de
Pombie

Soum de Pombie
2134 m

Cirque d' Anéou

Col du Pourtalet
1794 m

Monte La Raca

La Raca
2284 m

Canal   Roya

SPAIN

N
▲

0   1 km

On a beautiful day it's well worth considering leaving the Haute Route temporarily at this point and paying a visit to Refuge d'Ayous (see 'An easy summit: Pic d'Ayous', below), a mountain hut that offers a stunning view of the west face of the Pic du Midi d'Ossau, a forked mountain that dominates the landscape. The hut is delightfully situated near a beautiful lake called Lac Gentau (one of the three Lacs d'Ayous). There is no better place to admire the Pic du Midi d'Ossau than Refuge d'Ayous, and a night spent there is surely a night to remember.

How to reach the refuge: on the junction near Lac Castérau turn left and climb W to a pass. Cross the pass, pass a tiny pool and walk N along the east shore of Lac Bersau (2080m). Beyond the lake you walk alongside a few tiny lakes and go down in zigzags to Refuge d'Ayous (1960m).

Refuge d'Ayous is owned by the Parc National. Recently modernised, it provides 50 places, with meals available. Reservation necessary, tel. 05 59 05 37 00. Bivouac possible near the lake. There is a guardian in residence from mid-June to mid-September.

Isards thrive in the Pyrenees

too obvious at the start. The path eventually goes down steeper, bends a little N and reaches a junction west of Lac Castérau (signpost). Turn right, go down to the lake and pass it on its southern side.

Climb a few metres and go down NE on a somewhat eroded path to the floor of a valley. Beyond Cabane de la Hosse (1720m) you'll reach a *pista*. Cross the dirt road and the Gave de Bious (the stream on the other side of the dirt road) by a footbridge (1644m). Walk on more or less level terrain ENE to:

3.45 Cabane de Cap de Pount (1643m, a shepherds' hut). Here the Haute Route is faint. Try to find a small path a few metres north of the *cabane*. Climb steeply N in zigzags on this path, which is marked with cairns, arrive on a small plateau, and continue to climb until a plateau where the Cabane de Peyreget (1920m) is situated. Leave this shepherds' hut to the right and reach a well-worn path a few metres further on. Climb this path SE until the:

5.00 Lac de Peyreget (2074m). The path forks at the south side of this tiny lake. Turn left and climb E on a path marked with cairns close to the impressive Pic du Midi d'Ossau. The climb is not difficult, but some care is needed on a number of giant boulders that have to be crossed in the final stage of the climb.

5.45 Col de Peyreget (2300m). Go down E on rough terrain (no difficulties, however) to the small Lacs du Col de Peyreget. Beyond the lakes the path makes a sharp turn to the left and you go down to:

6.20 Refuge de Pombie (2032m), situated east of the charming Lac de Pombie. The hut is staffed from June until the end of September and belongs to the CAF. It has 48 places, plus 16 in a tent, tel. 05 59 05 31 78. Bivouac allowed on a designated terrain near the hut. The hut offers extensive views to the east, with high summits including the Balaïtous (3144m), the first 3000m summit you'll encounter. A large part of tomorrow's walk can be seen from here.

Variant: From Lac de Peyreget via the Col de l'Iou (2194m) to Refuge de Pombie

This very easy variant enables you to avoid the (certainly not difficult, but perhaps slightly unpleasant) climb to the Col de Peyreget. Climb from the lake S in zigzags to the Col de l'Iou

Crossing a field of gentians in the Vallée d'Ossau

(2194m). Turn left and walk E on the right side of pic Peyreget until you reach a junction. Turn left and go down N to Refuge de Pombie, which can be seen from afar.

AN EASY SUMMIT: Pic d'Ayous (2288m)

Height gain: 328m

Time: 1hr 45mins (1hr to reach the top)

The Pic Ayous isn't particularly high, but due to its situation on the ridge that separates the Ossau valley from the Vallée d'Aspe, this 'little' mountain deserves to be climbed. From the summit, far away in the west it's possible to see the limestone mountains such as the Pic d'Anie (2504m) and the Pic d'Ansabère (2377m) in the Lescun region, and in the south-west the quite impressive summits of the Bisaurin (2668m) and the Pic d'Aspe. But my guess is that you will be completely focussed on that one mountain in the east that dominates the scenery completely: the Pic du Midi d'Ossau. The best time to climb Pic d'Ayous is in the evening, when the sun shines on the Pic du Midi's west face. Sunset on the Pic d'Ayous after a bright summer's day is an experience to cherish.

0.00 Refuge d'Ayous (1960m). Follow the obvious path above the north shore of the Lac Gentau and arrive at a junction, where you find the GR10 trail. Turn left and climb W on a well-worn path and reach without difficulty the:

0.40 Col d'Ayous (2185m). Leave the GR10 and turn right. Climb NE on a path, staying left of a ridge. Arrive at a pass (2220m) and climb from there almost along the ridge until you reach the summit of the:

1.00 Pic d'Ayous (2288m). Return to the *refuge* on the same track.

DAY 12
Refuge de Pombie
to Refuge de Larribet

The first day of the
Haute Route that
might cause serious
problems. The high
passes that have to
be crossed at the end
of the day could be
covered with snow
early in the season.
Steep slopes with
rocks and scree,
snowfields and a tra-
verse of a rock face
(which is secured
with steel cables)
provide an exciting
day. Study the variant
at the end of the
route description and
the alternative route
described at the end
of day 13 before
leaving Refuge de
Pombie. The difficult
sections can be
avoided!

Route:	via the Col d'Arrious (2259m), the Col du Palas (2517m) and the Port du Lavedan (2615m)
Grade:	2
Time:	8hrs 10mins
Height gain:	1500m
Height loss:	1370m
Map:	Mapa Excursionista/Carte de Randonnées, 1:50,000, no 24: Gavarnie–Ordesa.

Note: Refuge d'Arrémoulit may be closed in 2004 due to modernisation. Information: CAF Pau, tel. 05 59 27 71 81, email: clubalpin-pau@wanadoo.fr

0.00 Refuge de Pombie. Follow the obvious path S that soon bends to the east and makes a few long zigzags. Follow a stream on your way down to Cabane de Pucheaux. Pass the *cabane* (1720m, a shepherds' hut) to the right. As soon as the *cabane* is passed, the route turns left and goes down to the floor of the valley. Cross the Gave de Pombie, turn right and follow the stream on a little way. Cross the stream again by a footbridge (1625m) just before you enter a foliage forest and go down E until you reach an open valley. Go down to the Gave de Brousset (1350m), cross the stream and after a short climb you'll meet the:
1.35 D 934, the road that links the Vallée d'Ossau with the valle de Teña in Spain by the Col du Pourtalet (small parking area, shepherds hut). Cross the road (you'll find Cabane de Caillou de Soques, a very basic shelter, near a stream), turn left and walk to a signpost on the other side of the road that indicates the climb to the Col d'Arrious and Refuge d'Arrémoulit (3hrs according to the signpost; we'll see!).

Follow a path that climbs in zigzags NE through a forest until you reach a bridge (1560m) on the Ruisseau d'Arrious at the edge of the forest. Cross the bridge and climb E in an open valley staying left and a little distance from the Arrious stream. Notice Cabane d'Arrious (1775m) on your right, on the right side of the stream. Cross the stream again and reach a so-called *fausse col* (it appears to be a pass, but the climb continues). Go through a small plateau, cross the stream once more and climb to the Col d'Arrious that you can now see ahead of you.

4.05 Col d'Arrious (2259m), where the path forks. Turn right and walk SE to the nearby Lac d'Arrious (2285m). The path immediately turns away from the lake (a turn to the left), crosses a kind of pass, turns right and approaches a rocky face that has been secured with steel cables. This so-called Passage d'Orteig is not too difficult, but impressive; it can be awkward for those who suffer from vertigo and dangerous in bad weather (see the variant at the end of the route description). Climb steeply above a deep abyss and finally, past the Passage d'Orteig, walk E in a chaos of boulders and go down a little to:

5.05 Refuge d'Arrémoulit (2305m; bivouac possible, but not ideal, on a designated area near the hut; in summer it could be difficult to find a suitable place for the tent), with a fine view on the largest Arrémoulit lake, which is dominated

Sheep grazing in the Vallée d'Ossau, near Caillou de Soques

109

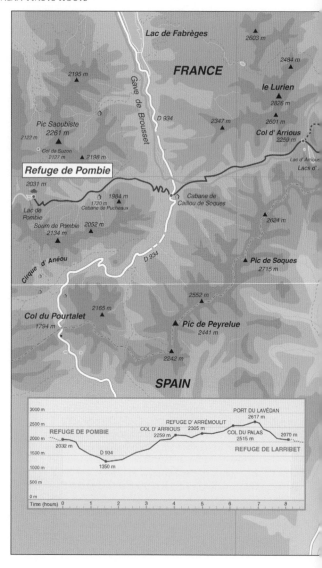

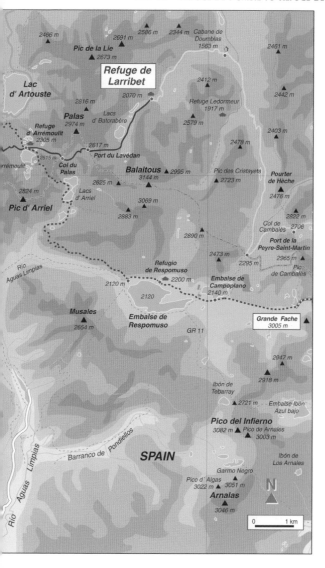

2466 m
2691 m
2586 m
2344 m Cabane de
Doumblas
1563 m
Pic de la Lie
2673 m
2461 m

Refuge de Larribet

Lac d' Artouste

2816 m
2070 m
2412 m
2442 m

Palas
2974 m
Lacs d' Batcrabère
Refuge Ledormeur
1917 m

Refuge d'Arrémoulit
2305 m
2579 m
2403 m

2617 m
Port du Lavédan
2478 m

rrémoulit
Col du Palas
2515 m
Balaïtous ▲ 2995 m
Pic des Cristayets
2723 m
Pourter de Hèche
2476 m

Balaïtous
3144 m

2824 m
2625 m ▲
2822 m
Col de Cambalès 2706

Pic d' Arriel
Lacs d' Arriel
3069 m
Port de la Peyre-Saint-Martin
2965 m Pic de Cambalès
2883 m
2890 m
2473 m
2295 m

Río Aguas Limpias
Refugio de Respomuso
2200 m
2120 m
Embalse de Campoplano
2140 m

Musales
2654 m
Embalse de Respomuso
2120
GR 11
Grande Fache
3005 m

2947 m
2918 m

Ibón de Tebarray
2721 m
Embalse Ibón Azul bajo

Pico del Infierno
3082 m ▲ Pico de Arnales
3003 m

Barranco de Pondiellos **SPAIN**
Ibón de Los Arnales

Río Aguas Limpias
Garmo Negro
Pico d' Algas
3022 m ▲ 3051 m

N

Arnalas
3046 m

Río Aguas Limpias
0   1 km

by the pyramid summit of Pic d'Arrièl (2824m). The CAF owns the hut. There is a guardian in residence from mid-June until mid-September, with meals available. 30 places in the hut and 18 in a tent next to the hut. Reservation necessary, tel. 05 59 05 31 79. Turn left after leaving the hut and climb NE on boulders and rocks through a narrow hanging valley to find a small tarn (Lac du Col du Palas). From the lake climb steeply through rocks and scree (the steep slope could be covered with snow early in summer) to the:

6.10 Col du Palas (2517m, on the French–Spanish border). Go down a short way on the east side of the pass and make

Shepherd at work east of the Pic du Midi d'Ossau

a traverse NE on rocks towards the Port du Lavedan. In some years the route can be covered with snow, even until mid-July.

6.55 Port du Lavédan (2615m), a narrow gap in the frontier ridge. You might be tempted to go down steeply in a deep gully, but it's better to go down carefully N on rocks, scree and (probably) snowfields towards the tiny Lacs de Micouléou (2300m), following the marks of the Parc National (white–red–white). The difficult part is over when you reach these lakes. Go down N to the Lacs de Batcrabère (the largest lake lies at 2180m) and pass the lakes, keeping them on your left-hand side. Beyond the lakes you reach the Brèche de la Garénère, a gap between rocks. Cross the gap (not difficult) or follow the path that goes around it and go down to the:

8.10 Refuge de Larribet (2070m), a CAF-owned hut staffed from June until the end of September. 60 places, tel. 05 62 97 25 39 or 05 62 95 89 96. Meals available. Overcrowded in summer: reservation necessary. Bivouac possible near the hut.

Evening romance above the Lac d'Arrious

Variant to Avoid the Passage d'Orteig

Go down NE in zigzags from the Col d'Arrious towards the Lac d'Artouste. Cross a tiny stream on a small plateau and go down until the path forks at about 2090m, which is well above the Lac d'Artouste. Turn right and follow a path that climbs in numerous zigzags to the Refuge d'Arrémoulit (2305m). This variant has a price: it makes the walk 20mins longer.

Note: Walkers who decide to spend the night in or near Refuge d'Arrémoulit and don't want to lose a day, can take the alternative route described at the end of day 13.

DAY 13
Refuge de Larribet to Refuge Wallon

A tough walk with Col de Cambalès as a serious obstacle. There is rough terrain and possible snow-fields (in early summer) on both sides of the pass. However, there are no problems in today's walk other than the pass. A delightful walk, with the romantic Vallon de Larribet, the Cambalès lakes and the arrival at the large Pla de la Gole with its old pine trees as highlights. A variant route from the Refuge d'Arrémoulit, avoiding some difficult sections of the route, is also described.

Route:	via the Col de Cambalès (2706m)
Grade:	1
Time:	8hrs 15mins
Height gain:	1200m
Height loss:	1350m
Map:	Mapa Excursionista/Carte de Randonnées, 1:50,000, no 24: Gavarnie–Ordesa

0.00 Refuge de Larribet. Go down NE in zigzags on a well-worn path to the floor of a small valley in which you'll find the Ruisseau de Larribet. Cross this stream and a few others and follow the Ruisseau de Larribet, keeping it on your right-hand side, until you arrive at the so-called Claou de Larribet (1740m, delightful place which looks like a natural garden; the place should be indicated with a signpost). Here you cross the Ruisseau de Larribet again and go down E between pine trees to the Vallée d'Arrens. The descent ends in this valley near:

1.15 Cabane de Doumblas (1563m, four places, useful but basic; sometimes in use by a shepherd), situated on the other side of the Gave d'Arrens. Don't go to the *cabane* but climb SE to the main path in the valley that leads S to the

Port de la Peyre-Saint-Martin (2295m). Climb this path and you'll soon reach a small plateau, in which the Gave d'Arrens quietly finds its way. Stay left of the stream while you cross the plateau, ignore the path that climbs to the unstaffed Refuge Ledormeur (1917m) and climb S. After a number of zigzags the path goes straight ahead S. Notice the Lacs de Rémoulis on your right (below) and keep climbing on a path that is very easy to follow. After a few short zigzags the path again goes straight ahead and reaches the:

4.00 Port de la Peyre-Saint-Martin (2295m), a large pass on the French–Spanish border that gives access to the Valle de Teña. Not exactly on the Port, but a few metres north of it, the final climb to the Col de Cambalès begins (signpost). Turn left and climb NE until the path forks at about 2400m. Don't follow the white–red–white marks that keep going in the same direction, but turn right and climb E on a path marked with cairns. Climb very steeply in zigzags on rough terrain (possible snowfields) to the:

5.15 Col de Cambalès (2706m, fine views on the east side of the Balaïtous, 3144m, with its small glacier, glacier de las Néous). On the east side of the pass go down very steeply a

Refuge Wallon

115

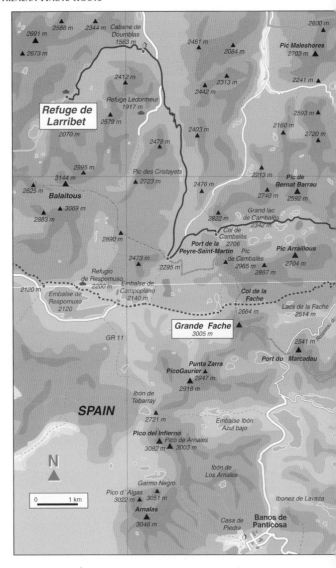

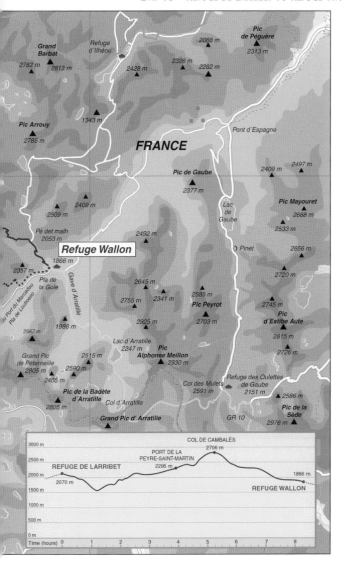

Pic de Péguère 2313 m

2068 m

Grand Barbat
2782 m 2813 m

Refuge d'Ilhéou

2428 m

2326 m 2282 m

Pic Arrouy
2785 m

1343 m

Pont d'Espagne

FRANCE

Pic de Gaube
2377 m

2409 m 2497 m

2409 m

2509 m

Pic Mayouret
2688 m

2533 m

Pè det malh
2053 m

Lac de Gaube

2492 m

2656 m

Refuge Wallon
1866 m

2720 m

Pinet

2357 m
Pla de la Gole

Gave d'Arratille

2645 m

2755 m 2341 m

2585 m

Pic Peyrot
2703 m

2745 m
Pic d'Estibe Aute
2815 m

du Port du Marcadau
Pla de Loubosse

2926 m

2925 m

2726 m

2567 m

1986 m

Lac d'Arratille
2247 m

Pic Alphonse Meillon
2930 m

Col des Mulets
2591 m

Refuge des Oulettes de Gaube
2151 m

2586 m

Grand Pic de Péterneille
2805 m

2515 m 2590 m

2405 m

Pic de la Badète d'Arratille
2805 m

Col d'Arratille

Grand Pic d' Arratille

GR 10

Pic de la Sède
2976 m

COL DE CAMBALÈS
2706 m

PORT DE LA
PEYRE-SAINT-MARTIN
2295 m

3000 m

2500 m
REFUGE DE LARRIBET
2070 m

2000 m

1500 m

1866 m

REFUGE WALLON

1000 m

500 m

0 m
Time (hours) 0   1   2   3   4   5   6   7   8

few metres, and turn left to go down NE on rocks and (possibly) snowfields for a short time. The route then bends to the right and descends E towards the Lacs de Cambalès. Pass the largest lake, the Grand Lac de Cambalès (2342m), leave two small tarns on your left side and go down ESE. Arrive at a small plateau called Pé det Malh (2053m), where you cross a stream before the path forks (signpost). Ignore the path that goes N to the Lac Nère, cross another stream and go down SE between pine trees on a distinct path to Refuge Wallon, situated on the north side of the Pla de la Gole.

8.20 Refuge Wallon (1866m). Owned by de CAF and staffed from June until the end of September. Meals available. 120 places, tel. 05 61 85 93 43 or 05 62 92 64 28. Bivouac allowed on a designated area on the plateau. Great place to stay for the night, but you won't be alone!

Variant
Refuge d'Arrémoulit – Refuge Wallon

This alternative route enables you to avoid some difficult sections of the Haute Route. It is a tough walk, but somewhat easier than the Haute Route via the Port du Lavédan and the Col de Cambalès. Snowfields tend to last long on the west side of the Col de la Fache, near the Lacs de la Fache. The final section of the climb to the Col de la Fache is steep. It's the only more or less difficult part of this variant. The →

Route:	via the Col d'Arrémoulit (2448m) and the Col de la Fache (2664m)
Time:	7hrs 45mins
Height gain:	850m
Height loss:	1300m
Map:	Mapa Excursionista/Carte de Randonnées, 1:50,000, no 24: Gavarnie–Ordesa

0.00 Refuge d'Arrémoulit. Walk from the hut to the northeast side of the lake and climb through a chaos of rocks SE (there are some cairns to guide you) to the Col d'Arrémoulit, a large frontier pass that can be seen from the *refuge*.

0.30 Col d'Arrémoulit (2448m). Go down steeply on the east side (in Spain!) of the pass towards the two northern lakes of the Lacs d'Arriël. Follow the cairns until you are between the two lakes. Turn right and walk S along the western shore of the lakes. Turn left as soon as you are past the lakes and meet a path south-east of the lakes. Turn right and follow the path, keeping a stream on your left-hand side. Pass a lake to the right and cross the stream just before passing another lake. Pass this second lake along its east side, cross the stream again and a few steps further cross it once more. Climb a few metres, just before a tiny lake with

←position of Refugio de Respomuso makes breaking the walk in two an attractive option.

Excellent places for a bivouac are to be found east of the giant Embalse de Respomuso

a dam, to the remains of a few buildings. Walk SE on a well-worn path that goes up and down high above the valley of the Rio Aguas Limpias to the large dam of the:

3.10 Embalse de Respomuso (= *dammed lake*, 2120m), where you'll meet the red–white marks of the GR11. Climb a little and walk above the northern shore of the lake. Cross the Barranco Respomuso and keep Refugio de Respomuso (2200m, open all year, 105 places, meals available, bivouac not allowed, reservation obligatory, tel. 974 490 203), a modern mountain hut, on your right. Leave the GR11 as soon as you are east of the lake, pass a few tiny lakes (excellent places for a bivouac) and arrive at the:

3.50 Embalse de Campoplano (2140m). Stay left of the unfinished dam as you walk along the southern shore of the lake (fine places for a bivouac on the east side of the lake). Cross the stream flowing from the lake and climb E on a path marked with cairns, keeping the stream coming from the Lacs de la Fache on your left. Early in the season large amounts of snow could cause some difficulties near the Lacs de la Fache. Keep the lakes (2514m) on your left-hand side and climb E on a steep slope (full of loose scree) to the:

5.40 Col de la Fache (2664m), a pass on the French–Spanish border that gives access to the Vallée du Marcadau. Go down E on an obvious path that is marked with cairns. Notice two lakes (also called Lacs de la Fache) on your right-hand side at some distance, and pass a third lake (2291m) on its south side. Cross a stream while passing this tiny lake and go down in a series of long zigzags to the Pla de Loubosso, in which you'll meet the Ruisseau (= *stream*) du Port du Marcadau. Cross a couple of footbridges, turn left and walk NE to the Pla de la Gole. Cross a footbridge on the Gave du Marcadau and go to the:

7.45 Refuge Wallon (1866m).

TEN CLASSIC SUMMITS

1: Grande Fache (3005m) from Refuge Wallon

Height gain: 1139m

Time: 6hrs 30mins (3hrs 30mins to reach the top)

Grade: F+

Should you decide to take the variant that leads to Refuge Wallon via the Col de la Fache (see day 13), then climbing the Grande Fache en route, one of the 212 Pyrenean summits that exceed 3000m, is worth the extra effort. Thanks to its height and its situation on the French–Spanish border the Grande Fache (Gran Facha in Spanish) offers superb views, in particular of the Balaïtous (3144m), the Picos del Infierno (3082m), the Pic du Midi d'Ossau (2884m, far away in the west), the Vignemale (3298m) and, of course, the enchanting Vallée du Marcadau. The climb is steep but not difficult. Should there be climbers above you, watch out for stonefall. Haute Route walkers who have followed the main route to Wallon are advised to consider taking a day off in order to climb the Grande Fache. The route description starts at Refuge Wallon.

0.00 Refuge Wallon (1866m). Gain the south shore of the Gave du Marcadau, where you'll find an obvious path. Turn right and climb W to the Pla de Loubosso (1940m), where the path forks. Ignore the path that goes S towards the Port du Marcadau, but cross a few footbridges to gain the west side of the Gave du Port du Marcadau. The path now climbs in a number of long zigzags and then goes WSW. Cross a stream near a tiny tarn (2291m) on your right, and notice a few lakes a little distance away on the left on your way up. Continue to climb W on a rather steep scree slope and arrive without any difficulties at the:

2.40 Col de la Fache (2664m). Leave the pass, turn left and climb S to gain the steep frontier ridge that leads to the Grande Fache. There are sufficient cairns on this western ridge to guide you. Here and there some easy scrambling will be necessary. Stay a little on the right (W) of the ridge and gain a secondary summit (Pointe Lagardère, 2990m). Go down a few metres and climb to the summit of the:

3.30 Grande Fache (3005m). Take the same route on your way back to Refuge Wallon.

DAY 14
Refuge Wallon to Refuge de Bayssellance

On a beautiful day this is a surprisingly easy walk without any real obstacles. A little care is needed on the rough terrain on the steep east side of Col des Mulets.

Route:	via the Col d'Arratille (2528m), the Col des Mulets (2591m) and the Hourquette d'Ossoue (2734m)
Grade:	2
Time:	7hrs 20mins
Height gain:	1400m
Height loss:	615m
Map:	Mapa Excursionista/Carte de Randonnées, 1:50,000, no 24: Gavarnie–Ordesa

0.00 Refuge Wallon. Go down gently E on a path for a few minutes to a junction near the place where the Gave d'Arratille meets the Gave du Marcadau (about 1800m). A signpost indicates the junction. Turn right, cross the Gave du Marcadau by a footbridge and walk through grass to the Gave d'Arratille. Cross the stream by a footbridge and follow the stream as you climb, initially between pine trees and later on a grassy slope, to the Lac d'Arratille. The path bends away from the stream and you climb ESE. After a surprising section where the route climbs in zigzags on large rocks that have been polished by ancient glaciers, the climb eases a little and then climbs in zigzags. Finally the Gave d'Arratille is reached. Cross the stream, and a few moments later you'll see the:
1.35 Lac d'Arratille (2247m). Walk S staying a few metres above the western shore of the lake. From the south side of the lake follow a well-marked path that climbs rather steeply SSE (early in the season snowfields could cause problems). During the ascent the path bends a little to the right and climbs S to the tiny Lac du Col d'Arratille (2501m). Keep the lake below on your right-hand side and go to the:
2.45 Col d'Arratille (2528m, on the French–Spanish border). What comes now is a short walk in the upper section of the

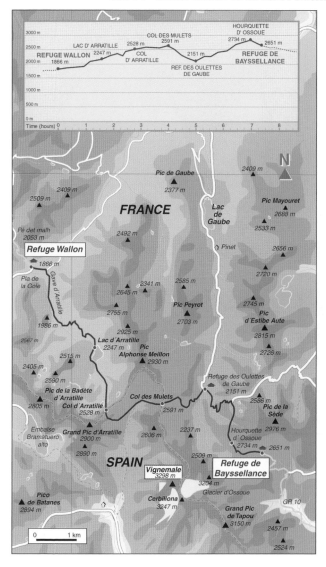

Bivouac at Oulettes de Gaube with a view of Vignemale's north face

Valle de Ara, in Spain. Turn left and walk NE on a more or less level path on the rocky southern slopes of Pic Alphonse Meillon. Finally climb steeply E to the border and reach the: **4.00 Col des Mulets** (2591m), which gives access to the Vallée de Gaube. Go down steeply on the east side of the pass, following paint flashes. Below the pass there is normally a large snowfield (except late summer), but if you follow the waymarks you'll avoid this snowfield, which could make the descent rather precarious. After the steep section go down in zigzags on a slope covered with stones to a bivouac area on the east side of a large bowl, out of which slowly runs the melt-water from the north face of the Vignemale. Go to the:

5.00 Refuge des Oulettes de Gaube (2151m), situated on a bluff and looking towards the famous north face of the Vignemale (3298m, highest summit on the border). The hut has 75 places and is staffed from mid-June until the end of September. Reservation necessary, tel. 05 62 92 62 97. You'll meet the red–white marks of the GR10 at the *refuge*.

Refuge des Oulettes de Gaube is the ideal place from which to admire the famous north face of the Vignemale. What a place to spend the night (bivouac possible and recommended)!

The Haute Route follows the GR10 until Gavarnie. Follow the obvious path that climbs initially S and then E in zigzags to a junction that's indicated by a signpost. Ignore the path that climbs steeply E towards the Col d'Arraillé (2583m, which gives access to the Vallée de Lutour) and climb gently S. The final metres of the climb to Hourquette d'Ossoue are steep and go through loose scree. In early summer you will encounter some snowfields on your way to the Hourquette d'Ossoue, but even then this climb isn't too difficult.

7.00 Hourquette d'Ossoue (2734m).
Go down E on the east side of the pass and walk through a barren landscape to the Refuge de Bayssellance, which can be seen from afar.

One of the summits of the Vignemale's north face, the Petit Vignemale (3032m), can easily be reached from the Hourquette d'Ossoue in less than an hour. Just climb the ridge S, staying a little to the left of it, to the top. Excellent views, especially of the Vallée de Gaube, the glacier d'Ossoue and the summits of the Cirque de Gavarnie.

Climbers on the Glacier d'Ossoue, with Vignemale in the background (3298m)

7.20 Refuge de Bayssellance (2651m, modernised in 2002, re-opened in 2003), the highest staffed mountain-hut of the Pyrenees. There is a guardian in residence from June until the end of September. 58 places, tel. 05 62 92 40 25. Reservation necessary. Nice view on the summits of the Cirque de Gavarnie. Bivouac possible near the *refuge*, but it's not ideal to pitch the tent here. Internet site: http://refuge.bayssellance.free.fr

TEN CLASSIC SUMMITS

2: The Vignemale (3298m) from the Refuge de Bayssellance

Height gain:	750m
Time:	5hrs 30mins; allow 3hrs for the ascent
Grade:	F+

The Vignemale is the highest mountain on the French–Spanish border. It's a mountain with several faces: its west face is a dark massif wall; the north face is a wonderful and impressive grey limestone cirque; and the Vignemale has a glacier-draped east side. In fact the Glacier d'Ossoue is the only ice field in the

Pyrenees that is still intact and has a tongue. The Vignemale is surrounded by a number of valleys that are among the most beautiful in the entire Pyrenees: *Vallée d'Ossoue*, *Vallée de Gaube* and *Valle de Ara*.

Thanks to the Pyrenean enthusiast and eccentric pioneer Count Henry Russell (in full, Count Henry Patrick Russell-Killough) the Vignemale has become a mountain of mythical proportions. Russell (1834–1909), who was born in Toulouse of a French mother and an Irish father, spend a lot of his time in the Pyrenees. He made a large number of new climbs, and wrote several books and articles, but it was his passionate devotion to one single mountain that made him famous: the Vignemale. He climbed the mountain 33 times and spent some 150 nights on the mountain.

In order to stay on or near the Vignemale for several days and nights Russell and his friends carved a number of grottoes. These grottoes still exist: tomorrow on your way down you'll notice the three Grottes Bellevue at about 2400m (one cave for himself, one for a guide and one in case a lady should arrive). Near the Col de Cerbilona (3195m, just above the glacier) there are the three very basic Grottes Russell, and only 17m below the summit lies the so-called Grotte Paradis, which was just for Russell himself.

Russell celebrated the Vignemale in a way that is perhaps hard to understand nowadays: he received friends, held dinner parties, celebrated a mass, built a huge cairn 3m high on the summit (as a result the Vignemale exceeded 3300m) and spent many days and nights on the summit or slopes of the Vignemale (the last time he stayed for 16 days). In Gavarnie, just outside the village, along the road to Gèdre, you'll find a statue of Russell, which only few visitors notice.

This is a climb that contains no major difficulties, but that has to be taken seriously. The Glacier d'Ossoue has lots of crevasses, so you have to take the necessary equipment: crampons, rope, ice axe. The final climb is a modest scramble on a steep slope full of loose rock. Pay attention to climbers ahead of you because there is a real danger of stonefall. Ask the gardian of Refuge de Bayssellance about the condition of the glacier. Especially in late summer there is only a small amount of snow on the glacier.

0.00 Refuge de Bayssellance (2651m). Go down for about 15mins on the obvious path that descends towards Gavarnie until you notice at around 2540m a small path on your right. (It's also possible to continue down to the Grottes Bellevue, 2420m. Just before the grottoes a path marked with cairns branches off to the right and climbs towards the glacier. Past the grottoes you'll soon find a tiny plateau on your left where you can pitch the tent for the night. Water available.) Turn right and follow this more or less level path next to a steep rocky slope. Walk SW towards the glacier, but don't go onto it, as there are a lot of crevasses. Climb

Dawn view from the Col de Cerbilona (3195m)

on rocks SSW, with the glacier on your right, until you find the place where most climbers start their walk on the glacier (usually somewhat to the south of the centre). At first the glacier is very steep, but soon the ascent eases and you climb more gently on an obvious track (sometimes several tracks). Notice the summits of Petit Vignemale (3032m), Pointe Chausenque (3204m) and Piton Carré (3197m) on your right, and walk to the place below the Pique Longue du Vignemale where the final scramble to the top begins. There are some cairns that will lead you to the summit of the:

3.00 Vignemale (3298m). Go back to the glacier and then turn right and follow a track that leads to the Col de Cerbilona (3195m), a broad saddle that offers superb views to the west. Just before arriving at the col you'll notice the three Grottes Russell. Follow the ridge S and gain without any problems the Pic de Cerbilona (3247m). The ridge makes a turn left. Go down E a little and after a short climb reach the Pic Central (3235m). Leave the ridge now and go down to the glacier. Find your way to the main track on the glacier and return to Refuge de Bayssellance. The excursion to the Pic Central will add about 45mins to the walk.

DAY 15
Refuge de Bayssellance to Gavarnie

Route:	via Barrage d'Ossoue (1834m)
Grade:	2
Time:	5hrs 20mins
Height gain:	200m
Height loss:	1485m
Map:	Mapa Excursionista/Carte de Randonnées, 1:50,000, no 24: Gavarnie–Ordesa

The Haute Route follows the GR10 all the way to Gavarnie. An easy walk on a well-worn path. No route-finding difficulties under normal conditions.

0.00 Refuge de Bayssellance. Go down mainly SE on a well-worn path until you see, next to the path on your left-hand side, the so called Grottes de Bellevue (2420m, three man-made primitive shelters cut out of the rock by the pioneer Henry Russell). Past the *cabanes* the path makes a curve to the right. Go down S in zigzags to a bowl in which a few streams, coming from the glacier d'Ossoue, have to be crossed. Go down after a short ascent to another bowl, in which a further few streams are crossed. Continue the descent along a steep rocky slope with the Gave d'Ossoue on your left-hand side until you reach the west side of a large plateau. Cross the Ossoue stream and walk E to the dam on the east side of:

2.00 Barrage d'Ossoue (1834m, bivouac possible on a designated area on your left; simple *cabane* that offers primitive emergency shelter). Cross a footbridge a few metres below the dam and climb gently SSE through grass to:

2.35 Cabane de Lourdes (1947m). Keep the *cabane* a little distance away on your right and cross the Canou stream by a footbridge. The GR10 now follows an almost level path that makes a large curve (N, SE and S) and reaches:

3.20 Cabane de Sausse-Dessus (1900m). Cross a stream by a footbridge and walk on a more or less level path for some time. Go down E, pass the remains of Cabane des Tousaous (1827m) and follow the path that goes down to the road (about 1700m) that links Gavarnie with the Col de

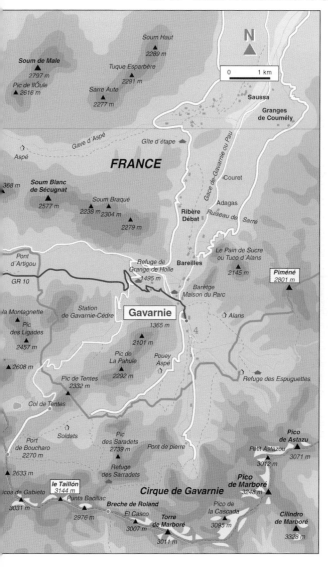

N

0   1 km

Soum de Male
▲
2797 m

Pic de lIÔule
▲ 2616 m

Soum Haut
▲
2289 m

Tuque Esparbère
▲
2291 m

Sarre Aute
▲
2277 m

Saussa

Granges
de Coumély

Gave d'Aspé

Gîte d'étape

Aspé

FRANCE

Couret

Gave de Gavarnie ou Pau

368 m

Soum Blanc
de Sécugnat
▲
2577 m

Soum Braqué
▲ ▲
2238 m 2304 m
▲
2279 m

Ribère
Débat

Adagas

Ruisseau de Sarre

Pont
d'Artigou

GR 10

Refuge de
Grange de Holle
▲
1495 m

Bareilles

Le Pain de Sucre
ou Tuco d'Alans
▲
2145 m

Piméné
▲
2801 m

Ja Montagnette

Pic
des Ligades
▲
2457 m

▲ 2608 m

Station
de Gavarnie-Cédre

Gavarnie
1365 m

Barètge
Maison du Parc

Alans

Pic de
La Pahule
▲
2292 m

▲
2101 m

Pouey
Aspé

Refuge des Espuguettes

Pic de Tentes
2332 m

Col de Tentes

Soldats

Pic
des Saradets
▲
2739 m

Pont de pierre

Petit Astazou
▲
3012 m

Pico
de Astazou
▲
3071 m

Port
de Boucharo
2270 m

▲ 2633 m

Refuge
des Saradets

le Taillón
3144 m

Cirque de Gavarnie

Pico
de Marboré
▲
3248 m

Cilindro
de Marboré
▲
3328 m

icos de Gabieto
▲
3031 m

Punta Bacillac
▲
2976 m

Breche de Roland

El Casco
▲
3007 m

Torre
de Marboré
▲
3011 m

Pico de
la Cascada
▲
3095 m

Looking back to Gavarnie

Boucharo. Turn left and go down this road towards Gavarnie. Notice on your way to the village Refuge de. Grange de Holle (1495m) on the left side of the road (tel. 05 62 92 48 77, owned by de CAF, opened all year except in November, meals available). Pass the *refuge* and its large parking area and pass another parking area on the right side of the road. About 150m past this area, where the road makes a turn left, leave the road. Ignore a signpost indicating Gavarnie and turn right, following the so-called Sentier du Turon des Clots. This obvious path descends gently SE and arrives finally at a junction (signpost; you are now on the path to the Col de Boucharo). Turn left, pass the little church and arrive in the centre of:

5.20 Gavarnie (1365m). Turn right at the next junction (supermarket) in the village and walk through Gavarnie towards the Cirque de Gavarnie. At the south side of the village you'll find the campsite, east of the Gave de Gavarnie. See for practical information on Gavarnie see the introduction to the next section of the route.

TEN CLASSIC SUMMITS

3: Le Taillon (3144m) from Gavarnie

Height gain:	1779m
Time:	10hrs; allow 5hrs 55mins to gain the summit
Grade:	F

Le Taillon is the most westerly summit of the Cirque de Gavarnie. Like all summits of the cirque, Le Taillon exceeds 3000m, but despite its altitude the ascent of Le Taillon presents no real difficulties in good weather. Scenically the route to Le Taillon is spectacular and contains many highlights, such as the famous Brèche de Roland (a gap in the Cirque de Gavarnie), the Grande Cascade and the views from the Plateau de Bellevue on the Cirque de Gavarnie. Theoretically this walk can be accomplished in one day, but it's better to make it a two-day excursion by spending the night at Refuge des Sarradets (reservations essential).

0.00 Campsite south of Gavarnie (1365m). Walk S on the dirt road with the Gave de Gavarnie on your right-hand side. Eventually you arrive at the:

1.00 Hotellerie du Cirque (1570m, close to the Cirque de Gavarnie; it's not a hotel but a bar). Continue towards the Cirque de Gavarnie and cross the river by a footbridge about 100m past the *hotellerie*. Follow a track SW that climbs a little and leads to the base of the cirque. Here the climb to Refuge des Sarradets really begins. Climb very steeply on the so-called Échelle des Sarradets, a sort of natural staircase that is quite impressive but not too difficult to negotiate. At around 2000m the path bends to the left and you climb, still steeply but without difficulty, SW. The route curves around the south slopes of Pic des Sarradets and you'll climb W through a chaotic landscape full of rocky terraces. The route is well marked with cairns and some ancient red marks. Find your way without further problems to:

4.00 Refuge des Sarradets (2587m). Staffed CAF hut with 60 places. Open from May to the end of September; meals available. Overcrowded in summer, reservation essential, tel. 06 83 38 13 24. Bivouac possible a little below the hut, but not ideal. Climb on a steep slope full of stones and scree towards the Brèche de Roland and arrive on a plateau from where the Brèche presents itself in all its glory. Climb on an obvious path through snow (in some years the snow vanishes in late summer, but there is still a small glacier – the Glacier de la Brèche) to the:

4.45 Brèche de Roland (2807m). Don't go down on the Spanish side, but turn right and follow a track W along the vertical walls of the Cirque de Gavarnie. Soon the so-called Le Doigt (*the finger*), a small rock pillar, comes in view. Go to this pillar, go round it on its north (French) side and follow the obvious path W on the east ridge of Le Taillon until you finally arrive at the summit of the:

5.55 Pic du Taillon (3144m). Enjoy the views and return on the same track to:

Cirque de Gavarnie as seen from Le Taillon (3144m)

7.25 Refuge des Sarradets. On the way back to Gavarnie, you take a different path. Follow the path NW that leads to the Col des Sarradets (2589m, classic view from here of the Cirque de Gavarnie and the *refuge*, and a nice view of Le Taillon, its glacier and Le Doigt). Go steeply down in a rocky area and carefully cross the melt-water of the glacier (follow the marks). Soon the path forks (signpost). Turn right, cross the melt-water once again, and go down N steeply on a scree slope. After a long zigzag the stream is crossed once more on a kind of balcony. A series of zigzags bring you finally to the floor of the Vallée de Pouey Aspé (1900m). Cross a stream and reach a junction. Turn right and walk ENE on a lovely track above the valley that descends gently and offers excellent views of the valley. Arrive on a junction at the so-called:

9.00 Plateau de Bellevue (1700m), a plateau that offers superb views on the Cirque de Gavarnie. Don't turn right but follow the path towards Gavarnie, which soon descends in zigzags. Continue N, go down once more in zigzags and walk finally N to the centre of:

10.00 Gavarnie (1365m).

Summits of the Cirque de Gavarnie in winter: Marboré (3248m) and Petit Astazou (3012m)

SECTION 3: GAVARNIE TO SALARDU
The Hard or the Easy Way to Salardu

On the second section of the Haute Route you walked for quite some time through the Parc National des Pyrénées Occidentales. If everything goes according to plan you'll leave the national park for good on the second day of section three, but you may find that you postpone your farewell to the national park, because the second stage is very long and demanding and the Barroude lakes, together with the massive Barroude wall, are one of the most beautiful places in all the Pyrenees to pitch a tent for the night.

The walk from Gavarnie to Salardu is said to be the most difficult part of the Pyrenean Haute Route. This is indeed a very tough section, whch serves the sensational trail Viados – La Soula – Portillon – Renclusa – Hospital de Vielha as the principal dish, where you have to face steep slopes full of scree and rocks, large snowfields and some remains of former glaciers, as well as lots of sections without path and a number of high passes. In fact the Col Inferieur de Literole (2983m) and the Coll de Mulleres (2924m) are the two highest passes of the entire Haute Route! Crampons and ice axe are necessary in early summer, but even in late summer when most of the snow has disappeared from the slopes this mountain gear can be useful.

This guide also offers an alternative to the main route – a **three day-variant** useful as an escape route in bad weather or as an alternative for those who don't want to carry crampons and ice axe all the way to the Mediterranean. This is the GR11 trail from Refugio de Viados to Hospital de Vielha (the route description follows day 24), which presents no major obstacles in summer. On the other hand, do not underestimate this variant, because there is a lot of rough terrain to be negotiated, especially in the Valhibierna region. Collado de Valhibierna is a high pass (2710m), and the walk from the pass to the Valle de Salenques has some steep sections that require care.

The time to make this important decision is at Refugio de Viados, where you arrive in the course of day 18 or 19. Study the main track and the alternative well in advance and consider your options carefully at Viados. Two things are decisive: your ability as a mountain walker in alpine landscapes and the weather forecast for the next couple of days. If weather conditions are favourable and you have what it takes to follow the main track of the Haute Route from Viados to Hospital de Vielha, then the 'easy way' shouldn't be an option. Remember that a choice for the Pyrenean Haute Route is a choice for challenge!

The charm of the main route is not only the fact that it is by far the most challenging section of the Haute Route, but also the remarkable landscapes it passes through. It offers an often frightening and intimidating landscape, an alpine wilderness with numerous 3000m summits, covered with snowfields and remains of former glaciers, enormous boulderfields and a number a high lakes, sometimes with ice floating in them. There are many highlights during this third section of the Haute Route – the view from Viados of the Posets west face; the Portillon region dominated by a dozen 3000m summits; the Lago de Literola, perhaps covered with ice; the beautifully shaped Lac du Milieu and Lac des Isclots filled with green water; and, of course, the snow-covered northern slopes of the Maladeta massif, with Aneto (3404m), the highest summit of the Pyrenees. This third section proves that you don't have to visit one of the national parks to have a splendid walk.

The guide also describes a Haute Route **escape route** at the end of day 21. This route leads to the village of Bagnères-de-Luchon (public transport to Toulouse/ Lourdes/Paris). Also described at the end of day 21 is an **alternative route** that leaves the main route and takes the Valhibierna route (GR11) to the Hospital de Vielha.

It's certainly worth considering taking a day off here and there to climb one or two beautiful summits. In this section the ascents of four **classic summits** are described: Piméné (2801m, day 16), Pic Perdiguère (3222m, day 20), Pico de Aneto (3404m, day 21) and the Montardo (2826m, day 24).

Gavarnie and the Cirque de Gavarnie

In recent times the village of Gavarnie has come to attract enormous amounts of tourists, both daytrippers and trekkers. It's certainly not the village itself that makes Gavarnie worth a visit, for Gavarnie is no more than a long street surrounded by bars, restaurants and souvenir shops. What brings tourists to Gavarnie is the giant natural amphitheatre that lies a few kilometres south of the village – the famous Cirque de Gavarnie. The vertical walls are more than 1500m high; from the valley floor to the top all the summits of the cirque exceed 3000m in altitude; and there are dozens of waterfalls, all relatively small except one – the Grande Cascade (422m), said to be the highest in all of Europe.

The main attraction for tourists in Gavarnie is a visit to the Cirque de Gavarnie, preferably on the back of a horse or mule. The simple walk to the Cirque de Gavarnie takes about an hour. As for trekkers, Gavarnie is an ideal base for a backpacking expedition. Options include the GR10 trail to the Vignemale region; a walk to Refuge des Sarradets to cross the French–Spanish border by the famous gap in the Cirque de Gavarnie, the Brèche de Roland (2807m); an exploration of the Ordesa National Park; or the start of the third section of the Haute Route!

The High Route pays a very brief visit to the Aigües Tortes National Park on day 24

Practical Information

Facilities in Gavarnie

Facilities in the village include Office du Tourisme (at the entrance of the village), Maison du Parc National (information available on the Parc National, especially on the Gavarnie region; there is always a weather forecast for the next few days at the entrance), post office, small supermarket, basic campsite south of the village (direction Cirque de Gavarnie), cash dispenser (beside the Maison du Parc and at the post office), hotels, restaurants, bars and souvenir shops.

There are two fine places for walkers to spend the night in the north section of the village: Gite d'étape Le Gypaete, 45 places, tel. 05 62 92 40 61 and Maison-refuge Jan Da Lo, 35 places, tel. 05 62 92 40 66, fax 05 62 92 40 27.
Gavarnie on the internet: www.gavarnie.com

Public Transport to Gavarnie

Take the Eurostar to Paris Gare du Nord. Take the subway to Gare d'Austerlitz and take the (night-)train to Lourdes. From Lourdes go by bus to Gavarnie. Take the SNCF bus (buy the ticket at the ticket-office in the station) to Luz-Saint-Sauveur (change bus in Pierrefitte-Nestalas), where the bus arrives at the tourist office. A private bus takes you from the office to Gavarnie. Buy the ticket on the bus. *Note:* in summer there are only two buses a day going to Gavarnie.

Facilities in Benasque

Facilities in the village include banks, cash dispensers, post office, supermarkets, souvenir shops, equipment shops, hotels, restaurants, bars and tourist office (weather forecast at the entrance). About 3km north of Benasque there are a few campsites close to the road, the A 139. Camping Aneto is probably the best of these – shady, with good sanitary facilities, washing machines, bar/restaurant, food shop (very expensive) and swimming pool. Maps for sale at reception. Internet: www.campinganeto.com, email: info@camping aneto.com, tel. 974 551 141 and fax 974 561 663.
Benasque on the internet: www.benasque.com

Salardu

For practical information see the introduction to the fourth section of the route.

Food

There are no opportunities to replenish food supplies, except at the end of day 17: at the petrol station close to Meson La Fuen there is some food available. Walkers who take the three-day variant route can buy food at Camping Aneto or perhaps (3km south of the campsite) at Benasque.

Maps
- Mapa Excursionista/Carte de Randonnées, 1:50,000:
- No 22: Pica d'Estats – Aneto
- No 23: Aneto–Posets
- No 24: Gavarnie–Ordesa

Accommodation: Contact Details

All numbers and other information on accommodation on the Haute Route is also given in the route description.

Day 16: Héas – Auberge de la Munia (05 62 92 48 39); Auberge Le Refuge (05 62 92 47 74)

Day 17: Refuge de Barroude (05 62 39 61 10); Meson La Fuen (974 501 047 or 974 501 170)

Day 18: Refugio de Viados – 974 506 082 or 974 506 163

Day 19: Refuge de la Soula – 05 62 99 68 40

Day 20: Refuge du Portillon – 05 61 79 38 15

Day 21: Refugio de la Renclusa – 974 552 106 (hut) or 974 551 490 (guardian)

Day 22: Hospital de Vielha – (tel. and fax) 973 697 052

Day 23: Refugi de la Restanca – 608 036 559; internet: www.restanca.com

Day 24: Salardu – Xalet Soler i Santalo (973 645 016) Refugi Rosta (973 645 308, fax 973 645 814)

Dawn view of the Cirque de Gavarnie from Espuguettes

DAY 16
Gavarnie to Héas

Route:	via the Hourquette d'Alans (2430m)
Grade:	2
Time:	6hrs 45mins
Height gain:	1150m
Height loss:	1000m
Map:	Mapa Excursionista/Carte de Randonnées, 1:50,000, no 24: Gavarnie–Ordesa

An easy walk on well-worn paths, with no route-finding difficulties under normal weather conditions. The final part is on road. The route provides excellent views of the Cirque de Gavarnie and a passing acquaintance with a lesser known cirque – the Cirque d'Estaubé.

0.00 Gavarnie (1365m). From the campsite south of the village follow the dirt road S on the east side of the Gave de Gavarnie. Ignore a path coming from the left and turn left after about 500m, just before a building (a signpost indicates 'Refuge des Espuguettes'), and climb an obvious track SE that soon enters the Arribama forest. Climb in zigzags until a junction near the border of the Parc National, just outside the forest, on the Plateau de Pailla. Turn left and climb in an open field towards the Refuge des Espuguettes, which is now visible. It's possible to climb in a straight line ENE to the *refuge*, but the ancient track (rather vague in places) climbs more gently, turns N and then ESE to arrive at the:

2.00 Refuge des Espuguettes (2027m), owned by the Parc National, 60 places, meals available, staffed from mid-June until the end of September, tel: 05 62 92 40 63. From here there are fine views of the Cirque de Gavarnie and the famous Brèche de Roland. Climb generally E in zigzags on a well-worn path until the path forks at 2260m. Ignore the path that climbs to the Piméné (2801m) (the route to Piméné summit is described at the end of this walk) and climb SE to the:

3.15 Hourquette d'Alans (2430m), which gives access to the Vallée d'Estaubé. Go down in short zigzags on the east side of the col (ignore a path on your right-hand side after a few zigzags) on an obvious path until the path forks at about 2160m. Ignore the path that goes SE to the Port Neuf de

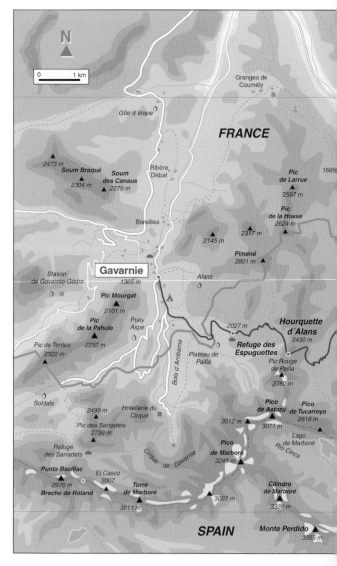

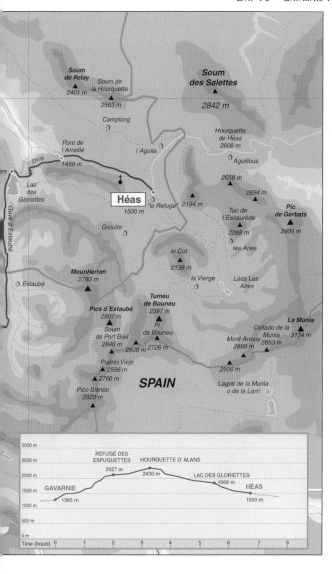

143

Refuge des Espuguettes and the Cirque de Gavarnie

Pinède and go down NE to the floor of the Vallée d'Estaubé. Stay left of the Gave d'Estaubé, leave the Parc National, and go gently down to the:

5.30 Lac des Gloriettes. Pass the dammed lake along its western shore and go down to the parking area below the dam. Go down NE on a small road (D 176) to the Pont de l'Arraillé (1459m), where you'll meet the D 922. Cross the stream, turn right (large Parc National information board) and walk SE for 2.2km on the road, which climbs a few metres, to the hamlet of Héas (1500m). Notice after 1.5km on your left La Chaumière, a bar with a small campsite (not very attractive – it's better to continue to Héas). In Héas it's possible to spend the night at Auberge de la Munia, 10 places, meals available, tel. 05 62 92 48 39. There is a small campsite called Le Cairn next to the auberge. Héas has no shops, just a few houses and a chapel. Walk through Héas and follow the road for some 300m to arrive at:

6.45 Auberge Le Refuge (simple accommodation, meals available, 20 places in a barn, open from June until October, tel: 05 62 92 47 74). Ask at Le Refuge if it's possible to pitch your tent.

TEN CLASSIC SUMMITS

4: Piméné (2801m) from Refuge des Espuguettes

Height gain: 787m

Time: 4hrs 15mins; allow 2hrs 15mins to the summit

Grade: F

Without doubt the Piméné offers one of the finest views in all the Pyrénées. It is not that the Piméné is high – its 2801m is rather modest in comparison with the many 3000m summits in the Gavarnie region – but it is the position of this mountain that makes it so special. Its place on the ridge separating the Vallée de Gavarnie from the Vallée d'Estaubé means that views from the summit are absolutely top class – including the cirques of both Gavarnie and Estaubé, the Monte Perdido (3355m) in the Ordesa National Park, the summits of the Cirque de Troumouse, the long, stretched valley of Gavarnie, the Pic Long (3192m) and other peaks in the Néouvielle region. Above all you can draw a straight line through the Vallée d'Ossoue towards the glacier-draped east face of the Vignemale (3298m).

This is an easy climb that contains no difficulties in summer. The final section is rather steep and requires a little care.

0.00 Refuge des Espuguettes (2027m). Follow the Haute Route trail to the Hourquette d'Alans until the path forks (2260m). Turn left and climb on a clear path in a number of long zigzags to the:
1.25 Col du Piméné (2522m). Follow a track through scree on the east side of the ridge and go around the Petit Piméné (2667m). Gain the ridge once again north of the Petit Piméné and climb steeply N on the ridge until you finally reach the:
2.15 Piméné (2801m). Follow the same track on your way back to the *refuge*.

Early morning view from Espuguettes on the Vignemale (ascent of the Piméné)

DAY 17
Héas to Parzan

A very long, exhausting walk, which in summer, when snowfields have disappeared, presents no real difficulties. It's a splendid walk, the last (partly) within the boundaries of the Parc National. Considering the length of today's walk, it might be a good idea to divide it in two. The Barroude lakes are a magical place to spend the night.

Route:	via the Hourquette de Héas (2608m), the Hourquette de Chermentas (2439m) and the Port de Barroude (2535m)
Grade:	1
Time:	9hrs 30mins
Height gain:	1500m
Height loss:	1600m
Map:	Mapa Excursionista/Carte de Randonnées, 1:50,000, no 24: Gavarnie–Ordesa

0.00 Héas. Just before Auberge Le Refuge (signpost) follow the path that climbs SE through the Vallon de Touyères to arrive after a minute at a junction. Turn left and climb gently NNE, then follow numerous zigzags on an obvious path. Notice a *prise d'eau* (with a footbridge on your left at 1750m) and climb, always staying on the right of the stream, to a small plateau in which the Ruisseau de l'Aguila flows. Ignore another footbridge (1880m) and on the other side of the stream you'll find the:

1.15 Cabane de l'Aguila (1900m), a basic but useful shelter with six places. Keep the stream on your left-hand side and pass the little Oratoire de Sainte-Famille. The path enters the Parc National, makes a turn to the right and climbs E a little way from the Aguillous stream. The path climbs in a number of zigzags and meets this stream on a small plateau. Notice Cabane d'Aguillous (2320m, useful but sometimes occupied by a shepherd) on the other side of the stream. Cross the Ruisseau d'Aguillous and climb E towards the ridge that hides the Hourquette de Héas. The path makes a number of zigzags and finally reaches the:

3.15 Hourquette de Héas (2608m), a well-hidden pass on the Crête (= *ridge*) des Aguillous. Go down NE carefully on the steep east side of the col. At 2450m the path forks. Don't turn left but continue to go down to approximately 2300m and climb E to the:

On the Hourquette de Héas (2604m)

4.00 Hourquette de Chermentas (2439m), where Refuge de Barroude is indicated. Go down on the east side of the pass for a short time and climb along the impressive rock faces of the Pic d'Aguillous (2851m). The path bends around the Pic d'Aguillous and reaches a junction (notice Pic de Gerbats on your right). Don't turn left but climb gently SE on an obvious path along the large Barroude wall and arrive at:

5.15 Refuge de Barroude (2373m), situated on a bluff and overlooking the largest of the two Lacs de Barroude. The hut is owned by the Parc National and has 30 places (of which 10 are in a tent). The hut is staffed from mid-June until mid-September, meals available. Reservation necessary, tel. 05 62 39 61 10. Bivouac possible near the lake. Follow the path that leads you to the east side of the lake. Cross a stream and climb S on a path that brings you to the:

6.00 Port de Barroude (2535m), on the French–Spanish border. Descend on the south side of the large pass to the floor of the Valle de Barrosa. Try to find the path that goes down in a few short zigzags. Then the descent eases somewhat and you go down SE. There isn't always an obvious path, but cairns and a few ancient red marks will guide you. The path eventually bends to the right and goes down S to the floor of the valley. Cross a stream, notice a *cabane* on your right (very basic, not useful) and finally reach the main stream in

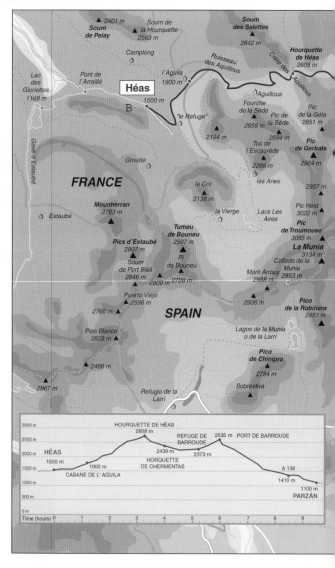

148

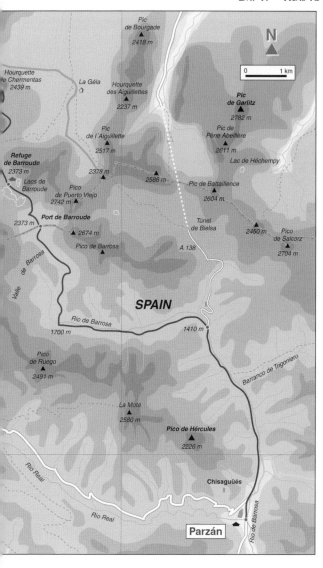

N

0   1 km

Pic
de Bourgade
2418 m

*Hourquette
le Chermentas
2439 m*

La Géla

*Hourquette
des Aiguillettes*
2237 m

***Pic
de Garlitz***
2782 m

Pic de
Pène Abeillère
2611 m

Pic
de l'Aiguillette
2517 m

Lac de Héchempy

***Refuge
de Barroude***
2373 m

2378 m

2586 m

Pic de Bataillence
2604 m

*Lacs de
Barroude*

Pico
de Puerto Viejo
2742 m

Port de Barroude
2373 m

Túnel
de Bielsa

2450 m

Pico
de Salcorz
2704 m

2674 m

A 138

Valle de Barrosa

Pico de Barrosa

SPAIN

Rio de Barrosa

1410 m

1700 m

Pico
de Ruego
2491 m

Barranco de Trigoniero

La Mota
2580 m

Pico de Hércules
2226 m

Rio Real

Chisagüés

Rio Real

Parzán

Rio de Barrosa

A dreamer's delight: Lac de Barroude and the Barroude wall

the valley, the Rio de Barrosa. Cross the stream (around 1700m), turn left and follow an obvious path E with the stream on your left-hand side. Eventually the path turns into a dirt road, which you follow E to the:

8.30 A 138 (1410m), the road that links de Valle de Bielsa (Spain) with the Vallée d'Aure (France) through the Bielsa tunnel. Turn right and walk SSE on the road for 5km. The road goes down gently. Notice on your way to Parzan an ancient customs house (1290m) and a power station (1200m), and take a look at the dirt road that leads to the Lago de Urdiceto (tomorrow's walk) after 3.5km. Don't turn right to the hamlet of Parzan, but walk on the A 138 to:

9.30 Meson La Fuen (hotel/bar/restaurant, 1100m), on the west side of the road, tel. 974 501 047 or 974 501 170 (certainly not the most attractive place to spend the night). Just before Meson La Fuen, on the other side of the road, there is a petrol station, with a bar/restaurant (not bad) and a shop (the Bodega, better than you might expect). Bielsa is another 2km along the road.

Parzan: no shops, but rooms may be available at Maria Lueros Ferrer, tel. 974 501 124.

DAY 18
Parzan to Refugio de Viados

Route:	via the Paso de los Caballos (2326m)
Grade:	2
Time:	7hrs 15mins
Height gain:	1500m
Height loss:	860m
Map:	Mapa Excursionista/Carte de Randonnées, 1:50,000, no 23: Aneto–Posets

0.00 Parzan. Climb N on the A 138 and turn right after 1.5km, before the Barrosa power station. Cross the Rio Barrosa and climb SE, then ENE on a dirt road, keeping the Barranco de Urdiceto below on your right-hand side. Take a short-cut before reaching the Urdiceto power station and continue climbing the dirt road for about 1km. Take a track on the right side of the dirt road, just before the dirt road climbs steeply in zigzags, and climb to the:

3.30 Paso de los Caballos (2326m). Leave the dirt road that climbs to the Lago de Urdiceto and walk E above the deep gully of the Barranco de la Solana, north of the multi-coloured Punta Suelza (2974m), until the path bends to the

Today the Haute Route follows the GR11 all day, so there are no route-finding difficulties. Unfortunately the climb to the Paso de los Caballos (11km on dirt road) is very disappointing. However, the second half of the walk leads through interesting landscapes, and the end of the day is perfect: a superb view from Refugio de Viados of the impressive west face of Pico de Posets (3375m), the second highest summit in the Pyrenees. An important decision has to be made at Viados – whether to leave the Haute Route for the three-day variant to Hospital de Vielha (see end of day 24).

Refugio de Viados and the Posets west face

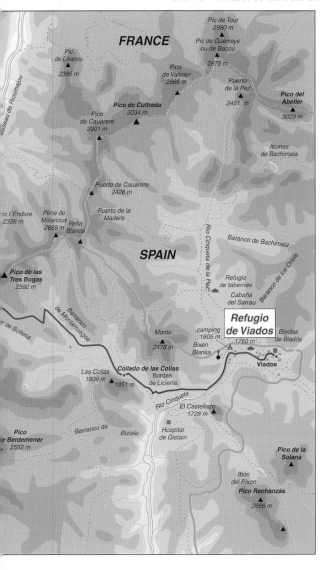

left. Go down to the valley through which the Barranco de Montarruegos runs. Cross the stream (2000m), turn right and follow the path SE that bends away from the stream and goes up and down a little. Notice a primitive *cabane* on your right on a hill and follow a quite new dirt road (that has unfortunately replaced the old track) to:

5.15 Collado de las Collas (1851m). Follow the dirt road that goes down in zigzags, keeping a *cabane* on your right-hand side, and walk to the Bordas de Licierte (1720m). Turn left and go down E to a junction in the Valle de Gistain (1540m, signpost GR11). Turn left and climb very gently NE for 1.3km (until Camping Forcallo) on a dirt road, keeping the Rio Cinqueta that runs through the valley on your right-hand side. After the building belonging to the Campamento Virgin Blanca (a holiday camp for children) and north of the place where the Rio Cinqueta de la Pez and the Rio Cinqueta de Anes Cruses meet (and thus form the Rio Cinqueta), cross the Rio Cinqueta de la Pez and arrive at:

6.45 Camping Forcallo (1580m, small, good facilities, bar, meals sometimes available if ordered well in advance), which is open in July and August. There's a choice of routes past the campsite. *Option 1:* Follow the dirt road until it forks, turn right and follow the dirt road all the way to Refugio de Viados. *Option 2:* Leave the dirt road past the campsite. Take a short-cut and arrive at the dirt road again. Take another much longer short-cut, notice a barn on your right and climb to the dirt road. Cross the dirt road once more and climb between pine trees to the back of:

7.15 Refugio de Viados (1760m, also called Biados or Biadors), private property. Staffed from mid-June until the last week of September, 70 places, meals available. Reservation necessary, tel. 974 506 082 or 974 506 163. Bivouac not allowed near the hut. Pleasant atmosphere in the *refugio* and a great view of the Posets west face.

DAY 19
Refugio de Viados to Refuge de la Soula

Route:	via the Port d'Aygues Tortes (2683m, also called Col Supérieur d'Aygues Tortes)
Grade:	1
Time:	6hrs 30mins
Height gain:	1000m
Height loss:	1070m
Map:	Mapa Excursionista/Carte de Randonnées, 1:50,000, no 23: Aneto–Posets

0.00 Refugio de Viados. Go down a few metres in front of the *refugio*, cross a stream and take the GR11 trail that climbs gently E along the Granjas de Viados (a number of barns). The large track soon turns into a path and arrives at a junction (signpost). Don't turn right (to Collado de Eriste and Refugio Angel Orus) but turn left and follow the path that turns to the valley of the Rio d'Añes Cruses. Stay left of the stream and climb NE gently staying high above the stream.

The route has recently been altered between Viados and the place where three streams meet and form the Rio Cinqueta d'Añes Cruses. There used to be a short steep section, the path used to pass close to the stream and several small ravines had to be crossed. Now the path stays well above the stream at all times and there are no awkward sections. My compliments to the GR11 workers responsible for these changes!

Eventually you'll notice a quite new *cabana* (shepherds' hut) on a bluff ahead of you. Go around this bluff on the right with the stream below in a deep gully and go down a few metres to the place where:

After an easy start on the GR11, there is a long section without path and waymarks. The climb to the Port d'Aygues Tortes is not too difficult under normal summer conditions. After a steep descent on the French side of the pass an easy walk through the Vallon d'Aygues Tortes leads to Refuge de la Soula. There is a three-day variant (see end of day 24) that avoids all the difficulties of the Haute Route's main track over the next four days.

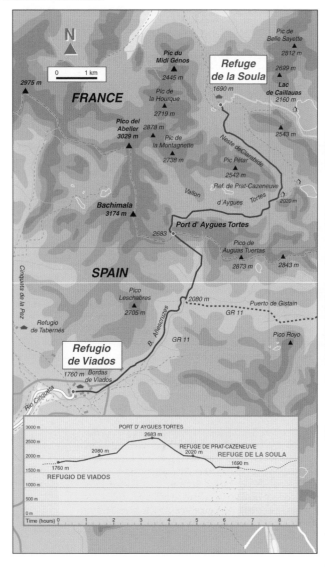

Sign on Refugio de Viados

1.30 three streams meet and thus form the Rio Cinqueta d'Añes Cruses (2080m, signpost). Notice an old *cabane* on your left in a field where sheep are often gathered. Cross the stream coming from the west, and the one coming from the north, and leave the GR11. From now on until the Port d'Agues Tortes there is no path and there are just a few cairns to guide you. Climb on a grassy slope NNE with a stream on your left-hand side. Beyond a small cascade in the stream and a short section of rocks you arrive at a small plateau. Keep right of the stream and turn left at the northern end of the plateau. Stay very close to the stream and climb steeply NW through scree. Cross the stream several times and climb NW on the right side of the stream (the Haute Route bends a little away from the stream) on a steep slope. Pass a tiny tarn and arrive at the:

3.25 Port d'Aygues Tortes (2683m), on the French–Spanish border. There is something like a path, marked with cairns, on the French side, but it may take some time to find it! Go down NNE in zigzags through scree on a very steep slope

You won't see them as you walk through the Vallon d'Aygues Tortes, but north of the path, a little higher, are a number of small lakes: the Lacs d'Aygues Tortes. There is no path leading to them, but for Haute Route walkers it wouldn't be difficult to find them. The largest lake, especially, is an excellent place to pitch the tent for the night. Recommended for walkers who prefer a *bivouac solitaire*!

Shepherd surrounded by sheep (confluence of three streams, 2080m)

until the floor of the Vallon d'Aygues Tortes is reached. Turn right and walk E through the valley, keeping a stream on your left-hand side.

Beyond a small dam in the stream, the path bends a little to the right. Walk through the south side of a plateau and go down a few metres to arrive at a small plateau at: **4.50 Refuge de Prat-Cazeneuve** (2020m), an unstaffed, solid *cabane* with eight places (sometimes used by a shepherd). Past the hut the path forks. Don't turn right (this path climbs to the Lac de Pouchergues) but go down in the valley, still on the right side of the stream. Notice a small cascade in the stream (here the descent is somewhat steeper), cross another stream and walk NW through the narrow valley of the Neste (= *river*) de Clarabide, surrounded by impressive steep slopes. Keep the stream on your left-hand side and follow a trail that goes up and down, cross several small plateaux and finally go down between pine trees to:
6.30 Refuge de la Soula (1690m), next to a power station. 60 places, staffed from June until the end of September, tel. 05 62 99 68 40. Bivouac possible near the hut. Certainly not the most attractive place to spend the night.

DAY 20
Refuge de la Soula
to Refuge du Portillon

Route:	via the Col des Gourgs-Blancs (2877m) and the Tusse de Montarqué (2889m)
Grade:	E
Time:	6hrs 15mins
Height gain:	1300m
Height loss:	430m
Map:	Mapa Excursionista/Carte de Randonnées, 1:50,000, no 23: Aneto–Posets

Snowfields, steep scree slopes, some sections on boulders and a few high passes make today's walk tough. The final section is very difficult and dangerous in bad weather. It leads to an impressive and remarkable alpine landscape with numerous 3000m summits.

0.00 Refuge de la Soula. Climb NE on a well-worn path. Pass a *cabane* and climb towards a narrow valley. The path bends a little to the right and climbs in numerous zigzags SE above the left of the stream coming from the Lac de Caillauas. Near the end of the climb to the lake, the path forks. Keep preferably left (the other path also leads to the lake) and climb to the lake. You'll arrive at the north side of the dam of the:

1.30 Lac de Caillauas (2160m). Cross the dam, climb a few metres and walk around the south side of the lake among alpenrose on a small path, staying about 20m above the water level. Beyond the lake you'll arrive at a small valley. Cross the stream coming down from the Lac des Isclots and climb E on a path marked with cairns that bends away from the stream. Arrive at the:

2.30 Lac des Isclots (2398m; *isclots* means 'tiny islands'). The lake is filled with icy water coming from the glacier of the Gourgs-Blancs; the water has a remarkable soft green colour. An excellent place to spend the night. Walk along the northern shore of the lake and climb on an obvious path SE to the:

2.55 Lac du Milieu (2510m). Cross a stream just before the Lac du Milieu and walk along the south side of the lake. Past the lake climb SE on rocky terrain and arrive at a tiny lake.

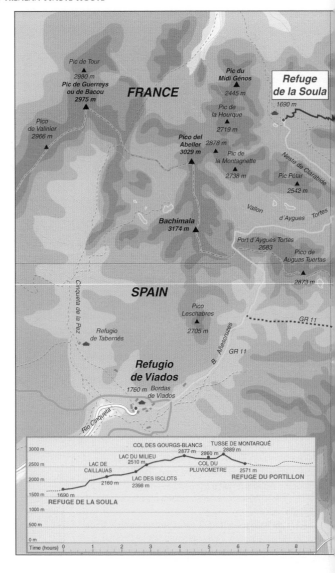

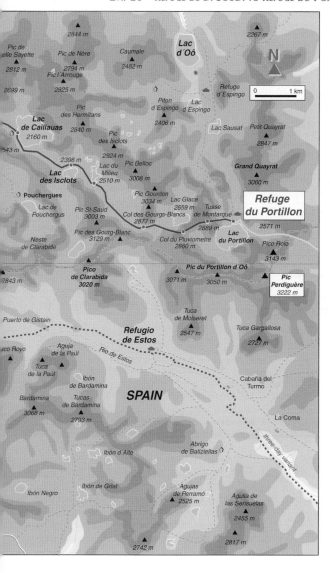

Walker near the Col du Pluviomètre (Pic des Gourgs Blancs in the background, 3129m)

Keep this lake on your left-hand side and climb SE on a very steep scree slope (the route is well cairned and therefore easy to find) towards the glacier of the Gourgs-Blancs, which is normally covered with snow. Due to the enormous amount of rocks on the ice, this glacier looks rather intimidating. Stay on the northern side of the glacier and climb gently through snow, ice and scree to the Col des Gourgs-Blancs, which is visible ahead of you.

4.10 Col des Gourgs-Blancs (2877m), a large pass between the Gourgs-Blancs (3129m) and pic Gourdon (3034m). The steep east side of the pass could be covered with snow, but in August there is probably only a small snowfield just below the col. Go down steeply and walk on boulders E high towards the south side of the Lac Glacé du Port d'Oo (2659m), which lies deep below in a bowl. Climb on boulders and on a large snowfield SE, staying high above the lake, to the:

5.00 Col du Pluviomètre (2860m), so called because of the rain gauge a few metres above the pass. Go down carefully NE on boulders to a pass (2795m) and climb (here and there a vague track, with a few cairns) to the:

5.30 Tusse de Montarqué (2889m). The summit is, in fact, a large plateau. Walk N on this plateau and find an obvious path that goes down E. This surprisingly easy descent ends at:

6.15 Refuge du Portillon (2571m, also called Refuge Jean-Arlaud), a modern hut situated near the dam of Lac du Portillon. 80 places, meals available, staffed from mid-June until mid-September, tel. 05 61 79 38 15. The hut is owned by the CAF. Bivouac possible a little distance from the hut. The rocky terrain is, however, not ideal for camping.

162

TEN CLASSIC SUMMITS

5: Pic Perdiguère (3222m) from Refuge du Portillon

Height gain: 642m

Time: 4hrs 30mins; allow 2hrs 30mins to reach the summit of Pic Perdiguère

Grade: F+

Pic Perdiguère is the highest of all the summits in the so-called Cirque du Portillon and therefore makes an obvious goal. Needless to say, due to its altitude and its position on the French–Spanish border Pic Perdiguère offers superb views: Lac du Portillon, all summits that form the Cirque du Portillon, valle de Estos and Pico de Posets, Pic Schrader (3177m, in the west) and the Maladeta massif. It's a rough climb through scree, boulders and snowfields.

This route is technically not difficult, but there is a lot of rough terrain to be tackled: slopes full of scree and boulders. The Vallon de Literole is normally covered with snow. In August it's possible to go around the snow (crampons and ice axe not needed), but usually the amount of snow is such that crampons and ice axe will be necessary.

0.00 Refuge du Portillon (2570m). Cross the dam of the Lac du Portillon. At the east side of the dam you'll find a path that climbs on a steep slope above the lake. Follow the path that leads to the Col Inférieur de Literole until the path forks. Turn right, go down a few metres on boulders and follow a line of cairns that climb gently SSW until you finally reach the floor of the Vallon de Literole. Turn left and climb steeply through scree, on boulders and possibly on snowfields ESE to a pass on the frontier, the:

2.00 Col Supérieur de Literole (3049m). Don't cross the border but turn right and climb steeply SSW (initially very steeply – care needed especially on the way down) on the ridge or a little to the right of it, to the summit of:

2.30 Pic Perdiguère (3222m). Adventurous walkers may be tempted to go down to the Col Supérieur de Literole and from there to climb N to the Tuca de Literole (3095m, secondary summit). Continue to climb on the ridge to Pico Royo (3121m), which should be reached without any problems. Continue to follow the ridge N as it becomes narrow and go over the Pointe de Literole (3132m) before going down to the Aiguille de Literole (3028m). Take great care on the very narrow Literole ridge! Don't follow the ridge all the way to the Col Inférieur de Literole, but leave it near the Aiguille de Literole. Go down steeply on a rocky slope and walk to the snowfield below the Col Inférieur de Literole (2983m). Turn left and go down W on the snowfield and then steeply through a slope full of rocks and loose scree (enough cairns to guide you). Eventually, find a vague track that leads you to the dam of the Lac du Portillon. This excursion (grade: F+) will take about an hour extra, but it's worth it!

DAY 21
Refuge du Portillon
to Refugio de la Renclusa

Rough alpine landscapes, snowfields and the highest pass of the whole traverse make this a difficult stage. Only experienced mountain walkers should walk from Portillon to Renclusa. In poor visibility route-finding problems are inevitable, especially in the uncompromising landscapes between Col Inférieur de Literole and the floor of the Valle de Remune. The east side of the Col Inférieur de Literole is very steep and always covered with snow. Until early summer ice axe and crampons are necessary. Recently only a tiny →

Route:	via the Col Inférieur de Literole (2983m)
Grade:	E
Time:	7hrs
Height gain:	900m
Height loss:	1330m
Map:	Mapa Excursionista/Carte de Randonnées, 1:50,000, no 23: Aneto–Posets

0.00 Refuge du Portillon. Cross the dam, turn right and walk a few metres along the lake. Turn left and climb steeply E on a small track marked with cairns. After a steep section through loose scree climb gently and without difficulty on a large snowfield to the:

1.15 Col Inférieur de Literole (2983m, on the French–Spanish border; the highest pass of the Haute Route). Go down carefully on the steep east side of the pass, which is probably covered with snow. Notice a tiny icy pool on your right (below), stay well above the large Lago de Literola and climb on rocks and snowfields to the ridge that separates the Valle de Remune from the Valle de Literola. Continue walking SE on rocks and snowfields, skirting the Forca de Remune (2945m) and arrive at a large pass:

2.15 Portal de Remune (2831m). Go down E through a chaotic granite wilderness towards the Pico de Remune. At an altitude of about 2600m the Haute Route bends to the left. Go down NNE, initially on boulders, later on a steep scree slope and arrive at the floor of the Valle de Remune in the:

3.00 Circo de Remune (2400m, tiny tarn, stream). Turn right and follow the right bank of the stream. Initially the stream flows through a narrow gorge, surrounded by steep rocky slopes. Cross carefully a few boulders and then cross the stream. The Valle de Remune then opens out and you go down gently ESE on an obvious path that follows (sometimes at a little distance) the left bank of the main stream. Cross a small plateau with a tiny lake at 2200m, and shortly after passing this plateau look out for where the path is marked with two red paint flashes. At 2130m a few streams coming from the left are crossed and at 1900m you reach a plateau, shortly before entering a pine forest. The track bends away for good from the main stream. Go down in the forest until you arrive at the:

4.45 road coming from Benasque (1800m) that ends here. Turn left and follow the road to about 70m from its end. Turn right, spot the foundations of few buildings on your right and go down in the Valle de Esera on a vague path. Cross a few side-streams and go NE through the valley with the Rio Esera on your right-hand side. Cross three streams on the marshy plateau by a footbridge and cross the Rio Esera by the fourth footbridge. Cross another footbridge and arrive at Hospital de Benasque (1760m), a large building, hotel/bar/restaurant, open all year, tel. 974 551 052; not really a place for walkers

← snowfield has remained in late summer (August), though crampons could still be useful. An escape route from the Refugio de la Renclusa, and a variant route for those who want to avoid the Coll de Mulleres (day 22), are also described.

Lac du Portillon

165

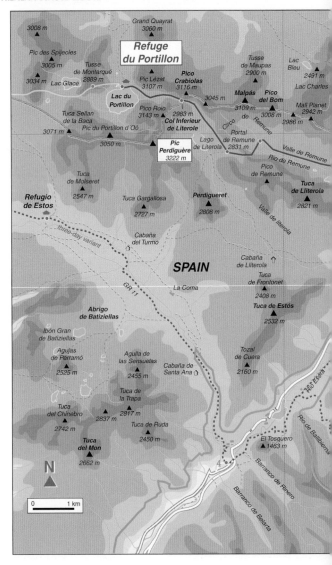

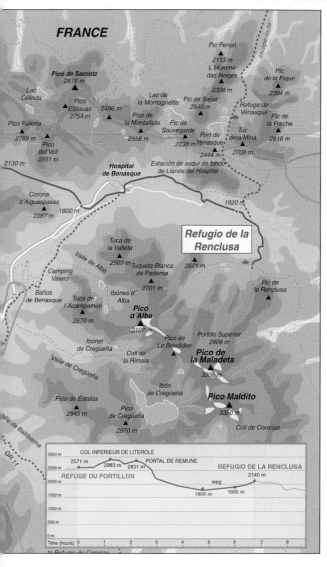

Looking down on Lago de Literola

to stay. (This is the starting point of the variant avoiding Coll de Mulleres, described below.) Don't go to the building and don't cross the river, but follow the stream to the right (yellow–white marks: you are now on the Sendero Geomorfologico de Aiguallut) for a few moments. Cross the stream again, follow the path between the stream and a stone wall and recross the Rio Esera by another footbridge. Turn right on a junction (signpost; take the path to La Besurta) and climb in zigzags on a path that enters a pine forest. The path climbs gently in the small forest and the landscape soon opens. Pass a small marshy plateau on the left and arrive soon at a much larger plateau: Plan d'Estan (1865m, indicated). Keep the plateau on your right and turn right at a junction (signpost). A few minutes later you reach the small road that runs through the Valle de Esera. Turn left, notice a shepherds' hut on your right after 100m (there is a rather faint path with yellow–white marks, starting past the *cabane*, that leads in a few minutes to the place where the road ends, so if you want, you can avoid the tarmac) and climb the road for around 15mins to the:

6.00 place where the road ends (1920m, La Besurta). Pass a bar, cross a side-stream and climb S between pine trees on a well-worn path. Cross a stream and arrive soon at a junction.

> For walkers who don't want to climb the Aneto and pre-
> fer to spend the night in the tent, it makes no sense to
> go to Refugio de la Renclusa. Turn left at the junction
> and follow tomorrow's route to the large plateau of
> Aiguallut. There are some good sites to be found on the
> east side of the plateau.

At the junction turn right and climb in zigzags to:
6.45 Refugio de la Renclusa (2140m, CEC owned), a logical base for the climb to the highest summit of the Pyrenees: Pico de Aneto (3404m). 110 places, overcrowded in August, meals available, staffed from the end of June to the end of September, reservation necessary, tel. 974 552 106 or 974 551 490. For years work has been in progress at Renclusa. The situation around the hut is rather depressing.

On the summit of Pic Perdiguère (3222m), with a view of the Posets (3375m)

TEN CLASSIC SUMMITS

6: Pico de Aneto (3404m) from Refugio de la Renclusa

Height gain: 1264m

Time: 7hrs 30mins; allow 4hrs for the ascent

Grade: F+

Pico de Aneto is the highest mountain in the Pyrenees, which explains why so many walkers try to reach the summit each summer. Refugio de la Renclusa makes a logical base for the ascent. In summer this hut is overcrowded, so it's essential to make a reservation. Make a very early start (about an hour before dawn) to make sure that you don't meet too many other walkers on their way to Pico de Aneto.

This climb contains no major difficulties, but it has to be taken seriously nonetheless. There is a rough climb to Portillon Superior, with a lot of boulders to tackle, and a long walk on the Aneto glacier (crampons, ice axe and rope needed). Close to the summit the so-called Puente de Mahoma has to be crossed: a very narrow horizontal ridge of about 30m. Not difficult, but it might be intimidating for walkers who suffer from vertigo.

0.00 Refugio de la Renclusa (2140m). Climb S on a path that is marked with an abundance of cairns. Sometimes there seems to be more than one path, but it doesn't matter which path you follow. To ensure that you go in the right direction, keep the Portillon ridge on your left-hand side. Don't go all the way to the Portillon Inférior (2745m), but climb SSW to an obvious gap in the Portillon ridge: **2.00 the Portillon Superior** (2908m), which offers fine views on Pico de Aneto. Go through the gap, go down a few metres and climb SSE on boulders and/or snowfields to reach the Aneto glacier (in early summer covered with snow; later in summer some parts of the glacier are snow-free). Keep climbing in the same direction (in late summer, when there's only a small amount of snow on the glacier, the safest way is to climb SSW in the direction of Pico Maldito and then to walk SE, close to the ridge, until you arrive at the Collado de Coronas), continuing on an obvious track to arrive at the:
3.15 Collado de Coronas (3196m). Climb a steep snow-slope until the climb eases somewhat, take off the crampons, and continue on until you arrive at the Puente de Mahoma, very close to the summit. Take care on this narrow ridge and finally walk to the summit of the:
4.00 Pico de Aneto (3404m), which has been decorated with a giant cross and all sorts of ornaments. Follow the same track on your way down.

Haute Route escape route
From Refugio de la Renclusa to Bagnères-de-Luchon

Grade:	2
Time:	4hrs 30mins; add 2hrs 20mins for the walk to Bagnères de Luchon
Height gain:	550m
Height loss:	1300m
Map:	Mapa Excursionista/Carte de Randonnées, 1:50,000, no 23: Aneto–Posets

A useful track for unfortunate walkers who have to go home. This is an easy route without any major obstacles in summer. Snowfields tend to last a long time on the steep northern slopes of the Port de Vénasque (sometimes until the end of June). Route finding is simple, and there are magnificent views of the north side of the Maladeta massif and a lovely walk along the Vénasque lakes.

0.00 Refugio de la Renclusa. Return to floor of the Esera valley. For a few minutes follow the road that goes down until you see a signpost that indicates the route to the Port de Venasque (Portillon de Benas) on your right (the first part of this route is not indicated on the map). Leave the road. Turn right and climb on an obvious path N. The path soon forks. Don't turn left (Ruta Hipica, white–yellow marks) but climb in zigzags N to a plateau that offers fine views of the Maladeta massif. The path forks on the plateau. Turn left and climb gently NW on an obvious path. The climb becomes a little steeper as you come closer to a small gap in the frontier ridge, the:

2.30 Port de Vénasque (2444m). Go down N in a number of zigzags and follow the path that descends to the Refuge de Vénasque, situated next to one of the so-called Boums (= *small, deep lake*) du Port de Vénasque. The hut (2250m) is owned by the CAF. 15 places in the hut; 15 in a tent. The hut is overcrowded in summer and a reservation is essential, tel. 05 61 79 26 46 (*refuge*) or 05 65 22 38 83 (*guardian*). Bivouac not allowed near the hut, but close to the highest lake. Go down in zigzags on an obvious path, cross a minor stream and work your way down to the main stream. Cross it and go down N in a long series of zigzags until you finally arrive at a junction. Ignore the *chemin de l'impératrice* that branches off to the left, cross a bridge and go down to the buildings of the:

4.30 Hospice de France (1385m). Turn left and walk to a parking area. From here you can walk all the way by road to Bagnères-de-Luchon, about 11km, but hitching is a good alternative.

Variant
Hospital de Benasque – GR11 Trail

This is a useful variant for those who want to avoid the awkward Coll de Mulleres (day 22).

Route:	from Hospital de Benasque via Collado de Valhibierna to the GR11 trail in the Valle de Benasque
Grade:	3
Height gain:	100m
Height loss:	400m

Follow the main route of day 21 all the way to Hospital de Benasque. Go to the road through the valley, turn right and follow the road until about 150m before a parking area. A path branches off to the left (there should be a signpost, but it had been destroyed in 2003) going to the Banos de Benasque. Leave the road, turn left and climb for a short while on this path (yellow–white marks). Walk SW on a path that goes up and down through pastures and between pine trees. Cross a small ravine and continue on a path that sometimes gets a little faint until on the floor of the valley you see a campsite (with hotel) near the road that gives access to the Banos de Benasque. Don't go down to the dirt road on your right below but keep on following the path. After a short descent and a short climb you cross a small ravine. Follow a level path on a stone slope until you arrive at the building of the Banos de Benasque (1680m). Go down on the road that gives access to the Banos de Benasque to a hairpin bend before reaching the valley floor. Leave the road, turn left and walk on a chaotic route (well marked, still yellow–white) SW until you finally arrive on a dirt road that runs through the valley. Turn left, cross the river by a bridge and go down gently SW on the road, with the river on your left-hand side. Recross the Rio Esera and arrive at the Puente de Creguena

(1468m). Cross the bridge and keep following the dirt road (100m after the bridge you'll find a water point on your left). Arrive at a very basic campsite (not really a place to spend the night) where the road forks. Don't turn right but continue in the same direction and you will soon arrive at a junction in a pine forest. You are now on the GR11. (For the route description to the Hospital de Vielha see the three day-variant from Estos to Hospital de Vielha at the end of day 24.)

DAY 22
Refugio de la Renclusa to Hospital de Vielha

Route:	via the Coll de Mulleres (2928m)
Grade:	E
Time:	7hrs 45mins
Height gain:	1000m
Height loss:	1500m
Map:	Mapa Excursionista/Carte de Randonnées, 1:50,000, no 23: Aneto–Posets

A magnificent stage that skirts the north side of the Maladeta massif and enters the Catalan Pyrenees. The crossing of the Coll de Mulleres should be attempted only in good weather conditions. The east side of the pass is extremely steep. Great care is needed on the initial stages of the descent.

0.00 Refugio de la Renclusa. Go down on yesterday's route to the junction (1980m). Turn right and follow a path that arrives at a level area. Turn right and walk SE on an obvious path to the so-called Forau de Aiguallut (also called the Trou de Toro), a deep hole into which the melting water flowing down from the Aneto glacier disappears. Pass the Forau de Aiguallut and a fine cascade (good view of the snow-covered summit of Aneto) and arrive on a large grassy plateau, the:

1.00 Plan d'Aiguallut (2050m). Cross the plateau SE until you reach a stream coming down from a higher level: the Valleta de Escaleta. Cross the stream and climb in a few zigzags to the Valleta de Escaleta. Cross this valley also SE and walk towards the remarkable twin peaks of Pico Forcanada, which you can't overlook. At the end of the

173

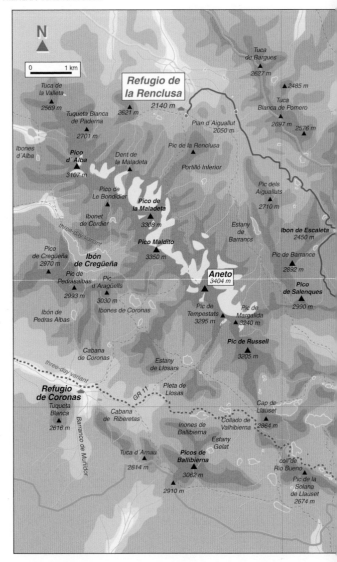

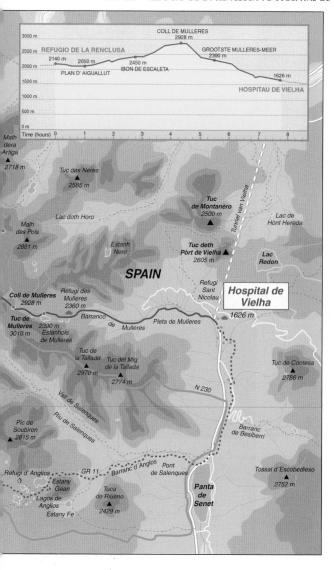

valley, the climb becomes steeper. The path, well marked with cairns, reaches a tarn (2320m). Pass the lake to the right, cross the stream that feeds the lake and climb to another lake that must be passed on the left side. Climb steeply in zigzags to the:

2.45 Ibon de Escaleta (2450m). Cross the outflow and climb steeply SSW on a slope that's covered with loose boulders. This steep section, which is well cairned and not difficult, ends at about 2600m. Notice a lake (2630m) on your right and take a good look at the summits south of you. Try to find the Tuc de Mulleres (3010m) and walk initially on polished boulders S towards the large pass south of the summit. The

Classic picture of the Aiguallut cascade and Pico de Aneto (3404m)

Haute Route, marked with a few cairns, then bends to the left and skirts the western slopes of Tuc de Mulleres to arrive at:

4.20 Coll de Mulleres (2928m).

> The Tuc de Mulleres is a 3000m summit that can easily be climbed from the Coll de Mulleres. Just climb S on boulders, staying on the west side of the ridge that leads to the summit (3010m). It takes about 15mins to get to the summit, which is decorated with a cross. There are excellent views of the Maladeta massif, the Besiberri ridge in the east and the Valle de Mulleres.

Don't go down directly on the extremely steep east side of the pass, but scramble N and then go down steeply to a bowl full of rocks. In late summer (August) there is probably only a small snowfield in the bowl, but in early summer snow could be lying close to the pass, which makes the descent rather precarious. There's now a choice of routes. It's possible to descend to the largest of the four Mulleres lakes, but my choice would be to descend steeply, but without difficulty, to the highest lake (2450m). Keep the lake at a distance on the right and walk E through the narrow valley to the:

5.35 largest Mulleres lake (2390m). Pass to the left of the oblong lake and of the next two lakes. (You will probably overlook the Refugi de Mulleres (2360m), an unstaffed solid shelter, painted orange, with places for about nine, situated on a rocky bluff on your left-hand side.) Beyond the last lake the route bends to the left and leaves the stream that cascades into the valley below. Go down in zigzags to the floor of this very rough valley and cross the valley E, staying left of the stream that here and there disappears. Past the valley the path goes down steeply for a few metres (this section needs to be taken carefully) close to the cascading stream (1855m). The descent then eases somewhat and you go down to the Pleta Nova de Mulleres, a flat grassy and marshy area. Keep on the left side of the plateau (it's possible to cross and recross the stream, but it is probably easier to stay left of it) and go down through a forest, in which you

The north face of the Maladeta massif

pass a beautiful cascade. Finally you walk, still on the left bank of the stream, on a broad track through the Pleta de Mulleres (a flat area) to the southern snout of the Vielha tunnel. Cross the road and walk to the:

7.45 Hospital de Vielha (1626m), also called Refugi Boca Sud and Refugi Sant Nicolau. 40 places, meals available, open all year (officially), reservation recommended, tel. 973 697 052. This *refugi* is often closed during the day, but should be open in the evening. The situation near the *refugi* has recently changed dramatically, because of the construction of a new tunnel. This work will continue until at least 2007! Walkers who want to spend the night in their tent are advised to continue for about half an hour (fine places in the Vall de Conangles) or to pitch their tent somewhere on the Pleta Nova de Mulleres. The situation around the *refugi* is unfortunately very depressing. Haute Route walkers deserve better!

DAY 23
Hospital de Vielha to Refugi de la Restanca

Route:	via the Port de Rius (2320m) and Collado d'Estany de Mar (2468m)
Grade:	2
Time:	7hrs 15mins
Height gain:	900m
Height loss:	500m
Map:	Mapa Excursionista/Carte de Randonnées, 1:50,000, no 22: Pica d'Estats – Aneto

A tough walk without any major obstacles, though a little care is needed on the steep east side of Collado d'Estany de Mar. The Haute Route follows the GR11 track to Estany de Rius. Today you'll pass several lakes. Unfortunately the water level of these lakes (the water is diverted by pipelines) tends to be very low in summer, making them less picturesque. But if you're lucky, and the water level is high, this will be a day you will never forget! A useful bad weather variant is also described.

0.00 Hospital de Vielha. Past the courtyard and a drinking trough for cattle you'll find a signpost indicating the GR11 track to the Port de Rius. Turn left and climb E in an open field on a small track. Cross a few streams (possibly dry in summer) and a path. The path bends a little to the right and arrives at a dirt road. Walk E on this road, which climbs gently until you reach a bridge on the Barranco de Conangles. Don't cross the bridge, but stay left of the stream. Cross the stream coming from Estany de Redo and climb E through a mixed forest (oak, beech, pine). Arrive at an open field with only a few small pine trees, cross several minor streams and climb N in zigzags. The obvious path bends eventually a little to the west. Ignore the path that's going to Estany de Redo (the path is indicated with a cairn) and climb NE to the:
2.15 Port de Rius (2320m). Keep walking NE and pass the large Estany de Rius along its northern shore. As soon as the lake is passed, leave the GR11 (but see below the optional GR11 continuation route to Refugi de la Restanca). Turn right and follow a line of cairns that leads S to Estany Tort de Rius. There isn't a clear path, and the cairns linger between smoothly polished giant rocks and some pools until the lake (2430m) comes in sight. It isn't be difficult to find the lake, even though there is sometimes more than one track and there are cairns everywhere. Keep the very long lake on your

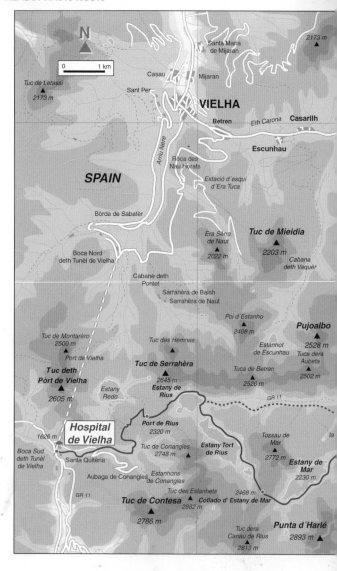

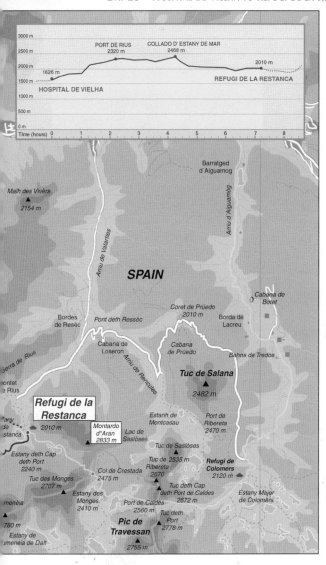

The sensational Estany de Mar

right-hand side and pass the lake on a route that goes up and down on rocky terrain. Beyond the lake you pass another lake (excellent places for a bivouac) and climb on a vague track SE to:

4.15 Collado d'Estany de Mar (2468m, named after the magnificent lake that lies ahead of you). Go down in zigzags to Estany de Mar on a very steep slope. Turn right and walk to the east side of the lake. Walk NE above the east side of Estany de Mar. This will take some time because of the many rocks that have to be crossed. At the north-east side of the lake pass a small tarn on your right and you'll arrive at a path with yellow waymarks. Go down NE in zigzags on this path to arrive on a small grassy plateau. Cross a side-stream and another stream and turn left. The path soon forks, and it makes little difference which route you choose. Go down to a stream, cross it and go down steeply between pine trees to the east side of Estany de la Restanca. Walk along the eastern shore of the lake to the:

7.15 Refugi de la Restanca (2010m), near the dam. 80 places, staffed from mid-June to the end of September, owned by the FEEC, meals available, reservation recommended, tel. 608 036 559. Internet: www.restanca.com. Bivouac not allowed near the lake or the *refugi*. If you continue along tomorrow's track for 45mins, you'll find some very fine places for the tent near Estany deth Cap deth Port.

Variant
*GR11 from Estany
de Rius to Refugi de la Restanca*

Route:	via Estany de Rius (2340m)
Grade:	2
Time:	4hrs 40mins
Height gain:	770m
Height loss:	390m
Map:	Mapa Excursionista/Carte de Randonnées, 1:50,000, no 22: Pica d'Estats – Aneto

The GR11 provides a useful bad weather variant, though you might be tempted to take this route even when weather conditions are in your favour because it leads much more quickly and easily to Restanca. However, you must not forget one thing: there is no doubt that the Haute Route is much more beautiful and spectacular!

2.40 East side of Estany de Rius. Cross the outflow and follow an obvious path that goes down E on the right side of the valley for about an hour. Pass the remains of a few buildings (possible water point) and continue E. Don't turn left at a junction but follow the path, which is almost level. Notice a *cabane* on your left below, climb a few metres and go down again in a side-valley. Cross a stream (1900m) and climb steeply until you overlook the Estany de la Restanca and the *refugi* (you are now on the place where the old *refugi* was situated, but there is nothing left of it). Go down to the dam, cross it and arrive at:
4.40 Refugi de la Restanca (2010m).

*Evening at the
Estany de Rius*

DAY 24
Refugi de la Restanca to Salardu

In good weather conditions an easy walk on well-worn paths, forest tracks and roads. The Haute Route follows the GR11 to Refugi de Colomers. The walk contains a brief visit to the Aigüestortes National Park, a visit that will inspire you to further exploration.

Route:	via the Col de Crestada (2475m) and the Port de Caldes (2560m)
Grade:	2
Time:	7hrs
Height gain:	600m
Height loss:	1340m
Map:	Mapa Excursionista/Carte de Randonnées, 1:50,000, no 22: Pica d'Estats – Aneto

0.00 Refugi de la Restanca. Follow the GR11 that climbs SE in zigzags and reaches a stream. Climb steeply along the stream, keeping it on your right-hand side, and arrive at the lovely Estany deth Cap deth Port (2240m, with fine places for a bivouac). Cross the small dam or walk below it and pass the lake along its northern shore. Climb SE on a somewhat chaotic slope covered with boulders and follow the GR11 marks that lead to the:

1.30 Coll de Crestada (2475m, also called Coll de Goellicrestada), situated on the border of the Parc Nacional de Aigüestortes i Estany de Sant Maurici. This col marks the beginning of the ascent of the Montardo d'Aran (see route description at the end of this walk). Go down in the park on the east side of the pass for a short while. Keep the sensational Estany des Monges (2410m) to your right and climb to an anonymous pass on a narrow ridge that offers fine views on the two Mangades lakes. A steep descent leads to the north side of the largest of the two lakes. Cross a stream, gain height E and arrive at the:

2.30 Port de Caldes (2560m, national park signpost), on the border of the national park, which you leave now. Go down E to the Port de Ribereta (2470m) on a flat area. Notice a tarn some distance to the right and go down SE in zigzags until you reach a stream. Follow this stream, staying close to it and keeping it on your right-hand side. Eventually the

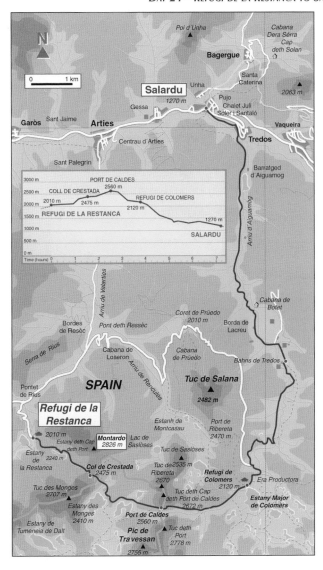

stream turns left. Cross the stream to avoid a few boulders and walk NE to:

3.45 Refugi de Colomers (2120m), overlooking the dammed Estany Major de Colomers. 40 places, staffed from mid-June to end of September, meals available, owned by the FEEC, reservation necessary, tel. 973 253 008. Leave the GR11 that crosses the dam. Don't cross the dam but go down N between pine trees. Cross a stream that comes out of a tunnel and go down to the floor of the valley, where you'll meet a stream. Follow the left bank of the stream to an open field (or cross the stream, follow the right bank and recross the stream when you arrive at an open field on your left side). Turn left and walk N on an obvious track through this level field. Notice a small lake on your right and, past the lake, go

Refugi de la Restanca and the lake

down steeply in zigzags until you arrive at a dirt road (1980m). Turn right and go down gently on this road through the Vall de Aiguamotx, taking short-cuts where possible. After about 20mins a signpost on the left side of the road indicates a path through the woods that leads to Bahns de Tredos (Camin dera Montanheta). Turn left, enter the pine forest and follow a path that goes up and down. Numerous simple wooden constructions have been made to enable walkers to walk through this enchanting but marshy wood without getting wet feet! Go down a few metres after a pass to a bridge on the main stream. Cross the bridge (fine place to relax) and arrive a few moments later near a *cabane*, again at the dirt road. Don't follow the road but go down on a path left of the road (with a beautiful cascade on your left-hand side; a popular place for tourists to relax). Follow the right bank of the main stream. Eventually the path becomes almost level. On emerging from the forest, you arrive at the:

5.45 Hotel/bar/restaurant Bahns de Tredos (1780m). Pass the building to the right and turn left past a parking area (a taxi service runs from here to the place where the final climb to Refugi de Colomers begins; price in 2003 was 3 Euros). Cross the stream and go down, generally N, on a small road through the Vall de Aiguamotx, taking short-cuts where possible. Pass a dammed lake after about 5km. Keep following the road for 500m past the dam until a signpost on your right indicates a path to the village of Tredos. Turn right (no harm done should you miss the path – the road you're on leads to Salardu). Go down in a forest to a junction of dirt roads, very close to Tredos. Turn left, following the road that goes down to Tredos. Enter the village, cross the Rio Garona de Ruda and turn left. Follow the right bank of the river until the next bridge and walk in the same direction (NW) on a small tarmac road until you again reach the road through the Vall de Aiguamotx. Turn right and walk to:

7.15 Salardu (1270m). Practical information about Salardu is given in the introduction of the fourth section of the Haute Route. In Salardu turn right and follow the main road (C 142, the road that leads to the Port de la Bonaigua) for about 100m. On the left side of the road you'll see Xalet Soler I Santalo. Open from June to the end of September, meals available, 105 places, owned by the CEC, tel. 973 645 016.

7: Montardo d'Aran (2826m) from Coll de Crestada

Height gain: around 400m

Time: 2hrs (1hr 10mins to gain the summit) from the Coll de Crestada

Grade: F

Just like the Piméné, it's not the altitude or the shape of Montardo d'Aran that makes this mountain so special. It is the superb views from the summit which, combined with easy access, attract numerous walkers each summer to the Montardo d'Aran. The dawn view from the Montardo is one of the finest experiences a Pyrenean walker can have, taking in all the summits of the Aigüestortes region, the Besiberri massif, long views north to the Vall d'Aran and the frontier ridge, the Maladeta massif and numerous lakes such as the Estany de Restanca and Estany de Mar. The ascent of the Montardo presents no difficulties – just enjoy an easy walk.

0.00 Coll de Crestada (2475m, also called Coll de Goellicrestada), situated on the border of the Parc Nacional de Aigüestortes i Estany de Sant Maurici. Go down in the park on the east side of the pass for a short while and arrive at a junction without a signpost. Here the ascent of the Montardo d'Aran begins. Follow a path (marked with cairns) that climbs N in numerous short zigzags until you reach a ridge. Cross the ridge, turn left and walk on a more or less level path towards the Montardo. Finally, climb steeply but without difficulty to the summit of the:

1.10 Montardo d'Aran (2826m). Follow the same track on your way back to the Haute Route trail.

GR11 from Viados to Hospital de Vielha (three-day variant)

Day 1
Refugio de Viados – Refugio de Estos

Route:	via the Puerto de Gistain (2572m)
Time:	5hrs 15mins
Height gain:	800m
Height loss:	670m
Map:	Mapa Excursionista/Carte de Randonnées, 1: 50,000, no 23: Aneto–Posets
Grade:	2

This variant avoids the difficulties of the Haute Route during days 19–22 (see maps for days 20–22).

An easy walk on well-worn paths. In early summer snowfields on both sides of the Puerto de Gistain could cover the track.

0.00 Refugio de Viados. Follow the Haute Route as described in day 19 to the place where three streams meet. Leave the Haute Route, cross the Barranco de Gistain and climb E (rather steeply at first and eventually more gently) on an obvious track to the:

3.10 Puerto de Gistain (2572m), which gives access to the Valle de Estos. On the pass the path makes a turn S to the right before descending E through the rough upper section of the Valle de Estos. Go down on the right side of the Valle de Estos through scree to the floor of the valley, cross a stream and go down gently on an obvious path that bends away a little from the Rio de Estos. The path leads to:

5.15 Refugio de Estos (1890m), well hidden until the last moment. 145 places, staffed all year, owned by de FAM, tel. 974 551 483. Meals available, but walkers can also cook their own meal in the *cocina libre*. Nice, cosy, modern *refugio*. Bivouac not allowed near the hut.

Day 2
Refugio de Estos – Pleta de Llosas

A very easy walk on path and dirt road. The route starts with a nice walk through the enchanting valle de Estos, followed by a somewhat disappointing and tiring walk on dirt road through the Valle de Vallibierna. The final hour of the walk, however, is worth every step.

Route:	via camping Aneto in the Valle de Benasque (1250m)
Time:	7hrs
Height gain:	970m
Height loss:	640m
Map:	Mapa Excursionista/Carte de Randonnées, 1: 50,000, no 23: Aneto–Posets
Grade:	2

0.00 Refugio de Estos. Go down SE on an obvious path, staying left of the Rio de Estos. Eventually cross the Palanca del Turmo (footbridge on the Rio de Estos) and follow the path over a level area to arrive in an open field at Cabana de Turmo (1750m). Pass the *cabana* on the right side, cross a pasture and go down gently on a dirt road. The road makes a few turns and crosses a secondary stream. Continue to go down SE through the Valle de Estos. Cross the Rio de Batisiellles, ignore the path that climbs W to the Valle de Batisielles and follow the dirt road. Pass Cabana de Santa Ana (1540m, on your right-hand side) and gain the left bank of the Rio de Estos by crossing the Palanca de Aiguacari (1450m). Continue the descent, pass the Embalse de Estos (1350m) and go down to a parking area. Leave the dirt road at a junction at Camping Chuise (on your left, not a recommended campsite), turn right and follow a dirt road for a short while, then go down on a track that branches off to the right to arrive soon at:

2.45 Camping Aneto (1250m, shady, good sanitary facilities, washing machines, bar/restaurant, an expensive food shop, maps for sale at the office, swimming pool), 3km north of the village of Benasque in the Valle de Benasque. Cross the Rio Esera that runs through the campsite and turn left. Follow a broad track, go under the Puente de San Jaime and arrive at a dirt road. Turn left and climb gently on this road. Cross a stream, don't turn left to Camping Ixeia and keep following the dirt road. Cross another stream and walk NE towards the dam of the Embalse de Paso Nuevo. The dirt road doesn't go all the way to the dam, but makes a surprising turn to the right. It's possible to follow the road, but it's better to take a short-cut, left of the road. Follow the GR11 waymarks and climb steeply between trees and shrubs until you again arrive on the dirt road. Turn left, walk along the dammed lake and continue until a junction, where a signpost indicates the GR11 track through the Valle de Vallibierna (if you continue in the same direction you'll soon arrive at a large campsite with basic facilities in an open area). Turn right and climb gently on a dirt road. Before entering the Vallibierna valley the dirt road climbs NE and SE, making a large hairpin bend (it's possible to take a short-cut, but this path can easily be overlooked) in a pine forest. Walk through the valley, with the Barranco de Vallibierna on your right-hand side deep down below. This walk needs no further description. Arrive at the:

6.15 Refugio de Coronas (1980m), a solid but unstaffed hut with 14 places at the point where the dirt road finally ends. Cross a few streams and follow a broad stone path that climbs initially NE on the left side of the Barranco de Vallibierna. Ignore the path that climbs N to the Lagos de Coronas and climb SE on the path that gradually becomes smaller. Arrive at a large open field, where the Barranco de Llosas gently runs, the:

7.00 Pleta de Llosas (2220m). Marshy in places, but with sufficient suitable places to pitch the tent. Excellent place to spend the night. Remarkable contrast between the plateau, surrounded by some old pine trees, and the impressive south side of the Maladeta massif.

Day 3
Pleta de Llosas – Hospital de Vielha

Without doubt one of the most beautiful sections of the entire GR11, through rough alpine landscapes decorated with numerous tarns that were left behind by the glaciers that once covered the Pyrenean mountains. A tough and tiring walk without any major difficulties in high summer. In early summer the track could be covered with snow near Collado de Vallibierna and the Coll de Rio Bueno. Care is needed on the rough terrain and some steep slopes.

Route:	via Collado de Vallibierna (2710m) and the Coll de Rio Bueno (2520m)
Time:	7hrs 25mins
Height gain:	800m
Height loss:	1400m
Map:	Mapa Excursionista/Carte de Randonnées, 1:50,000, no 23: Aneto–Posets
Grade:	2

0.00 Pleta de Llosas. Cross the stream as soon as you arrive on the plateau and climb SE along the Barranco de Vallibierna. Cross the stream and climb to the first of the: **0.45 Lagos de Vallibierna** (2432m). Climb a little and pass the lake along its northern shore, staying high above the water level. Follow past the lake the GR11 waymarks on giant boulders, pass close to a steep rocky slope, where a little care is needed, and climb on boulders E to the highest of the Lagos de Vallibierna (2484m, fine places for a bivouac). Pass the lake along its south side and climb steeply E on a rocky slope to the:
2.10 Collado de Vallibierna (2710m). Go down on the steep east side of the pass on rocks and scree (possibly on some snowfields) until the route bends a little to the right to avoid a rocky section. Go down SE between boulders and on grass to the upper section of a tiny valley where the path forks (signpost). Ignore the GR11 variant that goes S to the Lago de Llauset, turn left and walk to a stream. Cross the stream, climb with the stream on your left-hand side and soon arrive at the Lago de Cap de Llauset (2473m, with the remains of a small aeroplane in the water; offers excellent places for a bivouac). Walk S along its southern shore and after a short climb reach the:
3.20 Coll de Rio Bueno (2520m). Go down on the very steep east slope (full of scree and rocks) of the pass (snowfields early summer could make this descent rather

The Anglios region

precarious) to the Lagos de Rio Bueno, seen ahead of you. Pass the first two lakes along the southern shore, the third along its northern shore, and the fourth again along its southern shore. Go down on an obvious path to the:

4.10 Lagos de Anglios (2249m, also called the Lagos de Anglos), a few lakes situated in a large flat area. Pass the middle of the three largest lakes along its southern shore and arrive at a junction. Turn left, cross a stream and notice the unstaffed Refugio de Anglios (often used by fishermen) a little distance away on your left. Don't go to the hut, but cross a stream and go to the largest Anglios lake. Pass the lake on its eastern side and go down gently E on the right bank of the Barranco d'Anglios, through alpenrose and pine trees, until the path makes a turn left and goes down steeply NE, initially on a scree slope. Enter a forest and continue to descend steeply to the floor of the Valle de Salenques. Turn right and follow the right bank of the Rio Salenques until you are close to a road: the N 230. Climb a few metres and arrive at the:

6.00 N 230 (1430m; on the other side of the road you'll see the Embalse de Senet, often with a very low water level). Turn left, cross the Puente de Salenques and follow the road. Past a basic shelter on the right side of the road, and north of the Embalse de Senet, leave the road and turn right. Cross by a bridge the stream that runs to the lake, and arrive at a dirt road. Turn left and climb for a short while N. The road turns into a path that approaches the stream running through the valley. Keep the stream on your left-hand side and walk to Barranc de Besiberri, a side-stream coming from the east. Climb a few metres along this stream and cross it by a footbridge. Here the path becomes faint. Go down through grass to the main stream and arrive at a dirt road. Turn right, enter a forest and follow the dirt road to a junction. Don't turn right but keep walking N on a road that climbs very gently. Notice a picnic area on your left. Beyond this area the road forks. Take the right branch and soon the dirt road forks again. Keep right and climb gently until you arrive at a small stream. Cross this stream, and a footbridge a few seconds later, and walk W to the N 230.

> The GR11 track has been slightly altered here because of the construction of a new Viella tunnel. This work will continue until at least 2007. Small changes may be made in the years to come.

Notice on your left a Barcelona University building. Turn right and walk N along the road to the:
7.25 Hospital de Vielha (1630m), also called Refugi Boca Sud and Refugi Sant Nicolau. It is situated on the route of both the GR11 and the Haute Route.

194

SECTION 4: SALARDÚ TO L'HOSPITALET-PRÈS-L'ANDORRE
Eight Days Through a Mountain Wilderness

Unlike the GR10 and the GR11 – long-distance routes through the Pyrenees that have been nicely marked with red–white paint flashes – the Haute Route is not specifically waymarked, and as a consequence walkers find all sorts of marks on their way to the Mediterranean: paint flashes, signposts, cairns and border stones. Sometimes, in the few remote areas that still exist, walkers have to find their own way with a little help from a guidebook, map, compass or GPS. Perhaps most important of all, they have to rely on their own ability to stay on course in a true mountain wilderness.

The Haute Route often offers walkers a choice of routes, which enables them to create, to a certain extent, their own Haute Route. For example, compared with Georges Véron's original guide to the Haute Route, the route through the high mountains of the Pyrenees as described in Kev Reynolds's *Walks and climbs in the Pyrenees* shows remarkable differences. Obviously the choice of routes makes a difference. Here and there Haute Route walkers can make their traverse more arduous or, if they wish, somewhat easier. For the fourth section of the Haute Route I have chosen a route that traverses Spain and Andorra and pays only a brief visit to France. On the last day of this section the Haute Route descends to France, and in the final section the Haute Route stays in French territory most of the time.

The first thing that crosses my mind when I think of the walk from Salardú to l'Hospitalet-près-l'Andorre is that it is a walk without compromise in which trekkers not only face all sorts of natural obstacles but also have to confront themselves. They will encounter long and tough walks, in remote and inaccessible areas, with only one staffed mountain hut, practically no opportunities to replenish food supplies, just a few walkers to meet on the way, and lots of sections without path or good waymarking.

There is no doubt that this fourth section is by far the hardest of all. You have to give your very best in order to arrive finally at l'Hospitalet-près-l'Andorre, but there is another side to every coin, as you will find out. It's certainly the most rewarding journey as well. The Pyrenees always give the very best only to walkers who are willing to give the very best of themselves! This is not a walk that gives a few pleasant memories, but an overwhelming experience that you will carry with you and cherish for the rest of your life. A walk with a tremendous impact!

Walkers may wish to take a day off to climb one of the **classic summits** described in this section – Mont Roig (2868m, day 26), Pic de Certascan (2853m, day 27) and Pica d'Estats (3143m, day 29).

The guide offers several **variants** which enable walkers to avoid a few tough sections. The alternative route for day 25 is a long but very easy walk on a dirt road to the village of Alos de Isil. A variant on day 27 is included to allow walkers to replenish food supplies in Tavascan. Day 28 contains a useful short-cut to Estany de Sottlo for those who want to climb the Pica d'Estats (described at the end of day 29).

Day 25 is a very tough and difficult walk, and considering its length it might be a good idea to divide the walk in two. The two Estanys Rosari de Baciver are a logical place to pitch the tent for the night.

The Start Point: Vall d'Aran

Until a few decades ago the Vall d'Aran was an isolated valley, completely cut off from the rest of Spain. Surrounded by high, impenetrable mountain ranges (Maladeta, Besiberri, Encantats, Beret) the few inhabitants of the valley lived anonymously in small communities, each with its own Romanesque church, separated from Spain. Thus the valley developed its own character and even its own language. In the course of the 20th century, the isolation of the Vall d'Aran came to an end. The Vielha tunnel (1948) and the road to the Port de la Bonaigua made the Vall d'Aran accessible by road. The ski resort Baqueira-Beret, opened in 1964 and now one of the largest in the Pyrenees, has done the rest.

The once so picturesque Vall d'Aran has become a valley completely dominated by mass tourism. The changes have been dramatic. New villages have been created, and many old villages have been changed beyond recognition by extensive house building. A fine example is Salardu, which still has a lovely village centre (around the Placa Major) but is unfortunately surrounded by a great number of new buildings that dominate the scenery. You'll be happy to leave this valley behind, but don't forget to take a look back when you walk to the Plan de Beret: from a distance the Vall d'Aran, with the snow-covered Maladeta massif in the background, still looks very attractive!

Practical Information

Salardu

This old village situated in the eastern section of the Vall d'Aran has a lovely village centre around the Placa Major, with Romanesque church, but unfortunately the rest of the village is dominated by lots of new buildings. At the Place Major you'll find Refugi Rosta, a simple hotel and certainly a fine place to stay for walkers. There are small rooms for

Sunset at Estany de Baciver

'normal' guests and there is a dormitory for walkers. Good kitchen and excellent breakfast. (**Beware:** breakfast is served rather late. By the time you've eaten you'll be too late to finish the first walk in one day!) Open from late June until late September, 55 places, tel. 973 645 308, fax 973 645 814. The most logical place for walkers to spend the night is Xalet Soler i Santalo, a large *refugi* owned by the CEC. Open from June to mid-September, 105 places, tel. 973 645 016. Good meals available! Salardu also has a youth hostel: 180 places, tel. 973 645 271 and 934 838 363, fax 973 644 136. Internet: www.tujuca.com

Facilities in Salardu
Bank (with cash dispenser), supermarket, food shop, small tourist office next to the shop, hotels, restaurants, bars, public swimming pool. No campsites (there is one in the village of Arties, about 4km west of Salardu).

L'Hospitalet-près-l'Andorre
For information on this village, see the introduction to section 5.

197

Food

It's very difficult to replenish food supplies in this section of the Haute Route. In Alos de Isil, where you arrive on the first or the second day, there might be some food for sale at the local restaurant: bread, cheese and some canned food. Don't expect too much of it. There is an optional variant on the third day to the village of Tavascan, where you'll find a tiny food shop. On day six you can go to El Serrat in Andorra, but don't expect to find much more than bread and some snacks. On day seven, at last, walkers can visit the far from attractive village of Soldeu (3km south of Camping d'Incles), which has everything you might desire: food shops, banks, cash dispenser, hotels, restaurants, bars and post office.

Maps

- Mapa Excursionista/ Carte de Randonnées, no 22, 1:50,000: Pica d'Estats – Aneto
- IGN Carte de Randonnées, 1:50,000, no 7: Haute Ariège – Andorre

Warning: The Mapa Excursionista/Carte de Randonnées no 21: Andorra–Cadi contains numerous serious errors in the Andorra section of the Haute Route.

Accommodation: Contact Details

All numbers and other information on accommodation on the Haute Route is also given in the route description.

Day 25: no accommodation in Alos de Isil
Day 26: Refugi Enric Pujol is unstaffed
Day 27: Refugi de Certascan – 973 623 230, internet: www.certascan.com
Day 28: Refugi del Cinquantenari is unstaffed
Day 29: bivouac at Étang de la Soucarrane
Day 30: Refugi de Sorteny is unstaffed
Day 31: Camping Vall d'Incles
Day 32: l'Hospitalet-près-l'Andorre: *gite d'étape* – 05 61 05 23 14 and fax 05 61 05 23 19, email: gitedetape.lhospitalet@libertysurf.fr

DAY 25
Salardu to Alos de Isil

Route:	via the Tuc de Marimanya (2662m) and the Coll d'Airoto (2500m)
Grade:	1
Time:	9hrs 50mins
Height gain:	1500m
Height loss:	1490m
Map:	Mapa Excursionista/Carte de Randonnées, 1:50,000, no 22: Pica d'Estats – Aneto

A very long, very demanding route, including some stretches without path or marks, as well as rough terrain, a steep climb and a large section of boulders. One of the toughest stages of the Haute Route. Considering the length of this stage, it might be a good idea to make it a two-day walk – a bivouac near the two large Estanys Rosari de Baciver is recommended. The first part of the walk is not very exciting but offers superb views of the Maladeta massif. There is no water source along the route until La Basseta (about 7hrs 30mins along). A bad weather variant from Salardu to Alos de Isil is included at the end of the route.

0.00 Salardu (1270m). Follow the road that goes to the village of Bagergue until the junction where a road branches off to the small hamlet of Unya, which is nicely situated on a bluff. Turn left, cross the Riu Unyola by a bridge and turn right immediately. Walk past a few new houses to find a broad track that climbs gently NE (the GR211; you'll follow the red–white marks of this path until the Plan de Beret). Follow this track, cross the stream once again and climb along pasture and stone walls to the village of:

0.45 Bagergue (1419m). Pass the church and enter the village. Walk to the main street (the one from Salardu) that runs through the village, turn left and climb this road for a short while until you reach a high-tension pole. Walk under the cables and turn right. Ignore a private road on your right and walk between trees. Cross a stream and soon climb ESE in a few zigzags to a dirt road. Turn right and walk S on this gently climbing road. Ignore a dirt road that branches off to the right, and walk E now until you arrive at a road (that goes to the Plan de Beret). Cross this road and follow a dirt road NE, staying a little below the road you've just crossed. The dirt road climbs and finally reaches a large flat area:

2.20 the Pla(n) de Beret. Keep a *cabana* on your right-hand side (1890m, in use by a shepherd; it's also possible to walk along the back of the *cabana* on a dirt road – cross a grassy bluff and follow a track that leads to the road to Parking Orri)

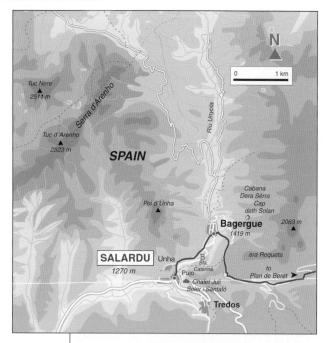

and continue to a road that leads to Parking Orri in the ski resort Baqueira-Beret. Turn right and follow the level road until the large parking area. Go through the entrance gate (tickets on sale in winter; look for 'Venta Billetes' sign) and descend a few metres. Walk under a ski lift to a dirt road and walk E. The road bends to the right; leave the road and walk to a bar with terrace (closed in summer). Keep to the right of the bar. The route becomes rather faint now. Walk SSE heading towards two small summits that are covered with pine trees. The left summit is the higher of the two. Soon you'll find a path that lingers between the two summits (although there's also a path that stays right of both summits – the two paths meet just behind the summits). After a short descent climb gently on an obvious path that approaches the stream coming from Estany de Baciver. The path then bends away from the stream, crosses a side-stream and climbs SE. Notice a small tarn a little distance below on your right and climb between pine trees to the dam of:

3.30 Estany de Baciver (2120m). Keep left of the dam, cross the stream (which has split into several minor streams) coming from the Estanys Rosari de Baciver and climb NE with the stream on your left-hand side. When you are above practically all the pine trees, the stream has to be crossed twice and you soon arrive at the first of the two large Estanys Rosari de Baciver (2315m). Walk along the lake, keeping it on your left-hand side, and do the same with the second lake (2320m). Both lakes are situated in an immense plateau, where horses and cows are sometimes grazing. Suitable places for a bivouac are not hard to find. As soon as

One of the Estany Rosari de Baciver and the Tuc de Marimanya (2662m)

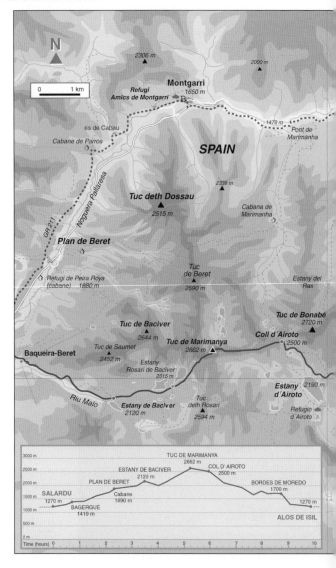

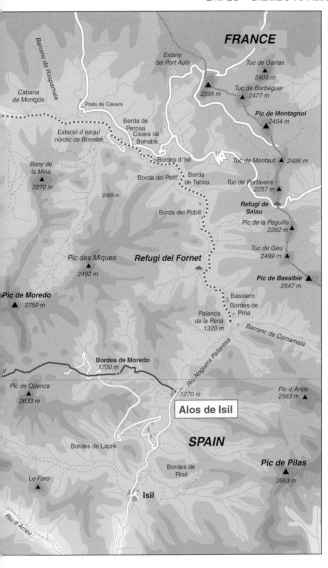

FRANCE

Barranc de Raspaimala

Estany
del Port Aula

Tuc de Garias
2409 m

Cabana
de Montgòs

Tuc de Barbéguer
2477 m

Prats de Clavera

2395 m

Pic de Montagnol
2454 m

Berda de
Perosa
Cases de
Bonabé

Estació d'esquí
nòrdic de Bonabé

Bordes d'Isil

Tuc de Montaut ▲ 2496 m

Bony de
la Mina
2270 m

Borda del Petit

Borda
de Tariou

Tuc de Portavera
2257 m

2065 m

Borda del Pubill

Refugi de
Salau

Pic de la Péguille
2262 m

Pic des Miques
2492 m

Refugi del Fornet

Tuc de Geu
2499 m

Pic de Moredo
▲ 2750 m

Pic de Bassibie ▲
2547 m

Bassiero
Bordes de
Pina

Palanca
de la Pena
1320 m

Barranc de Comamala

Bordes de Moredo
1700 m

Riu Noguera Pallaresa

Pic de Qüenca
2633 m

1270 m

Pic d'Arics
2563 m ▲

Alos de Isil

Bordes de Lapre

SPAIN

Lo Faro ▲

Bordes de
Risé

Pic de Pilas
▲
2653 m

Isil

Riu d'Arreu

you are past the second lake, walk in a straight line towards the Tuc de Marimanya. Initially on rocks, then on a very steep slope (no path, no marks), you climb to the summit. You reach the ridge just a couple of metres below the top of:

5.15 Tuc de Marimanya (2662m, execellent views especially of the Estanys Rosari de Baciver, the Maladeta massif and the ridge that marks the border with France, together with the Tuc de Maubermé (2880m) and Mont Roig, 2868m, the mountain you'll encounter tomorrow). Go down a little on the ridge and stay very close to it while climbing to the summit (2660m) NE of the Tuc de Marimanya. From the top you'll see the small Estany Gelat de Marimanya (2575m). Stay on the ridge, go down steeply and keep the lake on your left-hand side. Walk E towards the Coll d'Airoto, staying close to the Marimanya ridge. Keep to the right of a number of small tarns, the Estanys de Détras de Marimanya, and walk to the:

6.00 Coll d'Airoto (2500m). Go down SE on a steep slope towards a tiny tarn below the col. Don't go all the way to the lake, but go down towards the large Estany d'Airoto (2190m), initially through grass and later on giant boulders. Pass the northern shore of the lake, staying well above the water level and still walking on rocks. NE of the lake you climb steeply through grass until you meet a rather vague track that's marked with cairns. Turn left and climb on this path to a pass (2420m). Go down on the east side of the pass on rough terrain. There is no real path, but here and there you'll find a cairn. Find your way down to a tiny tarn called La Basseta (just before this lake you'll find a stream with good quality water). Walk along the southern shore of the lake (there are some fine places for a bivouac here), climb a few metres on a vague track and continue the descent in a narrow valley with the white limestone walls of the Pic de Quenca on your right. At an altitude of about 2100m you'll meet the Barranc de Moredo. Don't cross the stream but stay left of it and go down in zigzags on a path that meets a dirt road (1960m). From here you can clearly see the Bordes de Moredo (also called Bordes de Sebastia, comprised of a number of farmhouses – some are in a poor state, but some have recently been rebuilt), that the Haute Route is heading for. In order to save time, walk in a straight line (as far as possible) towards the buildings. Should you follow the dirt road, then walk to a junction just before the road crosses the Barranc de Moredo. Turn left and follow a dirt road to the:

8.45 Bordes de Moredo (1700m). Walk alongside the lowest buildings and continue NE on grass (no path) and soon arrive on a large ridge between two ravines. Find your own way down on a steep slope (but don't go all the way down to the stream), turn left, enter a small forest and cross, as you emerge from it, a stream (dry in summer). Follow some cattle tracks going E towards a stone wall near some trees. Continue to go down E, using several tracks, gradually approaching the Barranc de Moredo. Notice a small dam in the stream below and you'll soon arrive at an obvious path that brings you to:

9.50 Alos de Isil (1270m). There is no campsite or *gite* in the hamlet. The best thing is to go to the local restaurant (with bar and telephone) and ask if something can be arranged for the night. There are no shops in Alos de Isil, but you might be able to buy some food (bread, cheese, canned food) at the restaurant. There is a *refugi*/restaurant 3km south of Alos de Isil, in the village of Isil. If you prefer a bivouac, the best thing to do is to continue on tomorrow's route. There are some fine places to be found close to the Noguera Pallaresa in the first half hour of the walk.

Detail of a house in Alos de Isil

Variant
To Alos de Isil via the Montgarri Dirt Road

An easy route, in fact too easy for the Haute Route, but a useful alternative in case of bad weather.

Grade:	2
Time:	8hrs 30mins
Height gain:	650m
Height loss:	650m
Map:	Mapa Excursionista/Carte de Randonnées, 1:50,000, no 22: Pica d'Estats – Aneto

0.00 Salardu. Follow the Haute Route as described until the road on the Pla(n) de Beret. Don't go to Parking Orri, but walk to the main road on the plateau. Turn right and walk N on this more or less level road (or follow a path east of the road; this is the GR211, red–white marks). Pass Refugi de Peyra Roya (1880m, left of the road, not for walkers) after 1.5km and walk for 500m to the place where the road turns into a dirt road. There is a huge parking area here.

3.20 Parking area on the Plan de Beret. There is a choice of routes now. The shortest route is the dirt road to Montgarri. As this is an uninteresting walk (cars passing by all the time in summer), and you would be advised to take the route that stays left of the Rio Noguera Pallaresa. Enter the parking area and go to the north side of it, where you'll find a large track. Follow this track, which goes up and down a little through an attractive half-open landscape decorated with pine trees. Cross several minor streams, pass Cabana de Parros (on your left-hand side) and go down gently on the track that bends to the right and then swings down to a stream. Cross the stream by a solid bridge and climb a few metres to the remains of a house (Es Cabau). There is a junction behind the building. Ignore the GR211 that branches off to the left and keep following the broad track that goes down to the monastic church of Montgarri (dated 1117) that can be seen from afar.

4.50 Montgarri (1650m), romantically situated next to the Rio Noguera Pallaresa. Refugi Amics de Montgarri, a staffed *refugi*, open from June to mid-October, 40 places, meals

Montgarri

available, tel. 973 645 064 or 973 640 780, fax 973 645 900. Overcrowded in summer with tourists, and therefore not really a place for Haute Route walkers to stay. Cross the Rio Noguera Pallaresa by a bridge and follow a dirt road E. Ignore a path that branches off to a small *refugi* (Refugi Juli Amalot, 12 places, staffed from June to late September, meals available, tel. 608 998 436 – nice atmosphere in this well-hidden refugi!) and soon pass a farm/barn on the left. You'll arrive at a junction beyond the remains of the houses of Eth Dossau. Don't turn right (that is the dirt road to Pla(n) de Beret) but continue E on a dirt road (signposted 'Esterri', meaning Esterri d'Aneu) for about 18km. You won't need any detailed route description for this walk. The road crosses the Rio Noguera Pallaresa twice on your way to Alos de Isil – crossing it for the first time after 8km (1470m). Stay left of the river for about an hour, pass Refugi El Fornet (closed in summer) and recross the river. On the last section of the walk keep the river on your left-hand side. Notice about 2.5km before you get to Alos de Isil the small footbridge on the river: the Palanca de la Pena (1320m). This bridge marks the beginning of tomorrow's long climb to the Coll de la Cornella. As there is only informal accommodation in Alos de Isil it might be a good idea to pitch the tent somewhere next to the river instead of going all the way to the village. **8.30 Alos de Isil** (1270m).

DAY 26
Alos de Isil to Refugi Enric Pujol

Three passes have to be crossed in this tough stage. Due to the rough terrain, poor waymarking and the absence of a path here and there, it will sometimes be difficult to stay on course. Care is needed on the very steep east side of the Coll de la Cornella. The water in the lakes and streams on this stage is of poor quality, and will always need to be purified.

Route:	via the Coll de la Cornella (2485m), the Coll de Curios (2428m) and the Coll de Calberante (2610m)
Grade:	2
Time:	7hrs 25mins
Height gain:	1400m
Height loss:	400m
Map:	Mapa Excursionista/Carte de Randonnées, 1:50,000, no 22: Pica d'Estats – Aneto

0.00 Alos de Isil. Walk N on a dirt road that climbs gently and keep the Noguera de Pallaresa on your right-hand side. After about 45mins, when the road goes down a little, you'll notice the Palanca de la Peña (1320m) on the river. Cross the bridge, turn left and climb on a dirt road that winds up in a few zigzags. Keep a farm/barn on your right and follow the road to two other farms/barns (one much larger than the other) at 1450m. The dirt road ends at the buildings. Walk between the buildings, continue through grass for a few metres and turn right. Enter a forest, where you'll find a track. Climb through the forest, crossing several minor streams as you gradually approach the Barranc de Comamala, the main stream that runs through the valley. Walk SE through a more or less open valley after having left the forest and stay left a little distance from the Comamala stream. The path becomes faint at the end of the valley (about 1850m), where two streams meet. Cross the stream and climb S in zigzags between alpenrose to arrive at a:

3.30 tiny lake (2070m). Leave the lake on your right and climb E towards the Coll de la Cornella, passing two so-called *faux cols*. You'll reach the first at 2190m. Keep climbing steeply in the same direction to the second *faux col*

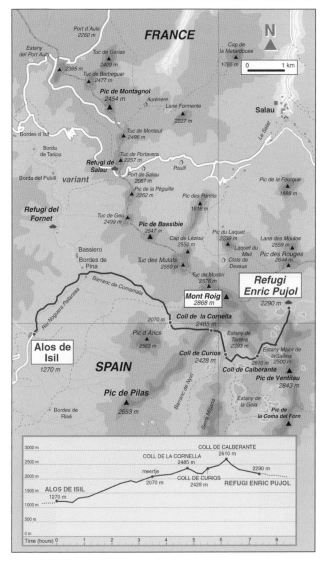

Ancient house in Alos de Isil

(2340m). The route, marked with cairns, makes several turns to avoid rocks as far as possible and then climbs to the:

4.45 Coll de la Cornella (2485m), a small gap in the ridge south-west of Mont Roig (also called Mont Rouch). Go down carefully on a very steep scree slope and walk E to the Estany de Tartera (2393m), which can be seen from the pass. Walk along the western shore of the lake and follow the cairns SSE to the next pass, the Coll de Curios. It's a simple climb, the pass being only 35m higher than the lake, on a scree slope.

5.30 Coll de Curios (2428m), a large pass. Don't go down to the two largest Calberante lakes, but climb E on a path marked with some cairns along a tiny stream to the highest and smallest Estany de Calberante (2490m). Walk along its southern shore and climb E on a vague track to the:

6.10 Coll de Calberante (2610m). Go down steeply to the large Estany Major de la Gallina (2500m) and walk around the lake. Walk along its northern shore until you've found the place where the descent to Refugi Enric Pujol starts. The *refugi* and the three Gallina lakes can be seen from here. Go down through a peculiar landscape of smoothly polished grey rocks towards the first two lakes (2380m). There are cairns everywhere, so there are several options. Walk N along the east side of the lakes towards the most northern Gallina lake (2275m) and cross its outflow.

> Crossing the outflow of the lake could be difficult for trekkers carrying a heavy rucksack. There is a place to cross the stream (that runs through a narrow, deep gully) a little lower. Should you not trust it, then the only option is to go all the way down to Estany de Llavera (excellent places for a bivouac), then cross the stream and climb back to the *refugi*.

Climb a few metres to:

7.25 Refugi Enric Pujol (2290m, also called Refugi Mont Roig). Refugi Enric Pujol is situated on a bluff, close to the imposing east face of the Mont Roig and overlooking the lake as well as the Estany de Llavera, down below to the east. The *refugi* is a solid, unstaffed hut, with places for nine. It's worth spending the night here.

TEN CLASSIC SUMMITS

8: Mont Roig (2868m) from Refugi Enric Puyol

Height gain:	578m
Time:	3hrs 15mins; allow 1hr 45mins to reach the summit
Grade:	F

From Refugi Enric Puyol the two summits of Mont Roig (also called Mont-Rouch) can be clearly seen: the French summit (2868m) and the Spanish summit (2864m). The east face of the mountain is quite impressive and has a narrow gully covered with snow practically all summer. The ascent is somewhat rough, but not difficult in summer, when snow has vanished from the slopes below the frontier ridge. There is no path that leads to the frontier ridge and just a few cairns here and there. The direction, however, should be obvious. A little care is needed on the ridge leading to the summit. The views from the summit are spectacular, but what will strike you most of all is the remarkable contrast between the fresh green French mountains and the much more barren Spanish sierras.

0.00 Refugi Enric Puyol (2290m). Gain height N and improvise as you work your way up through grass and rocks. There may be a few snowfields that have to be crossed. Finally climb through scree to reach a pass on the frontier ridge (2690m). Don't go into France, but turn left and climb SW on the ridge. Here and there you'll have to avoid a tiny rocky eminence on the ridge, but it won't be too difficult to reach the summit of the:
1.45 Mont Roig (2868m, the French call this the Mont Rouch de France), which is marked with a large cairn. Take the same route on your way down to the *refuge*.

DAY 27
Refugi Enric Pujol to Refugi de Certascan

Route:	via the hamlet of Noarre and the Coll de Certascan (2605m)
Grade:	2
Time:	7hrs 15mins
Height gain:	1050m
Height loss:	1100m
Map:	Mapa Excursionista/Carte de Randonnées, 1:50,000, no 22: Pica d'Estats – Aneto

A beautiful walk through inaccessible alpine landscapes, where only few trekkers come. Several sections have no path and no more than a few marks, but there are no major difficulties. The steep eastside of Coll de Certascan can, however, be covered with snow in early summer. Two variant routes for those who need additional food supplies are also described.

0.00 Refugi Enric Pujol. Follow the cairns along the stream and go down in the direction of Estany de Llavera. The path bends away from the lake and makes a turn to the left to go down steeply, staying very close to the stream that goes down in small cascades. Reach the upper section of a valley, stay left of the stream and walk SSE on polished rocks, occasionally on a path marked with cairns and some old red marks. Keep the stream on your right-hand side. Gradually the path bends away from the stream. After a short climb you'll reach a marshy plateau with some tiny streams. Cross the plateau, go down gently SE and enter a small forest with pine trees and birches. The descent ends in an open spot near the:

2.15 Riu del Port (1690m). Cross the stream by a footbridge, enter a forest (mainly birch) and walk for about 15mins S on an more or less level path until you arrive at a dirt road (that goes towards Tavascan). Go down S on this road until the first hairpin bend. Follow the road for about 20m and turn left (sometimes there are one or two cars parked here). Follow a separate path (ignore a larger track that doesn't arrive at Noarre) SSE through the woods and in a few minutes arrive at:

3.00 Noarre (1600m), a small hamlet that consists of a few (farm)houses in an open field, close to the Riu de Noarre.

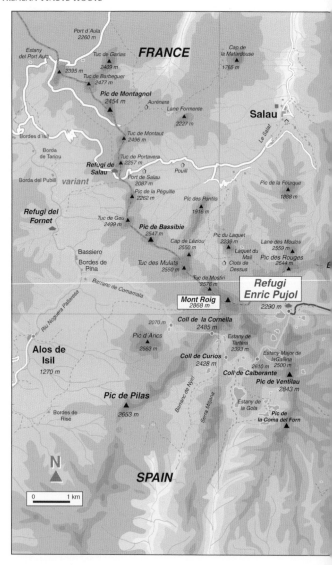

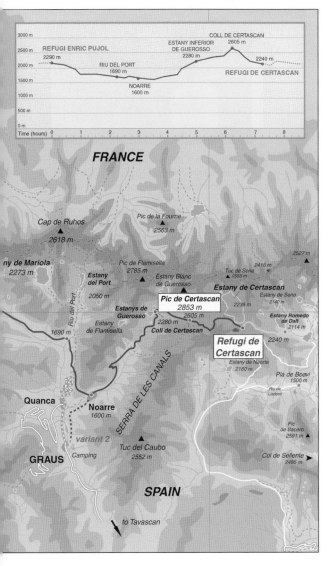

Refugi Enric Pujol and
Mont Roig (2868m)

Some buildings are in a poor state; others have recently been rebuilt and are now being used as summer residences. Noarre is remarkable for being completely cut off from what we call the civilised world. There is no road access to Noarre! The route from here is not obvious. Don't go to the Riu de Noarre but walk NE in the direction of the highest building (an isolated house that has been rebuilt) to find a path (ancient red marks) a few metres below it. Follow this path and climb gently NE between birch trees until you notice a cascade on your right-hand side at about 1850m. The path turns left and climbs in zigzags between pine trees. Cross the stream coming from Estany de Flamicella (about 2000m, just below a small cascade) and continue the ascent on a steep grassy slope. In a few minutes you'll arrive at a beautiful marshy plain, with a stream that winds through it. Notice the remains of a *cabana* on your left and walk along the plain keeping the stream on your right-hand side until you see some old paint flashes on the rocks on your left. Follow the marks and climb NE on a steep rocky slope decorated with numerous dead trees. The route gradually approaches the Riu dels Guerossos, which goes down in cascades. Climb steeply N on rough terrain to the small:

5.00 Estany Inferior de Guerosso (2280m). Cross the out-flow and climb steeply E until the path (that becomes faint sometimes) turns left and climbs N, with a stream on your left-hand side, to Estany Mitja de Guerosso (2350m). A little higher (2370m) you'll find estany Blau de Guerosso. Here the final climb to the Coll de Certascan begins. The route makes a sharp turn to the right and you follow a line of cairns as you climb straight forward ESE on rough terrain, but with no difficulties, to the:

6.15 Coll de Certascan (2605m), a small gap in the ridge south of the Pic de Certascan (2853m). Go down on the steep east side of the pass (there is possibly a snowfield just below the pass). The descent soon eases, the route turns left and you pass a snow-meter and a small tarn at a distance on the right. Cross a stream several times and walk towards the large Lac de Certascan. Near the lake (fine places for a bivouac) the path turns right. Walk above the southern shore of the lake on a path that goes up and down to:

7.15 Refugi de Certascan (2240m), which is surprisingly not situated at the lake, but a little hidden at a distance from it. Staffed from mid-June until the end of September, 40 places, meals available, owned by the FEEC, tel. 973 623 230. Internet: www.certascan.com

Variant 1
Via Tavascan to Pla de Boavi
(7hrs from Refugi Enric Pujol)

Grade:	2
Time:	7hrs
Height gain:	333m
Height loss:	1123m

A useful alternative for walkers who need to buy food supplies.

Follow the Haute Route as described for day 27 until you arrive on the dirt road coming from Tavascan. Go down gently all the way on this road towards Tavascan. On your way to the village you'll arrive at the tarmac road to Pleta del Prat. Turn left, pass the almost uninhabited hamlet of Quanca and pass a dammed lake on your left-hand side. Pass (at 1360m, near the barns of Graus) a small campsite (Camping Masia 'Bordes de Graus', 1360m, left of the road, with bar/restaurant and a *refugi*, excellent sanitary facilities, English spoken (one of the ladies in residence is of British origin); a nice place to stay, tel. 973 623 246 or 973 623 206). Keep following the road for 1.3km and cross the Riu de Tavascan by a bridge. From here it's 5km to Tavascan (also called Tabescan, 1167m). Tavascan is a simple mountain village with a remarkable contrast between old (church, the old dark houses, the ancient bridge on the Riu de Tavascan) and new (some newly built houses, hotels and a power station). All this makes Tavascan not too attractive. There are a few hotels (too luxurious for Haute Route walkers – Hostal Llacs de Cardos, tel. 973 633 046, Hostal Marxant, 973 635 051, and Casa Feliu, a bar that has also a few rooms available), bars, restaurants and a tiny foodshop. From Tavascan walk NE on a dirt road that climbs gently. After 6km the road forks. Don't turn left (that road goes towards Refugi de Certascan) but walk straight forward on a road that ends at the large flat area of Pla de Boavi (1500m), a popular place for tourists to have a picnic, but also suitable for pitching the tent for the night. At the east side of the plateau you'll find the Haute Route.

Variant 2
Noarre via Camping Masia 'Bordes de Graus' (1 day)

This variant allows you to replenish food supplies in Tavascan and return the next day to the main track of the Haute Route.

Grade:	2
Time:	4hrs 45mins
Height gain:	240m
Height loss:	630m

Follow variant 1 to Camping Masia 'Bordes de Graus', where you spend the night. The next day follow the ancient track from Graus to Noarre. Leave the campsite at the back by a large track that leads to a sports field below the camp-site. Leave the track almost immediately in a sharp curve and follow a path (a signpost indicates Noarre) upstream along the Riu del Port for a few moments until you arrive at a bridge. Cross the bridge and climb a few metres to find another signpost indicating Noarre. Turn left and follow an obvious path N between trees. Pass a dammed lake on the right, and past the lake the path turns right and makes a zigzag (notice a fine cascade in the Riu de Noarre on your left below). The path climbs NE now and approaches the Riu de Noarre. Follow the stream on the right for a few moments until you arrive at a footbridge (the kind of bridge they don't make any more!). Cross the bridge with care and follow the path that leads to the centre of Noarre. You are on the main track of the Haute Route again.

TEN CLASSIC SUMMITS

9: Pic de Certascan (2853m) from Coll de Certascan

Grade:	F
Height gain:	248m
Time:	1hr 10mins; allow 40mins for the ascent (from the Coll de Certascan)

The Pic de Certascan dominates the vast region between the Pica d'Estats (3143m) in the east and Mont Roig (2868m) in the west. This summit is worth the extra effort because of the extensive views it offers: all the summits of the Aigüestortes region, the Besiberri massif, the snow-covered summits of the Maladeta massif, the vertical east face of the Mont Valier (2838m) in France, Mont Roig, the Pica d'Estats, the Lac de Certascan and numerous sun-baked Spanish sierras! It's an uncomplicated, rough ascent in summer through a scree slope and finally on boulders.

0.00 Coll de Certascan (2605m) (see day 27 for access to Coll de Certascan). A few metres west of the pass you'll notice some cairns that indicate the climb to the Pic de Certascan. Climb steeply N on a more or less clear trail through scree and gain the ridge that leads to the Pic de Certascan. Stay close to the ridge as you climb to the summit. Go around the west side of a rocky eminence as the end of the climb approaches and finally climb on boulders to the top of the:
0.40 Pic de Certascan (2853m). Follow the same track on your way down to the Coll de Certascan.

DAY 28
Refugi de Certascan
to Refugi del Cinquantenari

This stage contains a short wilderness walk on the way down to Pla de Boavi, but generally it's a relatively easy walk without any major difficulties. The Haute Route again passes through great mountain scenery and encounters some of the most beautiful lakes of the region, including the Estany Romedo de Dalt. The Baborte lakes are a delightful place to spend the night. A short-cut from Coll de Sellente to Estany de Sottlo is described at the end of the route.

Route:	via Estany Romedo de Dalt (2114m) and the Coll de Sellente (2485m)
Grade:	2
Time:	7hrs 15mins
Height gain:	1200m
Height loss:	1000m
Map:	Mapa Excursionista/Carte de Randonnées, 1:50,000, no 22: Pica d'Estats – Aneto

0.00 Refugi de Certascan. Go down E to a small lake (2205m) and walk along its north shore. Continue to go down, keeping left of a stream that cascades down, and arrive at a junction. Don't go all the way down to a dirt road, but turn left and gain height on a path that climbs in a number of small zigzags (red marks). Near the end of the short climb, the path makes a surprising swing to the left and arrives at a pass on the Serra de Lluri (2250m). Go down on the east side to:

1.00 Estany Romedo de Dalt (2114m), a large lake with a few tiny islands (and excellent places for a bivouac). Walk along the south shore of the lake and go down SE on the right side of a stream towards Estany Romedo de Baix (2020m). Walk along the south shore of the dammed lake (there is a short rocky section that requires a little care) and walk to a dirt road coming from Tavascan. Walk to the dam of:

1.45 Estany Romedo de Baix (2020m) and cross it. Turn right immediately and go down S on a vague track, marked with a few cairns, keeping left of the Riu de Romedo. During this descent you cross a side-stream and arrive at an ancient *cabana*. Here the route becomes faint. Just continue to go down and you'll find hints of a path and some cairns. Eventually you have to cross the beautiful stream just below one of the many tiny cascades. The route soon bends away

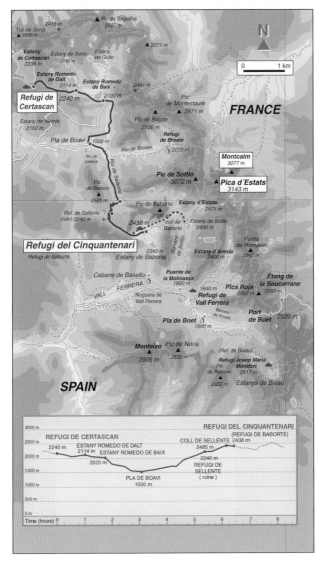

*Tiny islands in the
Estany Romedo
de Dalt*

from the stream, which disappears in a minor gorge. Find
your own way down in a forest (here and there are hints of a
path and a few cairns, but you are on your own now) and
work your way towards the stream. Follow it as you go down
to the eastern section of a large flat area, the:

3.05 Pla de Boavi (1500m). Cross the stream again, this time
by a footbridge (care needed!) and go SE on an obvious path
to enter a forest with large pine trees. Climb gently in
zigzags until you arrive at the Riu de Sellente. Cross the
stream and follow the path that bends away from the stream
and soon arrive at a junction. Don't go to the Vall de Broate
(another fine walk!) but turn right and climb SSE on a path
that approaches the Riu de Sellente. Cross the stream after a
rocky section (1800m) and climb above the west side of the
Riu de Sellente. Recross the stream at about 2000m and
walk along the east side of a large plateau in the upper

section of the valley. At the end of the plateau the path bends to the right, crosses several minor streams and goes up in a large zigzag to arrive at what is left of:

5.25 Refugi de Sellente (2240m), situated beside a small flat area. Cross a stream and walk S through the plateau. The route becomes faint, but as you climb SSE you'll find cairns that lead easily to the Coll de Sellente, a large saddle.

6.10 Coll de Sellente (2485m). Work your way down to the unstaffed, orange-coloured:

6.25 Refugi del Cinquantenari (2438m, also called Refugi de Baborte), situated on a bluff and overlooking the largest Baborte lake. The solid hut has places for about nine. Needless to say that there are lots of fine places to pitch the tent.

Short-cut: From Coll de Sellente to Estany de Sottlo

This is a useful short-cut for those who are interested in the ascent of the Pica d'Estats (see after day 29).

6.10 Coll de Sellente (2485m). Go down a few metres and turn left, finding your own way NE. Soon you'll find some kind of a track, rather faint in places, that climbs NE. Notice two tiny lakes on your right and continue to a much larger lake (giant rock in the water). Cross its outflow and keep the lake and another, much smaller lake, on your left-hand side. Climb NE on a steep scree slope without difficulties to the:

7.00 Coll de Baborte (2602m, Pic de Barborte, 2938m, is on your left). Go down steeply NE through a scree slope (a few cairns to guide you) to a tiny tarn below. Keep the tarn on your right-hand side, walk along the south side of another tiny tarn (2500m) and turn right. Go down ESE on a vague track (a few cairns here and there), cross a stream twice and arrive soon at the:

7.30 Estany de Sottlo (2392m), excellent bivouac places at the north side, but walkers who prefer a *bivouac solitaire* are advised to turn right and walk to the south side, where a few nice places for the tent can be found. The lake is an excellent base for the ascent of the Pica d'Estats. Follow the route to Pica d'Estats, described at 'Ten classic summits' (end of day 29), and follow the route in reverse to arrive at Refugi de Vall Ferrera in order to pick up the Haute Route.

DAY 29
Refugi del Cinquantenari to Étang de la Soucarrane

A relatively short and easy walk, mainly on well-worn paths. However, route finding becomes somewhat difficult during the climb to the Port de Boet. After having stayed in Spain for several days, the Haute Route pays a brief visit to France. You'll spend the night in your tent in the upper section of the Vallée de Soulcem, near the enchanting Étang de la Soucarrane.

Route:	via the Vall Ferrera and the Port de Boet (2509m)
Grade:	2
Time:	5hrs
Height gain:	700m
Height loss:	1050m
Map:	Mapa Excursionista/Carte de Randonnées, 1:50,000, no 22: Pica d'Estats – Aneto

0.00 Refugi del Cinquatenari. Go down towards the lake and walk along the eastern shore to the outflow. Don't cross the outflow but go down S rather steeply through grass and scree on a path that bends away from the stream. The descent then eases somewhat, the path approaches the stream and you continue to go down in an open valley. You'll arrive at a *cabana*:

1.00 Cabana de Basello, situated on the edge of a small plateau. The path forks here. Don't cross the stream, but turn left and go down towards a stone wall next to a pasture. Go down SE on a path that becomes a little faint now and then. Near the end of the descent to the floor of the Vall Ferrera the path broadens. Cross the Barranc de Sottlo that's coming from Estany de Sottlo and walk to the:

2.00 Puente de Molinassa (1800m), a solid bridge on the Noguera de Vall Ferrera. Cross the bridge and climb a few metres to reach a dirt road. Turn left and climb gently for about 15mins on the road until a signpost on your left indicates Refugi de Vall Ferrera. Don't turn left at the signpost but follow the road to arrive a few minutes later at a large plateau:

2.30 Pla de Boet (1900m), a beautiful flat area with places suitable for pitching the tent (you may have to pay a small fee in summer; unfortunately the Pla de Boet is often used

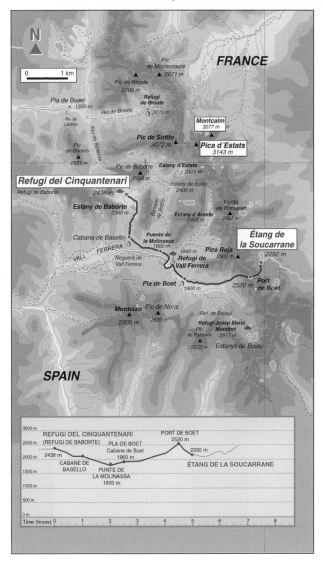

Should you want to go to the *refugi*, then turn left at the junction, cross the Riu de Baiau by a footbridge and climb on the right side of the Barranco d'Areste to the hut. Cross the stream just before you arrive at the hut (1940m). It takes about 10mins from the signpost to the hut. Refugi de Vall Ferrera is a staffed hut, owned by de FEEC, and is open from mid-June until the end of September. Many walkers use the hut as a base for the ascent of the Pica d'Estats (3143m), the highest summit of the Catalonian Pyrenees and one of the ten classic summits described in this guide (see end of day 29). Reservation necessary in summer. 35 places, meals available, tel. 973 620 754.

Bivouac at Estany de Sottlo (short-cut to Estany de Sottlo)

for summer camps). Leave the GR11, cross the Riu de Baiau, which runs through the Pla de Boet, by a few footbridges and climb to Cabana de Boet, a few metres above the plateau. Here you'll find a path that climbs E to the Port de Boet. Gradually the path becomes faint, but some old marks, cairns, cattle tracks and hints of a path will help you as you work your way up to a broad saddle on the French–Spanish border, the:

4.30 Port de Boet (2509m), south of the Pic de la Rouge (Pica Roya, 2902m). Enter France, ignore a path (yellow marks) that branches off to the right and go down NE on a well-marked path (yellow marks, cairns) on rough terrain. It offers no problems and you arrive at:

5.00 Étang de la Soucarrane (2292m). Bivouac possible next to this beautifully shaped lake, which is often visited by French fishermen.

TEN CLASSIC SUMMITS

10: Pica d'Estats (3143m) and Montcalm (3077m) from Refugi de Vall Ferrera

Height gain:	around 1350m for both summits
Time:	9hrs; allow 5hrs to reach the summit of the Pica d'Estats
Grade:	F (for both summits)

The Pica d'Estats is situated on the French–Spanish border, but this summit is regarded by the Catalonian people very much as their own mountain. The Pica d'Estats is the highest mountain of the Catalonian Pyrenees. On your way to the top you'll meet lots of Catalonian climbers. Next to the Pica d'Estats, on French territory, is Montcalm, highest summit of the Ariège and the most easterly summit that exceeds 3000m. It's a long and tiring climb from Refugi de Vall Ferrera, but this climb is worth every step. The Vall de Sottlo, with its lakes, cascades and all sorts of flowers, won't let you down. Estany de Sottlo (how blue can water be?) is a much used base for the climb by those who don't want to spend the night in the refugi (see the short-cut to Estany de Sottlo, described in the previous stage).

The ascent contains no major difficulties in late summer. In early summer, however, the French section of the climb could be snow covered, as could the slopes south of the Port de Sottlo, so take crampons and ice axe. →

0.00 Refugi de Vall Ferrera (1940m). Pica d'Estats is indicated with a signpost. Climb N in short zigzags on an obvious path. You reach a junction at around 2100m (signpost). Turn left and follow a path that climbs a little to a kind of pass (signpost). Walk NNW on a more or less level path that turns towards the Vall de Sottlo. Go down very steeply (care needed; rather awkward for walkers carrying heavy loads) a few metres and walk to the:

1.10 Barranc de Sottlo (2160m). Cross the stream by a footbridge and gain height on an obvious path with the stream on your right-hand side. Cross a beautiful plateau and climb energetically in a few zigzags. Soon after you have worked your way out of the valley, you reach the:

2.15 Estany de Sottlo (2392m), a large lake that offers a view on the Estats south face. Walk along the west shore of the lake, cross a small marshy area and climb towards the stream coming from Estany d'Estats (2471m). Climb with the stream on your right-hand side for a while, cross the stream and climb to the south shore of the lake. Cross the stream once more. Gain height above the west shore of the lake, cross a small plateau and climb N very steeply on a slope full of scree to the:

4.00 Port de Sottlo (2894m). Go down on the French side of the pass on a steep slope above the Étang de la Coumette (2736m) and gain height on a track that bends to the right. The route climbs through a gully, which may be covered with snow, and you arrive at the Col de Riufret (2978m). Turn left if you want to go to the Montcalm (3077m, there is a clear path going to the large summit) or turn right if you want to go to the Pica d'Estats (3143m). Climb without problems on a steep slope to gain the ridge that links Pica d'Estats with Pic Verdaguer (3131m, west of Pica d'Estats) and follow the ridge to the summit of:

5.00 Pica d'Estats (3143m), heavily decorated. Follow the same route on your way back to the *refugi*.

DAY 30
Étang de la Soucarrane to Refugi de Sorteny

Route:	via the Port de Rat (2540m)
Grade:	2
Time:	6hrs 15mins
Height gain:	1000m
Height loss:	1320m
Map:	IGN Carte de Randonnées, 1:50,000, no 7: Haute Ariège – Andorre

Again a stage without any major difficulties under normal conditions, but route finding is not always easy. Here and there the path becomes faint, and with only few marks it might be difficult to stay on course. On the Port de Rat you enter Andorra, where you walk for about two days. The Haute Route stays as much as possible in the mountains to avoid the 'civilised' world of Andorra.

0.00 Étang de la Soucarrane. Walk along the south shore of the lake to the outflow and cross it. Turn right and go down on a path with the stream on your right-hand side (notice an *orri* (ancient hut) on your left). The stream soon disappears and you arrive at a junction, which is not too obvious. Don't

Looking back to the Port de Boet and the Pic de la Rouge (2902m)

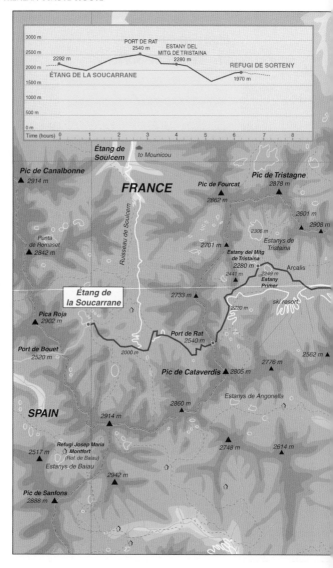

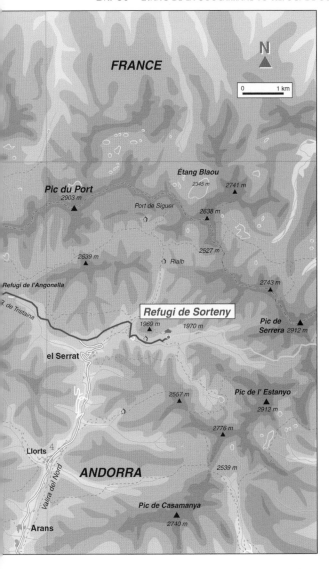

turn left to go all the way down to the valley floor, but turn right and walk on a small balcony to meet the stream again. Cross one stream, and another a few seconds later, and walk S on the path until you reach a dirt road in the upper section of the Vallée de Soulcem. This road runs through the valley, climbing in zigzags in the southern part, and finally makes a large swing to the east side of the valley. Work your way down to the place where this swing begins. Before you reach the Médecourbe-stream, you'll meet a path with yellow marks. Follow this path, cross the stream and go down to the dirt road. Follow the road, that climbs gently to the east side of the valley. After the first hairpin bend you'll find a path (cairns, yellow marks; also occasional ancient red marks) that climbs SE along the Ruisseau de Rat. Follow this path, keeping the stream on your right-hand side until the path turns to the left at about 2200m. Leave the stream, and on a path that's easy to follow climb N and, in the final stage, E to arrive at:

2.45 Port de Rat (2540m), which gives access to Andorra and offers a disappointing view of a ski resort. Go down in zigzags on the east side of the pass (snow tends to last on this side) until you arrive at a dirt road in the ski area. It's possible to follow this road, but it is better to take a more direct way towards the place where the road (coming from El Serrat) ends (large parking area, restaurant/bar), crossing the road a few times. Walk to bar/restaurant La Coma (opened in summer, self-service) and take the path around the back of the building. Gain height N on this obvious path until you see:

4.00 Estany del Mitg de Tristaina (2280m). Go down to the lake, cross a stream and climb a few metres to find an obvious path (that enables tourists to visit the Tristaina lakes). Turn right, walk along the north shore of Estany Primer and go down E carefully on a path that is a little exposed. Work your way down to a tiny dam (work is underway on a larger dam, which was almost finished in 2003) in the stream from the lakes, the Riu de Tristaina, and cross this. Go down on a large ski piste (ignore a dirt road branching of to the right) until you arrive at a road (1940m, large building on the other side of the road: Edifici Arcalis). Turn left and go down for 50m to a hairpin bend. Take a short-cut by following a stretch of the ancient road to El Serrat (no shops in this

unattractive village, just a few hotels), which you'll see on
your left and which descends very gently. Arrive at the road
again just past a bridge and follow the road for 2.4km. Turn
left at a junction and climb gently on a small tarmac road for
1.7km until you arrive at a new parking area where the road
ends and a dirt road (closed during the day) to the Vall de
Sorteny (this valley is a nature reserve: Parc Natural de la
Vall de Sorteny) begins. Follow this road for half an hour to
the place where it ends or take a short-cut after about 200m
(signpost, possibly with a squirrel on it). Go through a gate
and walk on a gently climbing path in a straight line for a
few minutes to the Refugi de Sorteny, seen ahead of you.
6.15 Refugi de Sorteny (1970m), a large, unstaffed hut with
places for 30. Water should be available next to the hut, but
the water point isn't always working.

DAY 31
*Refugi de Sorteny
to Camping d'Incles*

Route:	via the Collada dels Meners (2713m)
Grade:	2
Time:	7hrs 40mins
Height gain:	1100m
Height loss:	1230m
Map:	IGN Carte de Randonnées, 1:50,000, no 7: Haute Ariège – Andorre

A beautiful but tough
stage through a real
mountain wilderness
in the north of
Andorra. Route find-
ing is difficult during
the last four hours of
the walk: there are
very few marks and,
in some places, no
path or just a very
vague track.

0.00 Refugi de Sorteny. Walk ENE on a path, marked with
red–yellow paint flashes, left of a stone wall, and keep the
Riu de Sorteny at a distance on your right. Pass a small
marshy area and follow the obvious path that gradually
approaches the stream. Cross the stream at last at 2150m.
The path bends to the right and climbs in short zigzags to a
pass, the Pas de la Serrera (2231m). Go down a few metres
and follow the path that climbs gently SE. Notice a *cabana*

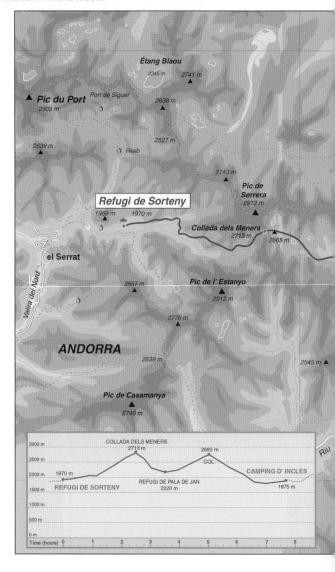

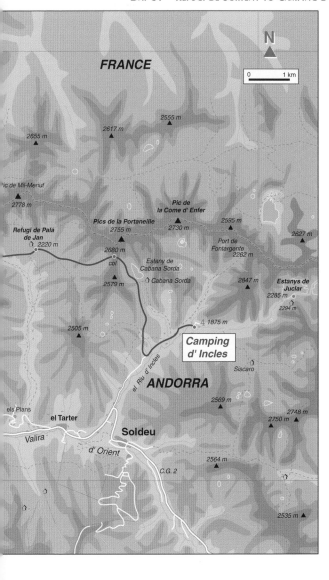

Looking down on the north section of the Vall d'Incles

on your right and continue climbing, with the Riu de Serrera on your right-hand side. Cross the stream at last and climb rather steeply, but without any problems, to the:

2.30 Collada dels Meners (2713m), also called Coll de la Mina, a small gap in the ridge between the Pic de la Serrera (2914m) and the Pic de l'Estanyo (2912m). In good weather you should have a clear view east of the ridge south of the Pic de la Portaneille (2755m), the second obstacle on today's walk. Go down on a steep scree slope on the east side of the pass. Notice Estany dels Meners (2619m) at a great distance on your left and go down on a clear track (red–yellow marks) to Estany de Ransol (2440m). Walk around the north side of the lake, staying well above it, and go down SE to arrive a few minutes later at:

3.10 a tiny tarn (2410m). Follow the obvious path that goes down SE in zigzags. Cross several streams before arriving at a small plateau. Cross another stream; don't go down to the floor of the Valle de Ransol, but follow a vague track in the grass that goes ENE to:

3.50 Refugi de Pala de Jan (2220m), also called Cabana Coms de Jan. It's a small, solid *cabana* that has been divided into two parts: one for the shepherd, the other (with places for two) for walkers. Here the route becomes faint. It is best to walk straight to the ridge in the east that separates the Vall de Ransol from the Vall d'Incles. Cross a stream east of the *cabana* and follow a vague track that heads east towards the ridge. Here and there you'll find some ancient red marks. At first the route climbs gently; in the final stage, however, you have to climb rather steeply to reach the ridge. It's not a difficult climb except near the end, when a small ravine has to be crossed and a little care is needed. Arrive on the ridge (about 2680m) not far from the Pic de la Portaneille, possibly with a fantastic view of Estany de Cabana Sorda. Go down SE on a steep grassy slope, out of sight of the lake. There may be a few waymarks, but basically you have to work your own way down. Near the end of the descent the Haute Route bends to the left and you walk towards the stream coming from Estany de Cabana Sorda. Don't cross the stream, but keep it on your left-hand side. Soon the stream disappears in a deep gorge, and you enter a pine forest and go down S on an obvious path towards the floor of the Vall d'Incles. Near the end of the descent the path turns left and you go down in an open valley to reach a small road in the valley. Turn left and follow this tarmac road for 1.5km. It leads to the northern end of the Vall d'Incles, where:

7.40 Camping d'Incles (1875m) is found. Nicely situated near the confluence of a few mountain streams, but unfortunately it has very poor facilities, and the bar (which also used to be a restaurant) sells only a few cold drinks. There's no food for sale. To buy food you have to go to the ugly, touristy village of Soldeu, 3km south of the campsite. There are hotels, restaurants, bars, a post office, a bank, cash dispenser and a few small supermarkets in the village.

Auberge d'Incles

DAY 32
Camping d'Incles
to l'Hospitalet-près-l'Andorre

This fourth section of the Haute Route ends with a nice walk along numerous lakes in Andorra and the Haute Ariège. The Haute Route leaves Andorra at the Port de l'Albe and stays in France for several days. Today there is some rough terrain to negotiate, especially on the north side of the Port de l'Albe, but the walk contains no major difficulties.

Route:	via the Port de l'Albe (2539m)
Grade:	2
Time:	6hrs 20mins
Height gain:	700m
Height loss:	1140m
Map:	IGN Carte de Randonnées, 1:50,000, no 7: Haute Ariège – Andorre

0.00 Camping d'Incles. Cross the Riu de Juclar and climb gently on a dirt road with the stream on your left-hand side. Don't turn right at a junction, indicated with a signpost after 15mins (the path leads to the unstaffed Refugi de Siscaro), but soon recross the Riu de Juclar by an old bridge (picnic area). Climb NNE on an obvious path (yellow marks from here to the *refugi*), initially on the left side of the stream. The path bends away from the stream but returns to it. Cross the stream by a footbridge near a small cascade. Climb steeply, with the stream now on your left-hand side, and soon the path bends away from the stream and arrives at a flat, marshy area. Cross the plateau and cross the stream once again by a footbridge. Walk upstream along the stream, cross the stream once more, and as you get very close to the first of the Estany de Juclar (2285m) the path seems to fork. The left path climbs to the small dam on the lake; the other climbs steeply to Refugi de Juclar. It doesn't really matter which one you follow, as both lead to the:

1.30 Refugi de Juclar. I found this rather large unstaffed hut (2294m) in excellent shape in 2003. Fine places to pitch the tent. Follow the path (yellow marks) E above the south shore of the lake, go down a few metres and turn left to follow a track between the two lakes. Climb NNE to a large pass: Collada de Juclar (2442m). Don't cross this pass but climb NE towards the:

2.30 Port de l'Albe (2539m), where you'll enter France. Go down NE on a steep slope full of stones and scree (not difficult but a little care is needed) to the beautiful Étang de l'Albe (2355m). Walk along the west shore of the lake, staying well above the water level. The Haute Route then bends a little to the left and goes down N on a small path, marked with some cairns. Pass a few tiny tarns and go down E rather steeply, but without problems, to the large:

3.45 Étang de Couart (2230m). Unfortunately the water in this lake is diverted by pipelines, and as a result the water level can be low. Walk along the south shore of the lake (the route along the north shore contains a short difficult section, should the water level be high). From the east side of the lake work your way SE through a rather chaotic landscape full of rocks to a large pass: the Couillade de Pédourés (2251m, 4hrs 15mins). Go down ESE on a clear path to:

4.30 Étang de Pédourés (2165m), which has a small dam on the east side. Walk above the north shore a little distance from the lake and go down SE through a small valley along the Ruisseau de Val d'Arques. Notice Cabane de Brougnic (2070m, a shepherds' hut) at a distance on your left and go down to a small dammed lake. Continue to go down SE until

Cloud reflection in one of the Estany de Juclar

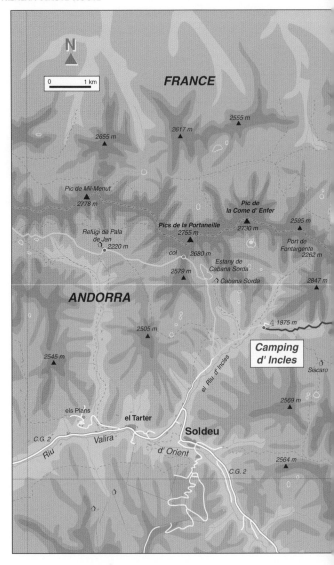

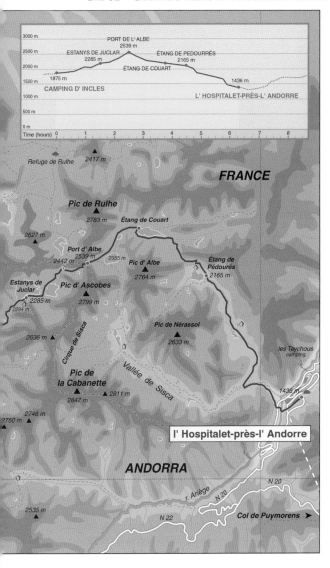

you arrive at an old stone bridge on the stream. Cross the stream, go down S on an obvious path, walk underneath a pipeline and arrive at a footbridge on the Ruisseau de Sisca (1740m). Cross the bridge and go down ESE to the village of l'Hospitalet, walking twice below the pipeline of the EDF (Electricité de France). Arrive at a road near the village. Cross the road and follow a small road that crosses a stream, the railway and a pipeline. Enter the village of:

6.20 l'Hospitalet-près-l'Andorre (1436m). Walk along the church and just keep on walking through the village to find the *gîte d'étape*. For more information about l'Hospitalet see the introduction to section 5 of this guide.

Signpost in l'Hospitalet-près-l'Andorre

SECTION 5:
L'HOSPITALET-PRÈS-L'ANDORRE TO BANYULS-SUR-MER
Through the Eastern Pyrenees to the Mediterranean Sea

The first stage of the Haute Route began with a warning, and so does the final part: don't underestimate the last stages of the Haute Route – for several reasons. First, the walk from l'Hospitalet-près-l'Andorre to Banyuls-sur-Mer is a long walk. The ten stages (some quite long) described in this section make it the longest of the five. Secondly, there are a few serious obstacles to be tackled.

The most difficult mountain appears on the second day: Pic Carlit, at 2921m the highest summit of the eastern Pyrenees. The impressive west face of Pic Carlit might well intimidate you, but fortunately there is an easy variant by which you can avoid Pic Carlit (described after day 34). Other high but less difficult obstacles are found on the fourth day (day 36), a classic walk in the Catalonian mountains that involves a long and (when conditions are favourable) quite easy walk on the frontier ridge, reaching an altitude of 2861m (Pic de Noufonts). On the sixth day (day 38) you finally have to face one of the most famous mountains of the Pyrenees: Pic du Canigou (2784m). The Haute Route leads to the summit of the Pic du Canigou!

Furthermore, the weather conditions in the eastern Pyrenees could turn the final section into a severe battle. Beyond the Carlit massif the influence of the Atlantic Ocean wanes, and the climate gradually becomes Mediterranean. In short, this means heat and drought. Especially on the last three days the high temperatures and the fact that there are practically no water points along the route can make mountain walking a rather unpleasant activity. All you can do is make a very early start in order to take advantage of the relative coolness of the early morning and refill water bottles at every possible occasion.

Overall, this last section of the Haute Route is a long walk that is not suitable for beginners and demands a thorough preparation. For Haute Route walkers walking the entire route, the walk from L'Hospitalet-près-l'Andorre to Banyuls-sur-Mer is a final test.

How will you feel as you enter the streets of Banyuls-sur-Mer? You will probably have mixed feelings – happy and relieved because everything has gone well, but at the same time there will be a sense of disappointment because a great journey is ending and you'll finally have to go home. You'll be assailed by all sorts of emotions, memories and thoughts as you make your last footsteps towards the Mediterranean Sea. Kev Reynolds, in his classic book *Classic walks in the Pyrenees,* couldn't have expressed better the feelings of Haute Route walkers as they arrive at Banyuls: 'And as you stand there with the water lapping against your legs you'll be tormented by a kaleidoscope of impressions that will take weeks to sift into some semblance of order. But by then you'll be planning your next trip. For trekkers are incurable dreamers.' So dream on about the Pyrenees, the over-whelming environment, the many highlights, the hard moments, the difficulties you have meet on your way and, who knows, about future adventures in the Pyrenees.

This section describes two so-called **consolation walks**, which have been included for those who were forced to avoid two major obstacles – Pic Carlit and Pic du Canigou. Walkers who avoid the hard climb to Pic Carlit on day 34 and follow the GR10 to Bouillouses can make the classic climb of Pic Carlit (2921m) from Bouillouses the next day (without heavy loads). This is an easy but very fine walk that includes a lovely circuit along a dozen lakes in the Désert du Carlit. It will add an extra day to your journey, but it will be a day to savour. Should you have followed the GR10 on day 38 – which doesn't visit the summit of Pic du Canigou (2784m) but goes around the mountain by a safe route – then it's worth considering the second consolation walk for the next day, a climb of this famous mountain from Cortalets. The route described is not just the classic route to the summit, but an exciting circuit via the Porteille de Valmanya and the Crête de Barbet.

Practical Information

L'Hospitalet-près-l'Andorre

Due to the railway, the traffic on the N 20 and the power sta-tion the tiny village of l'Hospitalet-près-l'Andorre, where the final section of the Haute Route starts, is far from attractive. But for various reasons walkers should not avoid l'Hospitalet. In the first place l'Hospitalet can easily be reached by public transport. There is a railway service from Paris to Latour-de-Carol. This train (a night-train that arrives early in the morning in l'Hospitalet – ideal for making an immediate start!) also stops in l'Hospitalet-près-l'Andorre. Secondly, there is a basic campsite north of the village, a tiny food shop, a post office, a cash dispenser, a hotel and a *gite d'étape* (open all year except November, tel. 05 61 05 23 14, meals available). Furthermore l'Hospitalet-près-l'Andorre lies at 1436m. Not a bad altitude to start a walk in the Pyrenean mountains!

Public Transport to L'Hospitalet-près-l'Andorre

As mentioned above there is a railway service from Paris to Latour-de-Carol. This night-train also stops in l'Hospitalet early in the morning. It's also possible to catch the TGV from Paris to Toulouse. There is a railway service from Toulouse to l'Hospitalet, and a bus service from Ax-les-Thermes (15km north of l'Hospitalet) to Andorra. Ax-les-Thermes is a good place to replenish food supplies.

Mouflons in the Carlit region

Public Transport from Banyuls-sur-Mer to Paris

There is a train service from Banyuls-sur-Mer to Paris.

Food

Replenishment of food supplies is possible in Bolquère (day 35, small shop), Amélie-les-Bains (day 39) and Le Perthus (day 41). There is the option to spend a number of nights in a mountain hut or a *gite d'étape*, which reduces the amount of food you need to carry for this section of the Haute Route.

Maps

* IGN Carte de Randonnées, 1: 50,000, no 8: Cerdagne-Capcir

- IGN Carte, 1:25.000, 2249 ET Font-Romeu
- Mapa Excursionista/Carte de Randonnées, 1:50,000, no 20: Puigmal – Costabona
- IGN Carte de Randonnées, 1:50,000, no 10: Canigou
- IGN Carte de Randonnées, 1:50,000, no 11: Roussillon

Accommodation in Banyuls-sur-Mer

It's a long walk from the beach to one of the two campsites in Banyuls. Go back on the GR10 trail to the tunnel underneath the railway. Don't go through the tunnel, but turn left and follow the road along the railway until you reach another tunnel underneath the railway. Turn right, go through the tunnel and go straight ahead. There is a choice of campsites. Turn right to Camping de la Stade (tel. 04 68 88 31 70), close to the sports stadium, or continue to a roundabout. Turn right and walk to Camping Municipal 'La Pinède' (which I prefer), on your right. There is a supermarket on the other side of the road.
Camping Municipal: email: camp.banyuls@banyulssurmer.com, tel. 04 68 88 32 13, fax 04 68 88 32 48.

There are numerous hotels, including the basic and not too expensive Hotel Pension Canal (tel. 04 68 88 00 75, fax 04 68 88 13 85, email: hotel.canal.ringot@wanadoo.fr, single rooms start at 25 Euros), in the Rue Dugommier, and Hotel Le Manoir (tel. 04 68 88 32 98, rooms start at 34 Euros, internet: www.hotellemanoir.com, open from June to October), in the Avenue du Maréchal Joffre.

Internet: www.banyuls-sur-mer.com (with a good English version)
Tourist information, email: otbanyuls@banyuls-sur-mer.com (Tourist Office)

Accommodation: Contact Details

All numbers and other information on accommodation on the Haute Route is also given in the route description.

Day 33: Refuge des Bésines – 05 61 05 22 44 (hut) or 05 61 64 44 73 (guardian);

Day 34: Chalet/refuge des Bouillouses – tel and fax 04 68 04 20 76; Auberge du Carlit – 04 68 04 22 23; Hotel des Bones Hores – 04 68 04 24 22

Day 35: Eyne – Cal Païe (04 68 04 06 96, fax 04 68 04 06 97); Gîte du Presbytère – 04 68 04 72 72

Day 36: Refugi d'Ull de Ter – 972 192 004 (hut) or 938 679 361 (guardian)

Day 37: Refuge de Mariailles – 04 68 05 57 99 or 04 68 96 22 90; email: mjordronneau@wanadoo.fr

Day 38: Chalet-Refuge des Cortalets – 04 68 96 36 19 (hut) or 04 68 96 18 90 (CAF-Prades); Gîte d'étape de Batère – 04 68 39 12 01

Day 39: Amélie-les-Bains: Hotel Residence Jeanne d'Arc – tel. 04 68 87 96 96, fax 04 68 39 06 07 and Hotel Le Canigou (tel. 04 68 39 00 68, fax 04 68 87 89 78)

Day 40: Las Illas – *Gîte d'étape* – 04 68 83 23 93 or 04 68 83 41 70; Bar/restaurant dels Trabucayres – 04 68 83 07 56

Day 41: Col de l'Ouillat – 04 68 83 62 20, fax 04 68 39 43 21, internet: www.ot-leboulou.fr/alberes.htm

Day 42: Banyuls-sur-Mer, see the information above.

DAY 33
l'Hospitalet-près-
l'Andorre to Refuge des Bésines

The final and longest section of the Haute Route begins with a very simple, short walk to a modern staffed hut.

Route:	via Étang des Bésines (1973m)
Grade:	3
Time:	3hrs
Height gain:	700m
Height loss:	50m
Map:	IGN Carte de Randonnées, 1:50,000, no 8: Cerdagne–Capcir

0.00 l'Hospitalet-près-l'Andorre (1436m). Should you have spent the night at the campsite, walk back to the village along the N 20, cross the railway and turn right just before Hotel du Puymorens. Enter the village, pass the *gîte d'étape* and turn left. Walk to a signpost that indicates the route to Refuge des Bésines. Leave the village and climb on a path that reaches the N 20 near a hairpin bend.

> In 2003 this section of the road was closed. Nowadays the traffic passes l'Hospitalet on the west side. There may be further changes to this stretch of road in the future.

Cross the N 20 and climb once more to the road that you follow now until the next curve.
0.30 Hairpin bend in the N 20 (1536m). Leave the N 20 and follow the path (red–white marks from the GR107) that climbs gently NE. Don't turn right at a junction, and a little later walk below two tiny cascades. Arrive at a pass (about 1800m) where a signpost indicates the *refuge*. In an open landscape the path bends to the right and goes down to a stream. Cross the stream and climb E until you reach an ancient railway (not in use; it was used when Étang des Bésines was being dammed). Let the railway guide you to:

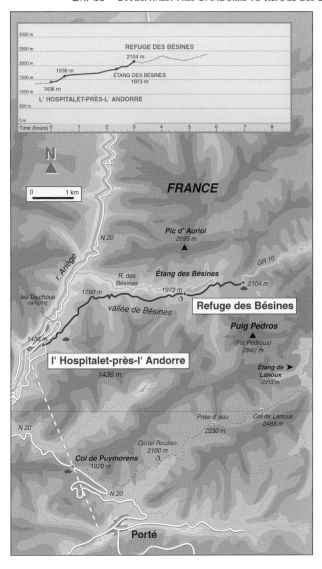

*Snow in June at
Refuge des Bésines*

2.25 Étang des Bésines (1973m). The path arrives at the small dam on the west side of the lake. Just before the lake there's a shepherds' hut, with a small room for walkers. Walk along the south shore of Étang des Bésines and walk E through the beautiful flat area east of the lake (notice a small *cabane* on the north side of this plateau). Cross a stream by a footbridge on the east side of the plateau and climb between some pine trees to:

3.00 Refuge des Bésines (2104m). A modern hut, staffed from June to the end of September, owned by de CAF. 55 places, tel. 05 61 05 22 44.

Advice
Take a good look at the next stage, which is very long and strenuous, and contains the difficult ascent of Pic Carlit (2921m). I strongly recommend that you continue on from the *refuge* and complete the first part of tomorrow's stage today. My advice is to walk to Estany de Lanoset, on the east side of the Col de Coume d'Agnel, and pitch the tent for the night there. It's about two hours' walk from Refuge des Bésines.

DAY 34
Refuge des Bésines
to Barrage des Bouillouses

Route:	via the Col de Coume d'Agnel (2470m) and Pic Carlit (2921m)
Grade:	1
Time:	7hrs 25mins
Height gain:	1100m
Height loss:	1200m
Map:	IGN Carte de Randonnées, 1:50,000, no 8: Cerdagne–Capcir

A long, tough stage with Pic Carlit as an obstacle that should be taken seriously. There are very steep slopes on both sides of this mountain to negotiate. Pic Carlit is always awkward for heavily loaded backpackers, especially the west face, which looks rather intimidating. Fortunately there is an alternative track (described at the end of the walk) that enables you to avoid Pic Carlit.

0.00 Refuge des Bésines. Follow the GR10 trail NE until it arrives on a small plateau with a stream running slowly through it. Don't cross the plateau but stay on the north side of it. Continue to climb NE until you reach a tiny lake (2350m) in a rocky area. Walk along the south shore of the lake and follow the red–white marks of the GR10 on rocks and stones as you climb to the large:

1.30 Col de Coume d'Agnel (2470m, snow tends to last well into summer just below the pass). Go down on an obvious path towards the north side of a giant, dammed lake: Étang de Lanoux. On your way down you pass Estany de Lanoset. Keep the lake on your left-hand side and walk to the Étang de Lanoux. Follow the path on the north side of the lake. The path goes up and down and arrives at a shepherds' hut, Cabane de Rouzet. Leave the GR10 (unless you prefer the easy variant described below), which climbs E to the Portella de la Grave, and follow a well-worn track above the east shore of Étang de Lanoux (2213m). The path goes up and down and arrives finally, before you reach the dam on the south side of the lake, at a very basic *cabane*. Leave the *cabane* on your right and go down a few metres to the Ruisseau des Fourats. Cross the stream and climb E on a path marked with cairns and some red paint flashes. Cross the stream once more and climb left of it to the small:

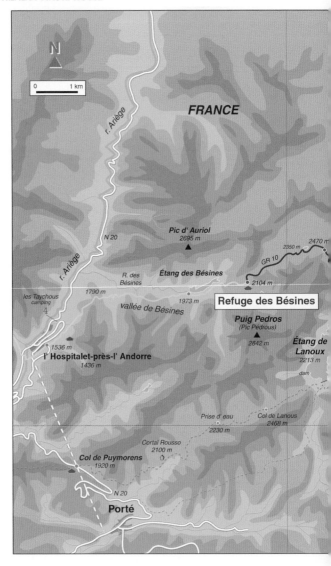

252

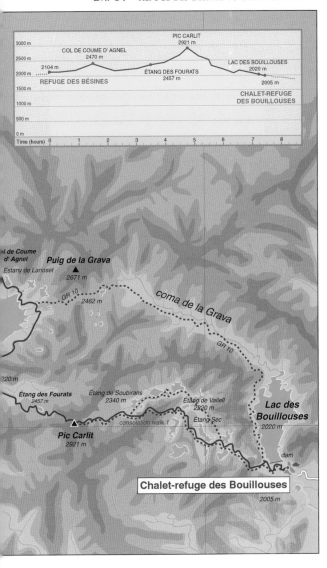

3.30 Étang des Fourats (2457m). Walk along the south shore of the lake E straight ahead to Pic Carlit. It's an unpleasant, rather awkward climb that is very steep and requires the use of both hands and feet in the final stage, when you are above a nasty section of boulders. A vague track and some cairns guide you to a pass (2910m), just below the summit of Pic Carlit. From here, climb from the pass to the highest summit of the eastern Pyrenees:

4.45 Pic Carlit (2921m). Go down, probably together with numerous tourists, on a very steep scree slope on the east side of Pic Carlit and soon arrive on a ridge. Continue to go down on this very steep ridge, using your hands here and there. On finally leaving the ridge, the route bends a little to the left, crosses a tiny stream at a place where snow tends to linger and go down E in zigzags without any problem on a stony slope. The stones eventually turn into grass. The path forks (2370m). Don't turn left on a path that descends to Étang de Soubirans (2340m), but walk to the tiny Étang de Vallell (2220m) and keep the lake on your left-hand side. Go down SE after a short climb to the Étang Sec and Étang de la Comassa. Walk between the lakes and, a little later, between Étang Noir and Étang del Viver. Continue to go down in a pine forest ESE to the dam of another giant lake:

7.15 Lac des Bouillouses (2020m). Pass a hotel/bar/restaurant to the right (des Bones Hores, tel. 04 68 04 24 22, which has has a dormitory for walkers), and walk on the dam (if open) or on a dirt road just below the dam (notice on your right a small tourist office) to:

7.25 Chalet-Refuge des Bouillouses (2005m), SE of the Lac de Bouillouses, beside a small road (D 60) coming from Mont-Louis, past a few buildings belonging to a *colonie des vacances*. The *refuge* is owned by the CAF, staffed from June until late September and has 45 places. Meals available, tel. and fax: 04 68 04 20 76. Reservation necessary. Auberge du Carlit also offers accommodation for the night (20 places, tel. 04 68 04 22 23).

Variant
GR10 Avoiding Pic Carlit

Route:	via the Col de Coume d'Agnel (2470m) and the Portella de la Grave (2426m)
Grade:	2
Time:	6hrs 10mins
Height gain:	650m
Height loss:	750m
Map:	IGN Carte de Randonnées, 1:50,000, no 8: Cerdagne–Capcir

The GR10 trail from Refuge des Bésines to the Lac des Bouillouses is a logical, easy and beautiful alternative to the awkward and strenuous climb of Pic Carlit. It is an easy walk on obvious tracks, which are marked with the red–white paint flashes of the GR10.

0.00 Refuge des Bésines. Follow the Haute Route until Cabane de Rouzet (see day 34). Stay on the GR10, turn left and follow an obvious path that climbs E towards the Portella de la Grave, which can be seen from far. The easy climb, straightforward on a sometimes eroded path, ends at the:

3.00 Portella de la Grave (2426m), a large saddle south of the Puig de la Grave (2671m). Go down steeply on the east side of the pass (possible snowfields just below the pass). The track soon bends a little to the left, eases somewhat and goes down ENE to a small lake:

3.20 L'Estagnol (2297m). North of the lake the GR10 bends to the right. Cross a stream and go down gently SE on a path in an open landscape with the Ruisseau de la Grave below on your left all the time. As you come closer to the Lac de Bouillouses more and more pine trees fill the valley. Cross several minor streams on your way down. Notice on your left a large delta-like marshy plateau with numerous streams running slowly through it. Climb a few metres and you'll see today's second giant lake, the:

5.20 Lac des Bouillouses (2015m). Go down towards the lake and soon arrive at a junction. Turn right and walk along the lake, which has a length of 3km. The path goes up and down between pine trees and finally arrives at the SW side of the lake. Pass a hotel/bar/restaurant on the left (des Bones Hores, tel. 04 68 04 24 22, which has a dormitory for walkers) and walk on the dam (if open) or just below it (you'll pass a small tourist office that has information on the Carlit region). Walk to the:

6.10 Chalet-Refuge des Bouillouses (2005m), SE of the Lac des Bouillouses, beside a small road (D 60) coming from Mont-Louis, past a few buildings belonging to a *colonie des vacances*. The *refuge* is owned by the CAF, staffed from June until late September and has 45 places. Meals available, tel. and fax: 04 68 04 20 76. Reservation necessary. Auberge du Carlit also offers accommodation for the night (20 places, tel. 04 68 04 22 23).

Consolation Walk 1
From Chalet-Refuge des Bouillouses to Pic Carlit Summit

This walk involves an ascent of the Pic Carlit (2921m) and a lovely circuit through the Désert du Carlit along a dozen lakes. The ascent is easy, although the final section of the climb is steep and requires the use of hands. A very early start is recommended because of the huge number of tourists that visit the Carlit region every day.

Grade:	F
Time:	5hrs 30mins; allow 3hrs to gain the summit
Height gain:	around 1000m

0.00 Chalet-Refuge des Bouillouses (2005m). Return to the SW side of the Bouillouses dam. Ignore the GR10, keep Hotel des Bones Hores on your right and walk S to a large signpost that indicates where fishing is allowed. Enter a pine forest, climb W and go through a marshy area until you arrive at a junction (2143m). Turn right, keep Estany Nègre at a distance to your left and walk NW along the west side of the beautiful Estany del Viver. Climb a few metres, pass a few lakes that have been overgrown by plants and arrive at Estany de les Dugues (2236m). Cross the outflow at the west side of the lake and follow the obvious path NW to Estany de Castella. Walk W and keep the Estany de Trebens (2306m) and Estany de Sobirans (2340m) on your right-hand side. Climb a little and arrive at a junction. Turn right and climb W on a scree slope until you arrive at a:

2.10 stream (2598m, possible snowfield). Cross the stream and walk to the ridge that leads to the summit. Climb this

Dawn in the Désert du Carlit (Estany de Llat)

very steep ridge W, using your hands here and there, and finally climb through a scree slope very steeply to a pass (2910m), just below the summit. Without any problems you'll reach the summit of:

3.00 Pic Carlit (2921m). Follow the main track of the Haute Route on the way down to Bouillouses (see the route description for day 34).

DAY 35
Barrage des Bouillouses to Eyne

Route:	via the village of Bolquère and the Col de la Perche (1579m)
Grade:	3
Time:	4hrs 45mins
Height gain:	100m
Height loss:	550m
Map:	IGN Carte de Randonnées, 1:50,000, no 8: Cerdagne–Capcir. Because the Haute Route is not very well marked on this map, I recommend that you use IGN Carte 1:25,000, 2249 ET: Font-Romeu as well.

A short, easy walk on tracks, road and dirt road. An attractive first hour, but unfortunately the rest is less interesting.

0.00 Chalet-Refuge des Bouillouses (2005m). Go down for a few minutes on the D 60 until you notice a footbridge on the

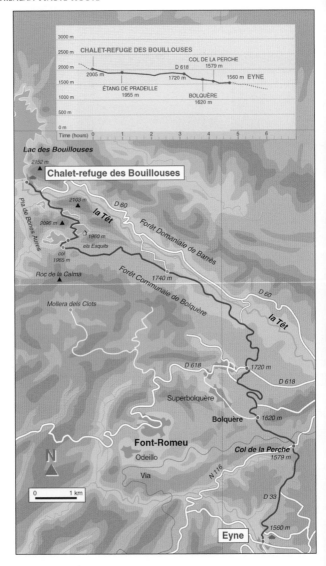

right side of the road. Leave the road, cross the bridge and follow a broad track. After about 50m the path forks. Leave the GR10, turn left and climb through a pine forest on a path with yellow marks. Notice Étang Racou at a distance on your right, and a little later go down steeply to the lovely Étang Long (Estany Llong). Walk along the south shore of the lake and go down between pine trees to the much larger Étang Noir (Estany Nègre). Turn right, walk along the west shore of the lake and follow the marks SW to the next large lake:

1.00 Étang de Pradeille (1955m, Estany de la Pradella). Haute Route and GR10 meet again S of Étang de Pradeille

*Island in the large
Lac des Bouillouses*

on a broad track. Turn left and follow this track (in fact more of a dirt road) E. It climbs initially a little and then goes down. Ignore the path that branches off to the Col del Pam (indicated with a signpost) and keep walking in the same direction. Cross a ski piste, walk under a ski lift and follow the dirt road until you arrive at a junction. Leave the GR10 to the right and follow an almost level old road, which is closed to traffic. You finally arrive at a picnic area with a snack bar (probably closed in summer) at a road:

3.10: the D 618. Turn left and follow the road (see on your left a parking area) for about 100m. Leave the road, turn right and follow a track SW, with a pine forest on your left-hand side. Ignore a path (yellow marks) on your left, enter the forest and just follow the most obvious track. After 10mins arrive at the D 10c, where the Haute Route meets the GR10 once again. Turn left and follow the GR10 as you walk on the road. Take a short-cut after about 300m and go down on the road that leads to the village of:

3.55 Bolquère (1620m). The GR10 takes a sort of short-cut in the village then returns to the main road (if you turn right here you'll find a small food shop, opposite the post office). Turn left and walk SE on the D 10. Cross a railway and soon arrive at the:

4.10 Col de la Perche (1579m, hotels, bars and restaurants but no shops). Cross the N 116, leave the GR10, which branches off to the left, and follow the D 33 for about 3km until you arrive at the hamlet of:

4.45 Eyne (1560m). There are no shops in the village, but there is a magnificent gite in the upper section of Eyne: Cal Païous (30 places, tel. 04 68 04 06 96; fax 04 68 04 06 97, excellent meals available. Reservation is necessary, at least a week in advance!!). Gite du Presbytère, tel. 04 68 04 72 72. Information on the Eyne nature reserve can be obtained at the Maison de la Réserve, below in the village.

Advice

Take a good look at the next long and quite hard stage (**height gain: 1700m**). My recommendation is not to stay in Eyne but to continue on and pitch the tent somewhere in the Vallée d'Eyne, for example near the remains of Cabane de l'Orri de Baix (2040m).

DAY 36
Eyne to Refugi d'Ull de Ter

Route:	via the Col d'Eyne (2683m), the Col de Noufonts (2652m), the Col de Noucreus (2796m), the Col de Tirapitz (2781m) and the Col de la Marrana (2535m)
Grade:	1
Time:	8hrs 15mins
Height gain:	1700m
Height loss:	1050m
Map:	Mapa Excursionista/Carte de Randonnées, 1:50,000, no 20: Puigmal–Costabona

A delightful stage that contains a long walk on a high ridge that forms the French–Spanish border. A true classic walk in the Catalonian mountains! Once all snow has disappeared, which should be the case in summer, the walk is surprisingly easy and contains no real difficulties. It follows the GR11 from the Col de Noufonts to Refugi d'Ull de Ter.

0.00 Eyne. Go down through the village to the road that links Eyne with the village of Llo. Walk S on this road, cross a stream by a bridge and turn left just before a parking area on the left side of the road. Walk S between some pastures on a track that leads to the Réserve Naturelle de Vallée d'Eyne (just follow the signposts). Soon you'll enter a forest, and the path climbs a little steeper. The path goes up in zigzags and eventually approaches the stream that runs through the Vallée d'Eyne. Don't cross the stream, but keep it on your left-hand side and gain height on an obvious path. Notice at an altitude of 2040m on the other side of the stream what is left of:

2.00 Cabane de l'Orri de Baix (2040m). Continue to climb, with the stream on your left-hand side, until a place (about 2300m) where another stream meets the stream you have been following. Cross the stream and climb through grass between the two streams. Cross a minor stream coming from the right. The grass turns into scree as you work your way up to the Col d'Eyne. The last part of the climb is rather steep but not difficult. Near the end the path bends to the right and climbs S to the:

4.10 Col d'Eyne (2683m), also called the Col de Nuria and the Col d'Eina. It's a broad saddle on the French–Spanish border between the Pic de Nuria (2794m) and the Pic d'Eina

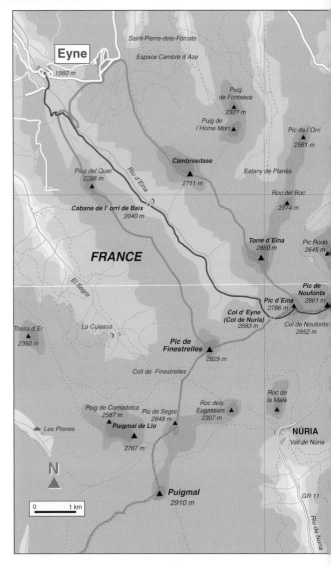

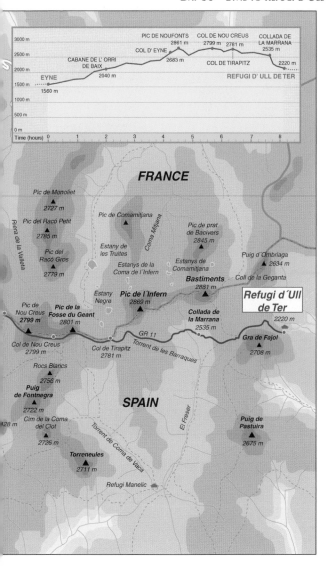

Walkers on the frontier ridge near the Pic de Noufonts

(2786m). Turn left and walk NE on a track towards the Pic d'Eina. Don't go all the way to the summit, but keep it at a distance to your left. Follow the frontier ridge and climb through scree on a track to today's highest point:

4.50 Pic de Noufonts (2861m). Go down carefully on the rather steep frontier ridge and arrive at the Col de Noufonts (2652m). Notice a *cabane* of stone on the pass and find the red–white marks of the GR11, which you will follow to Refugi d'Ull de Ter. Don't turn right (that path goes down to Nuria) but stay on the ridge and climb steeply, but without any problems, towards the Pic de la Fosse du Geant. Beyond a kind of pass the path, still on the ridge, goes up and down and arrives at the:

5.40 Col de Nou Creus (2799m). It won't be difficult to recognize the pass: there are nine small crucifixes to be found on the pass, which in French is called Col des Neufs Croix. Don't turn right to go down but stay on the ridge. Go down to the Col de la Vaca (2726m) and climb rather steeply towards the Pic de la Vaca (2826m). Don't go all the way to the top, but go around the summit. For the first time since the Col d'Eyne the path bends significantly away from the frontier ridge to go to a pass situated SE of the Pic de la Vaca:

6.25 Col de Tirapitz (2781m). Go down steeply in Spain on a path that makes a sharp curve to the north. Notice a round *cabane* at a distance to your left and go down E. Cross several minor streams before you reach the floor of the so-called Circo de Freser (2450m). Notice a variant of the GR11 coming from the right (from Refugi de Coma de Vaca) and climb from here E on rough terrain and arrive without any problems at the:

7.40 Collada de la Marrana (2535m), situated between the Puig de Bastiments and the Pic Gra de Fajol. Go down initially NE rather steeply in the Circo d'Ull de Ter (unfortunately partly ski resort). The descent eases somewhat and finally you go down ESE through an area that's severely scarred with ski pistes. The path gets lost a little here, but it won't be difficult to find Refugi d'Ull de Ter.

8.10 Refugi d'Ull de Ter (2220m), owned by the CEC (internet: www.cec-centre.org), staffed from mid-June until late September. 52 places, tel. 972 192 004 (hut) or 938 679 361 (guardian), meals available.

DAY 37
Refugi d'Ull de Ter to Refuge de Mariailles

Today the Haute Route stays remarkably high for a long time: above 2200m. Also remarkable is the fact that several large plateaux have to be crossed. Near Roc Colom the route bends away from the French–Spanish border and goes NE towards the last high obstacle before the Mediterranean: the Pic du Canigou (2784m). Today you can admire the mountain; tomorrow you'll have to face it! Be aware that route finding can be very difficult today in poor visibility. Under normal conditions, however, all should go reasonably well.

Route:	via the Porteille de Mourens (2383m) and the Pla Guilhem (2300m)
Grade:	2
Time:	7hrs 15miins
Height gain:	600m
Height loss:	1110m
Map:	Mapa Excursionista/Carte de Randonnées, 1:50,000, no 20: Puigmal–Costabona

0.00 Refugi d'Ull de Ter. Go down NE on the GR11 track until after about 20 minutes you reach a road (2080m) that links the village of Setcases with the ski resort of Vall Ter. Leave the GR11, turn left and climb on this road for 15mins to the large parking area of Station de Vall Ter (2170m). The route from here is not obvious, and you'll have to search for it behind the buildings. Ignore a large track and climb NE on a small path above a stream that runs through a small ravine on your right-hand side. Gradually the path approaches the stream, which you cross at an altitude of 2285m. Don't turn left to go to the Porteille de Mantet, but climb rather gently E on a small path until you arrive at the:

1.15 Porteille de Mourens (2383m), situated on the French–Spanish border. The Porteille gives access to the first large plateau: the Pla de Coma Armada. Walk ENE through the grass on a more or less level track. The track is rather faint here and there, but fortunately the route has been marked with a line of large flat stones that have been set into the ground. Follow these marks that bend around the Puig de la Losa (2456m) and without any problems you'll reach the:

2.15 Porteille del Caillau (2387m), situated south of the next plateau, the Pla de Campmagre. Walk E on a more or less level and distinctive track and go around the Roc Colom

(2507m, the last frontier summit higher than 2500m). East of this mountain you arrive at a point that gives a fine view of the little cirque between the Roc Colom and the Pic de Costabona. Don't go down steeply in this cirque, but walk NE on a vague path. After a short steep descent you'll reach the Porteille de Rotja (2377m, small *cabana* on the other side of the pass). Keep the Porteille on your right-hand side and walk along the sharp, white ridge of the so-called Esquerdes de Rotja. Keep close to this pointy ridge as you walk on a sometimes very vague track (here and there marked with cairns and a few paint flashes). Eventually the Haute Route bends a little away from the ridge, but turns back to it and arrives on the ridge at:

4.25 Collade des Roques Blanches (2252m, a signpost indicates the pass), situated on the border of two nature reserves – Reserve Naturelle de Py and Reserve Naturelle de Prat de Mollo. During the ascent to the pass the path becomes faint and you'll have to improvise a little as you work your way up. Fortunately the pass can easily be recognised from a distance: there is a dirt road that leads to the Collade des Roques Blanches. There is a junction of dirt roads on the pass. Don't cross the pass, but follow the dirt road that climbs gently NE towards today's last large plateau: the Pla Guilhem (2300m). On this plateau the road makes a turn left and goes down NW. Leave the road (in poor visibility it's safer to follow the road) and walk N on a track to arrive at a huge cairn. Keep the cairn on your left-hand side and walk to a small *cabane*:

5.45 Cabane du Pla Guilhem (2265m). In addition, a short distance away you'll find a solid, unstaffed hut with places

Large cairn on the Pla Guilhem

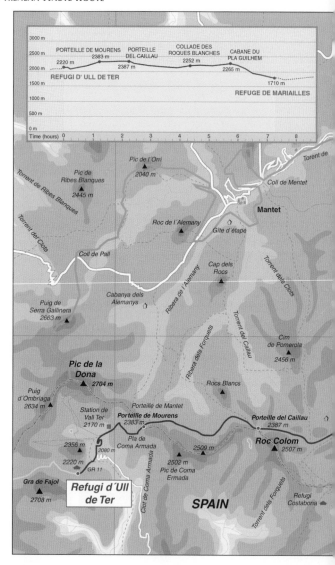

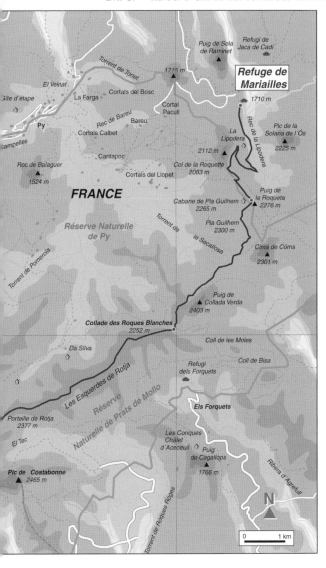

Refuge de Mariailles

1710 m

Puig de Sola de Raminet ▲

Refugi de Jaca de Cadí ⌂

Torrent de Tonet

1745 m

El Veinat

Gîte d'étape ⌂

La Farga

Cortals del Bosc

Cortal Pacull

Rec de la Lipodera

La Lipodera ⌂

Pic de la Solana de l'Ós ▲ 2225 m

Rec de Bareu

Bareu

Py

Cortals Calbet

2112 m ▲

Campelles

Cantapoc

Col de la Roquette 2083 m

Roc de Balaguer ▲ 1524 m

Cortals del Llopet

Puig de la Roqueta ▲ 2276 m

FRANCE

Cabane de Pla Guilhem 2265 m ⌂

Réserve Naturelle de Py

Pla Guilhem 2300 m

Torrent de

Cima de Cóms ▲ 2301 m

la Secallosa

Torrent de Pomerola

Puig de Collada Verda ▲ 2403 m

Collade des Roques Blanches 2252 m

Coll de les Moles

Da Silva ⌂

Coll de Bisa

Refugi dels Forquets

Les Esquerdes de Rotja

Réserve

Els Forquets

⌂

Porteille de Rotja 2377 m

Naturelle de Prats de Mollo

El Tec

Les Conques Châlet d'Aceceuil ⌂

Puig de Cagallops ▲ 1766 m

Ribera d'Agetull

Pic de Costabonne ▲ 2465 m

Torrent de Roques Roges

N

0   1 km

for twelve (no water). Improvise as you go down NNW and arrive at the dirt road again near the Col de la Roquette (2083m). The road goes down in a few long zigzags to the floor of the small valley of the Ruisseau de la Lipodère. Follow the road – or, better, take a few short-cuts – to the floor of the valley and walk N on the road to Refuge de Mariailles. Near the end of the walk you arrive at a junction of dirt roads. Here you'll see the *refuge*, but also on the right side of the road is a *refuge forestier* (solid building but closed to walkers) and (out of sight), about 100m S of it, a *cabane* (in very bad shape). Follow the road or walk in a straight line through the grass to:

7.15 Refuge de Mariailles (1710m). Staffed practically all year, 55 places, tel. 04 68 05 57 99 and 04 68 96 22 90. Email: mjordronneau@wanadoo.fr (reservation necessary in summer).

DAY 38
Refuge de Mariailles to Mines de Batère

A very long and strenuous walk that contains the last high obstacle of the Haute Route: the Pic du Canigou (2784m). The route goes over the top of this famous mountain. It's not a difficult climb in summer, when snow has disappeared from the slopes of the Canigou. The final section of the climb, however, is very steep and needs →

Route:	via the Pic du Canigou (2784m), the Col des Cortalets (2055m) and the Col de la Cirère (1731m)
Grade:	1
Time:	9hrs 15mins
Height gain:	1400m
Height loss:	1600m
Map:	Mapa Excursionista/Carte de Randonnées, 1:50,000, no 20: Puigmal–Costabona

0.00 Refuge de Mariailles. Walk back to the *refuge forestier*, where a signpost indicates the route to the Pic du Canigou. Leave the dirt road, turn right and follow a level path that goes parallel with the road. After having crossed the Ruisseau the Llipodère (1686m) by a footbridge the path bends to the left and climbs gently NE. Cross a minor stream after a short section SE and continue to climb NE to the Col Vert (1861m, difficult to recognize but indicated by a signpost), where you arrive at a gate. Go through the gate and climb E on the clear path, passing several gates, and go finally down a few metres to the Ruisseau de Cady (1964m, confluence of two streams). Cross the stream and walk for about 15mins NW on the GR10 trail. Leave the GR10 at a junction (signpost), turn right (there is a bad-weather variant that starts here, see below) and climb on a path (yellow marks). You'll arrive at:

2.00 Cabane Arago (2123m, three places, very basic, water point). In the Vallon de Cady the path climbs gently NE. The path has been marked with yellow paint flashes and with wooden posts with a yellow top and the route is therefore very easy to follow. Cross a tiny stream before you arrive at a kind of plateau, where the path climbs gently in long zigzags. It's possible to take a number of short-cuts instead of following the path that climbs in zigzags, thus creating a more direct route to the Porteille de Valmanya (2591m). Only the last part of the climb to the Porteille is rather steep and involves walking on rough terrain. A few metres below the Porteille you arrive at a junction (no signpost). Ignore the path that branches off to the right (to the Porteille de

← the use of hands in places. The descent from the top to Refuge des Cortalets (the classic route to the summit) is easy. This long walk can easily be cut in two by spending the night at Chalet-Refuge des Cortalets. A bad-weather variant from Refuge de Mariailles to Chalet-Refuge des Cortalets is described at the end of this day stage.

View from the Brèche Durier, close to the summit of the Canigou (2784m)

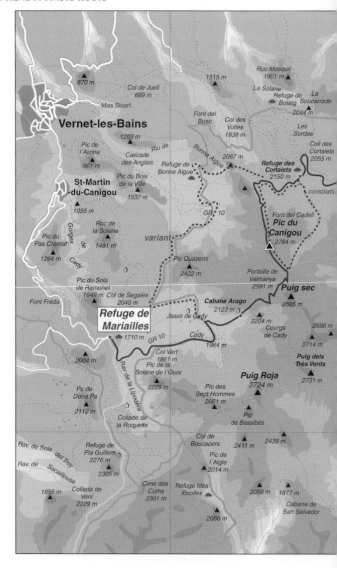

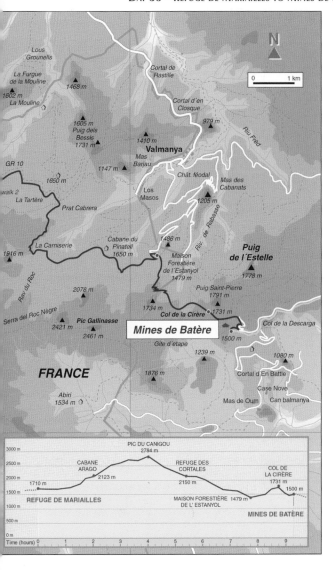

Valmanya, also yellow marks) and follow the path that stays below the Porteille. Climb NW on rocky terrain towards the Pic du Canigou until you reach a *cheminée* (natural staircase of stone, 2696m) and climb carefully through this so-called Brèche Durier to the top of:

4.00 Pic du Canigou (2784m), large crucifix, *table d'orientation* and various decorations. You won't be the only person on this peak that offers massive views of the eastern Pyrenees. The descent to Refuge des Cortalets presents no difficulties. Go down N in zigzags on an obvious path (yellow marks) through a slope full of loose scree. Keep the north ridge of the Canigou on your right-hand side on your way down to the Pic Joffre (2362m). Keep this summit also on your right-hand side, and past the summit the path makes a sharp turn to the right to soon reach the GR10 trail (signpost: 15mins to Cortalets). Go down generally E on an obvious path by Alpenrose to the small Lac des Cortalets (2164m), which in summer is an unattractive pool. Keep left of the lake and follow the path to:

5.20 Chalet-Refuge des Cortalets (2150m). Owned by the CAF, 85 places, staffed from June until late September, meals available. Overcrowded in summer, reservation necessary, tel. 04 68 96 36 19 (*refuge*) and 04 68 96 18 90 (CAF Prades-Canigou). There is also an unstaffed *refuge* that's open all year. A bivouac is possible a little distance from the hut. From the hut the Haute Route follows the red–white marks of the GR10 all the way to Mines de Batère. Follow a dirt road that goes down N (or take a path at the back of the *refuge*) and arrive after 15mins at a junction on the Col des Cortalets (2055m). Turn right and go down gently SE on a dirt road. After 4km, at Prat Cabrera, where the road makes a sharp curve to the left, you leave the road. On your right side you'll find a clear and generally level path on the steep slopes of the Canigou massif. Follow this magnificent trail, the so-called Balcon du Canigou. Walk S initially, then E, cross a few streams and arrive at Cabane du Pinatell (1650m, possibly closed, very basic), on your left below the path. The path stays more or less level for a while and then goes down in a few zigzags through a forest to the:

7.45 Maison Forestière de l'Estanyol (1479m), where the climb to the Col de la Cirère begins. Turn right past the building and climb S, rather steeply in places, between pine trees. After a pass and a short descent you cross a stream. The path bends to the left and climbs gently ESE to the:

8.45 Col de la Cirère (1731m, just above the trees). Go down ESE on a path until you reach a dirt road. Turn right and go down on this road until you arrive at a tarmac road. Follow this road for a few minutes. It will lead you to:

9.15 Gîte d'étape de Batère (1500m), left of the road and offering fine views. There is a bar/restaurant/hotel next to the *gîte*. Open all year, 35 places, tel. 04 68 39 12 01. No meals available in the *gîte*.

Variant
The GR10 from Refuge de Mariailles to Chalet-Refuge des Cortalets

Grade:	2
Time:	6hrs
Height gain:	850m
Height loss:	420m
Map:	Mapa Excursionista/Carte de Randonnées, 1:50,000: no 20: Puigmal–Costabona

This is a useful variant in case of very bad weather, as the GR10 trail curves around the Canigou.

0.00 Refuge de Mariailles. Follow the route as described in day 38 until the junction after crossing the Ruisseau de Cady. Don't turn right but follow the GR10 that climbs gently N. The path crosses a few giant rock slopes (very easy) and bends W to go to the:

2.10 Col de Segalès (2040m). This is hard to recognize, but fortunately there is a signpost that indicates the pass. Don't turn left (yellow marks), but walk NNE on a path that climbs a little until 2100m, then becomes almost level and finally goes down a little to the:

2.45 Col de la Jasse d'En Vernet (2047m). Go down NE on an obvious track until you arrive at an open area full of rocks and boulders. Cross this area, called Les Conques (1880m), with care, as the boulders are not always stable. Go down to cross another rock slope (Roc dels Isards, 1820m) and go

Snow-covered mountains in early May (GR10 trail between Marialles and Cortalets)

down WNW to a dirt road (1740m). Walk N on this practically level dirt road to:

4.15 Refuge de Bonne Aigue (1741m), an unstaffed hut with a water point (not always working). Leave the hut on your left, below, ignore a path branching off to the left (to Vernet-les-Bains) and continue on the dirt road for about 50m. Leave the road, turn right and climb energetically ESE in a number of zigzags between pine trees. Arrive at an open field, where you pass a beautiful *orri* (Casteille, ancient *cabane*, 1966m) on the left. Continue to climb, and the path makes a swing to the left and arrives at a rocky bluff (excellent views from here). The path turns to the right and climbs gently SE until you arrive finally near Fontaine de la Perdrix (2253m) at a junction. You are now on the main track of the Haute Route again. Turn left and follow the Haute Route, which in 15mins reaches:

6.00 Chalet-Refuge des Cortalets (2150m).

Consolation Walk 2
The ascent of Canigou from Cortalets

Grade:	F
Time:	4hrs
Height gain:	771m

0.00 Chalet-Refuge des Cortalets (2150m). Go back on the GR10 trail to the junction near the Fontaine de la Perdrix (2260m). Don't turn right, but leave the GR10 and continue to climb W on an obvious path (yellow marks). Go around the Pic Joffre (2362m) and climb S along the north ridge of the Canigou. The path always stays a little to the right of the ridge and finally climbs in a number of zigzags to the summit of the:

1.45 Pic du Canigou (2784m), giant cross, *table d'orientation* and other decorations. Splendid views in good visibility from the Mediterranean to the Carlit massif. Go down S through the so-called Brèche Durier (very steep but not difficult). Hands are required here and there. When the base of the *brèche* is reached, follow the path SE on the right of a ridge. The rocky path descends gently. Notice a lovely narrow *brèche* on your left and continue to a junction (no signpost) a few metres below the Porteille de Valmanya. Turn left and climb to the:

2.45 Porteille de Valmanya (2591m), a large pass that offers fine views. Turn left and climb NE on a well-worn path (yellow marks) on the right of a ridge until you finally reach the ridge at a pass at 2712m (fine view of the vertical east face of the Canigou). Go down NE on the ridge on a path that stays a little to the left of it. The path leaves the ridge at about 2500m to go down N. Notice a giant cairn next to the path and enter a pine forest at 2350m. Go down NNW until you arrive at:

4.00 Chalet-Refuge des Cortalets (2150m).

For those who were forced to take the GR10 to Cortalets, this walk offers the ascent of the Canigou from Cortalets and a surprising return to Cortalets by the Crête de Barbet.

This is a beautiful circuit without any major difficulties – only the descent in the Brèche Durier requires a little care (steep; use of hands is needed here and there; certain of risk of stonefall). This walk can easily be accomplished (by those without heavy loads – you can leave heavy rucksacks at the refuge!) in the morning, and in the afternoon you could follow the Haute Route to Batère.

DAY 39
Mines de Batère
to Amélie-les-Bains

Not a spectacular walk, but a short, easy and pleasant one, mainly on dirt roads. The Haute Route goes all the way down to Amélie-les-Bains (220m), where palm trees greet you. Relax in this friendly village in the afternoon and take a deep breath for tomorrow's climb to the Roc de Frausa.

Route:	via the Col de Descarga (1393m) and the Col de Formantère (1133m)
Grade:	3
Time:	4hrs 45mins
Height gain:	100m
Height loss:	1380m
Map:	IGN Carte de Randonnées, 1:50,000, no 10: Canigou

0.00 Mines de Batère. Go down on the road for about 700m and arrive at the Col de Descarga (1393m), where the road makes a sharp curve to the right. The Haute Route and GR10 leave the road on the col. Turn left, leave the GR10 (which branches off to the right to go down to Arles-sur-Tech), and climb gently on a dirt road. After half an hour you'll notice on your left, above the road, the remains of the Tour de Batère (1439m). Near the tower the road starts to go down. Follow the road, ignore a road after 100m that branches off to the right and don't turn left at the second hairpin bend. Go down E now on the dirt road that passes below a ridge on your right-hand side. You'll arrive at the:

1.40 Col de Formantère (1133m, also called the Col de Croix de Fer), where several dirt roads meet. Go down in the same direction, now with a ridge on your left-hand side. Walk under a high-tension cable and pass what is left of the former mines of Formantère. Past the buildings the road bends to the right and goes down S in a few zigzags. Go down E again and ignore a dirt road coming from the left. Go down E on the broad ridge after a few zigzags until, in a forest, you reach the:

2.45 Col de la Redoute (875m, also called Col de la Reducta), junction of dirt roads. Follow the broad dirt road that goes gently down S. Don't turn right at the second sharp curve, but continue to go down until you reach a tarmac road. Follow this road SSE, notice a few houses on your right below, and walk until the road makes a large curve to the left. Leave the road at this curve, turn right and walk towards a TV antenna. Pass the antenna and go down on a path (yellow marks) to a dirt road. Turn left, follow the dirt road for about 50m, and turn right (a signpost indicates Amélie). Go down rather steeply ESE on a path through woods and shrubs. Ignore the path that branches off to Montbolo, and a little later take the left path on the junction 'Amélie–Arles' (signposted). Go down to the first house of Amélie-les-Bains, where the path makes a sharp turn right. Walk on a level path and enter the village. Turn left immediately and go down through the village. Pass a small park (on your right), cross the River Tech and turn left. Walk along the river until you arrive at a small roundabout (take notice of tomorrow's climb to the Roc de France, that starts here). Turn left and keep following the Tech until you finally arrive at the campsite of:

4.35 Amélie-les-Bains (220m). A small village with hotels, casino, bus service to Perpignan, banks, cash dispenser, post office, supermarket. Not a bad place to relax for half a day. There are several basic and not too expensive hotels in Amélie, such as Hotel Residence Jeanne d'Arc (tel. 04 68 87 96 96, fax 04 68 39 06 07, rooms for one start at 18 Euros)

Looking back to the village of Amélie-les-Baines

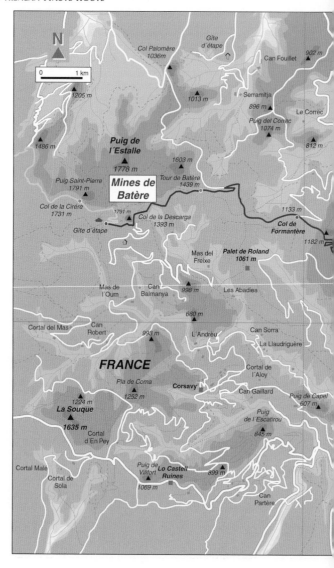

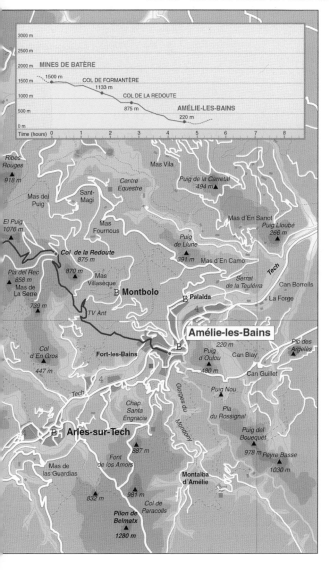

and Hotel Le Canigou (tel. 04 68 39 00 68, fax 04 68 87 89 78, rooms for one start at 16.76 Euros).

Amélie-les-Bains on the internet: www.amelie-les-bains.com

Tourist office, email: omtt.amelie@little-france.com

DAY 40
Amélie-les-Bains to Las Illas

This walk involves the last long climb of the entire Haute Route. On a hot summer's day the climb to Roc de Frausa (also called Roc de France), on the French–Spanish border (offering superb views especially of the Canigou massif), is quite hard. After a brief visit to Spain the Haute Route returns to France, where you can spend the night in the quiet hamlet of Las Illas.

Route:	via the Roc de Frausa (1450m), the Col du Puits de la Neige (1250m) and the Col de Lly (713m)
Grade:	2
Time:	6hrs 30mins
Height gain:	1400m
Height loss:	1070m
Map:	IGN Carte de Randonnées, 1:50,000, no 11: Roussillon

0.00 Amélie-les-Bains. Walk back from the campsite to the small roundabout in the village. Turn left between a garage and Parking Général De Gaulle (Roc de France is indicated). Climb S on a small road for about 100m until you reach a gate. Don't go through the gate but turn right just before it (Roc de France is indicated on a tree). Gain height on a path that climbs initially rather steeply along a wall and then through a forest. Shortly after a spot that offers a very fine view back on Amélie-les-Bains, you arrive on a junction. A signpost indicates Roc de France. Don't turn right but climb on a path which is marked with yellow paint flashes. The climb eases significantly as you come closer to Can Felix, a large farmhouse.

2.00 Can Felix (782m). Don't go through the gate that gives access to the farm (don't even think about it) but follow the marks on the right side of the building and the fence. As you pass the land that belongs to Can Felix the Haute Route joins

the GR10 trail. Turn left and follow the red–white marks on
your way to Roc de Frausa. On your way up you'll pass the
remains of the Cortal de la Garrigue (900m; keep the farmhouse on your right-hand side), the Col Ric (961m) and the
Pic de la Pourasse (1272m; the Haute Route stays on the
right of this summit). At an altitude of 1300m, and very close
to the frontier-ridge, your route bends away from the GR10,
which branches off to the left and goes E through the lovely
beech forest known as the Bois de la Marquise. The junction
is indicated with a signpost.

> In poor visibility it makes no sense to go to the Roc de
> Frausa. Just follow the GR10, which leads without any
> problems to the Col du Puits de la Neige, and from
> there follow the Haute Route.

Climb S on a small path to the frontier (don't pay attention to
a path with blue marks on your right side). When you are
close to the border, just above the trees, the Haute Route
bends to the left. Keep a small rock face on your right-hand
side, the Roc de Frausa Occidental (1417m), and climb to
the highest summit:
4.00 Roc de Frausa Oriental (1450m, today's highest point).
Walk E on the frontier ridge, pass an antenna on the left and
keep a small concrete road that leads to the antenna on your
right-hand side. Go down on the ridge, initially through
open landscape and then through a beech forest. In the

*Cork-oak trees in the
Eastern Pyrenees*

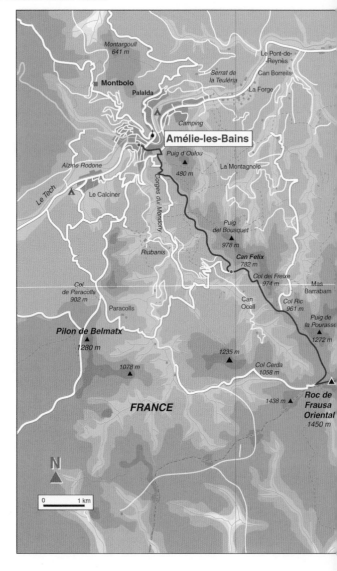

284

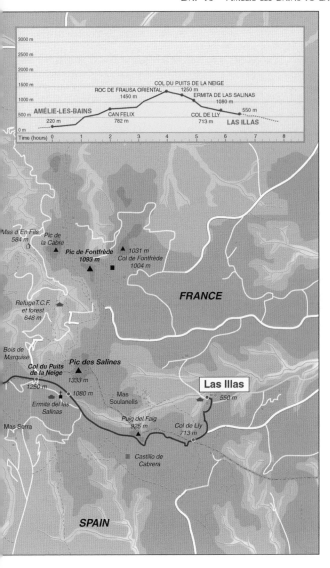

forest you have to improvise, because there's no path and not more than a few marks. Just follow the ridge on your way down to the:

4.30 Col du Puits de la Neige (1250m). On the Spanish side of this pass, on the left side of the road that leads to the antenna on the Roc de Frausa, you'll find a signpost that indicates the route to the Ermita de la Salinas. Go down SE on an obvious path between trees and shrubs until you arrive, within sight of the *ermita*, on a dirt road. Follow this road to the *ermita*.

4.50 Ermita de las Salinas (1080m). Meals and drinks may be available in summer, when the *ermita* is open for tourists. For the rest of the year the building is closed, but there is a basic *cabane/refuge* for walkers (12 places). Walk along the building and follow a path to a useful water point about 100m E of the *ermita*. Turn right just before the water point and for 15mins follow a path with red marks until you reach a dirt road. Turn left and walk SE on this road. Notice the ruins of Castillo de Cabrera at a distance on your right. Beyond the ruins the road makes a large curve to the left and goes NE to the:

5.55 Col de Lly (713m). Make sure you don't miss the Col de Lly, which is found between border stone no 557 and the remains of a house at a place where the road touches the border. There's a fence on the border. Go through a gate and go down NNE on a path that's marked with yellow paint flashes. Go down in the forest until you arrive at a dirt road. Keep walking in the same direction until the route forks. Leave the road, turn left and go down on an obvious path to the hamlet of:

6.30 Las Illas (550m). Bar/restaurant, *gite d'étape*, but no shops. The *gite d'étape* is situated next to the Mairie. Should the door be closed, then call on Mme Martinez, who lives a few houses N of the *gite*. There are no meals available in the *gite*, but you can cook your own meal in the well-equipped kitchen, tel. 04 68 83 23 93 or 04 68 83 41 70. Reservation recommended in summer: there are only 16 places. Open from April until late September. Bar/restaurant dels Trabucayres also seems to have a few rooms available, tel. 04 68 83 07 56.

DAY 41
Las Illas to Col de l'Ouillat

Route:	via the Col du Perthus (280m)
Grade:	2
Time:	6hrs 30mins
Height gain:	1000m
Height loss:	570m
Map:	IGN Carte de Randonnées, 1:50,000, no 11: Roussillon

An unpleasant walk on road, track and dirt roads. The Haute Route follows the GR10 trail today, so route finding is quite simple. There are lots of supermarkets in Le Perthus, the last point at which to replenish your food supplies. Col de l'Ouillat is a fine place to spend the last night before you arrive at Banyuls-sur-Mer. The views from the pass on the Canigou massif are magnificent. There is a nice atmosphere in the Col de l'Ouillat *gite*.

0.00 Las Illas. Walk past the monument for victims of the First World War and follow a dirt road NE until you arrive at a road. Follow, with the GR10, the so-called Route de Manrell that climbs in zigzags alongside the houses of Super Las Illas. You finally arrive at the Col de Figuer (685m, signpost). Turn left and walk NE on a dirt road. Keep alert to the GR10 marks and ignore several other dirt roads. Soon the dirt road enters a beautiful beech forest, where you'll find a water point on your right. Don't turn left as you emerge from the forest but follow the 'main' dirt road to a farm: Mas Nou (667m). Keep the farmhouse on your left-hand side, ignore (after about 45mins from Mas Nou) the dirt road that branches off to Maureillas, and continue on dirt road until the:

2.25 Col Priourat (459m), not easily identified, but you'll find border stone no 565 on your right. Continue on the dirt road for about 1km. Turn right where the road makes a hairpin bend and walk SE to Mas Roelofs (360m). Near the farm you'll find the dirt road that leads to Le Perthus. Follow this road all the way down, keep Fort de Bellegarde (built in 1679) on your right-hand side and in Le Perthus go down to the main road that runs through the frontier village.

3.40 Col du Perthus (280m). Le Perthus is, in fact, no more than a long street (N 9), with numerous shops, supermarkets, restaurants and hotels. It is overcrowded, noisy and certainly not a place to stay for a long time. Walk to the north section of Le Perthus and take the D 71 that branches off to the right (Col de l'Ouillat is indicated). Walk under a giant viaduct

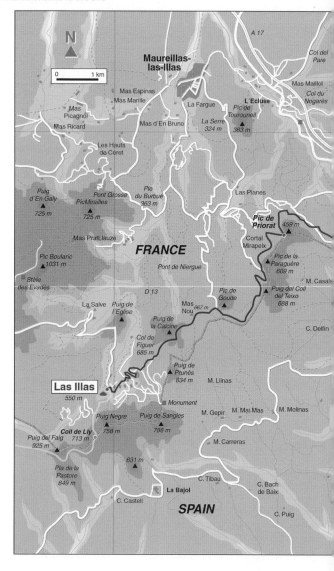

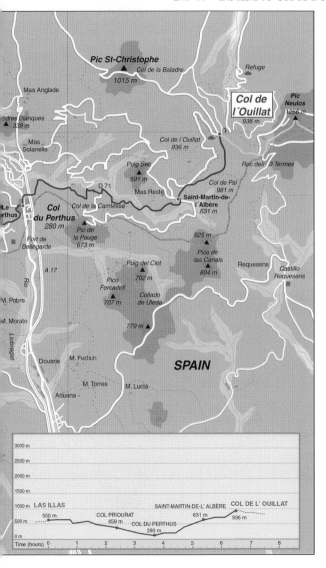

Early morning view from the Col de l'Ouillat in spring

(autoroute A 17) and follow for about 5km the quiet D 71 that climbs gently. Water bottles can be filled at one of the water points along the road (for example at the Fontaine Sainte Marie, dated 1885). Beyond Mas Reste, on the left side of the road, leave the road and turn right. Climb E on a broad track, which turns into a more regular path, until you see the tiny hamlet of:

5.25 Saint-Martin-de-l'Albère (631m) ahead of you. Work your way up to the hamlet, pass the church and follow the road that gives access to Saint-Martin until you return to the D 71. Follow the road for a short while until you pass a curve. Notice a small parking area on the left side of the road and leave the road. Turn right and climb on a path through a forest to a house. Keep the building on your right-hand side and climb until you return to the road. Cross it and walk E through a rather chaotic forest that has been mutilated with a series of dirt roads. Keep alert to the GR10 marks as you walk on these roads. Eventually you'll find a path which leads again to the D 71. Cross the road and follow a path, which is rather faint in places but well marked, ENE in an open landscape until the path forks and a signpost indicates the *gite d'étape* on the Col de l'Ouillat. Turn left and walk N through a forest to the:

6.30 Gite d'étape on the Col de l'Ouillat (936m, also called chalet de l'Albère), situated next to the road along the Foret Domaniale des Alberes. (About 100m past the *gite* there is a picnic area with a water point on the left side of the road.) The *gite* is open all year, with 40 places (in the chalet and a building next to the *gite*), meals available, tel. 04 68 83 62 20, internet: www.ot-leboulou.fr/alberes.htm

DAY 42
Col de l'Ouillat
to Banyuls-sur-Mer

Route:	via the Pic Neulos (1256m), the Pic des Quatre-Termes (1156m) and the Pic de Sailfort (981m)
Grade:	2
Time:	8hrs 25mins
Height gain:	700m
Height loss:	1680m
Map:	IGN Carte de Randonnées, 1:50,000, no 11: Roussillon

A tough stage, but without any major difficulties. The final walk of the Haute Route involves a long walk on the frontier ridge. In poor visibility route finding could be difficult in places. A stylish end to the Haute Route that follows the GR10 trail all the way to Banyuls.

0.00 Col de l'Ouillat. The GR10 to Banyuls-sur-Mer is indicated on a signpost near the *gîte d'étape*. Follow a path that climbs energetically SE through a pine forest. Finally the path arrives at the small road that gives access to the buildings and large antenna on the Pic Neulos. Don't walk on the road, but follow a path just above it along a fence on the border and walk to Pic Neulos (1256m). Go clockwise around the fence on the top. East of Pic Neulos you go down on the French side of the border on a path that approaches a dirt road. Keep the road below on your left-hand side and walk E until you arrive at:

1.30 Refuge de la Tagnarède (1045m; unstaffed, rather basic shelter, owned by the CAF, 12 places), next to a forest and very close to the border. Walk SE on a path between the dirt road on your left and the Pic Pragun (1052m) on your right. Arrive at the Col de Pragun (1010m) and follow the ridge, or keep a few metres left of it, as you walk to the:

2.00 Col del Faig (988m), border stone (crucifix) no 584. Walk SE through the grass to the Col de l'Orry (974m) and climb ENE. Keep a beech forest on your left and the Puig de la Basses (1073m) on your right. Go down to the Col de l'Estaque (border crucifix no 586). Keep the dirt road on

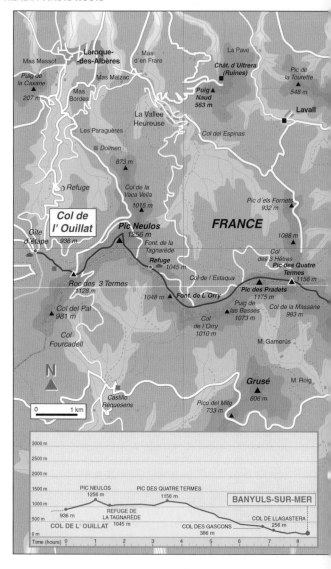

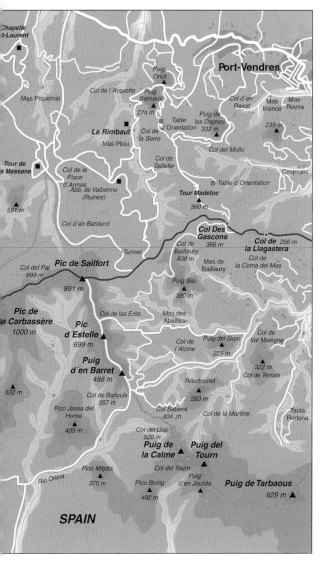

your left, don't pay attention to the GR10 marks and climb ENE on the frontier ridge to the:

3.30 Pic des Quatre-Termes (1156m). Walk clockwise around the summit and go down steeply on the ridge to the Col de la Massane (983m). Continue in the same direction to the Pic de la Carbassère (1000m), where the route bends to the left. Arrive at the Col del Pal (899m) and climb, generally E, to the:

4.50 Pic de Sailfort (981m). Take a short break here, because the views of the Côte Vermeille are magnificent. Go down E on a steep ridge, avoiding rocky sections. During the descent, at a kind of pass, the route bends a little to the left and follows a ridge. Stay a little to the left and below this ridge, and go down gently NE to arrive at a pass that can be seen from afar:

6.10 Col de Baillaury (418m). A dirt road crosses the col. From here you can follow a more or less level dirt road to the Col des Gascons, but the best thing to do is to take the path that climbs NE. Cross a ridge soon (456m, Col de Formigou) and walk on an almost level path along a steep slope above the dirt road. Arrive at a junction on a ridge, turn right and go down steeply to the:

6.55 Col des Gascons (386m). A small road (D 86) touches this pass. Turn right and go down on the road for about 50m. Turn left and take two short-cuts (**beware:** the path is very steep and eroded) to arrive once again at the road. Leave the road again and follow a path that passes a water point. The path reaches the road, which you follow this time. Notice a *table d'orientation* on your right and continue for a few metres until the road turns right. Here you are on the:

7.20 Col de Llagastera (256m). Leave the road, take dirt road no AL 73 (indicated – the right one) and climb E towards the Puig Geraud. Ignore a dirt road that branches off to the left and cross the ridge. Go down towards Banyuls (you can see the village from here) and soon take a short-cut on your right. Continue to go down on what appears to be the main dirt road and arrive at a house (Corral Nou). Here the road makes a sharp turn to the right. Follow the road until you find a path on the right side of the road. Go down on this path, which touches the road once (where the road makes a sharp turn left), and arrive finally on a small road. Cross this road, follow a dirt road and turn right at the next

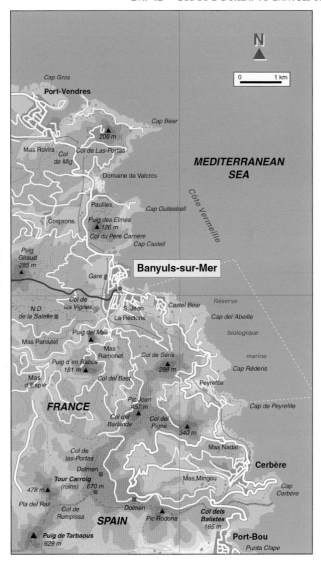

N

0   1 km

Cap Gros

Port-Vendres

Cap Béar

206 m

Mas Rovira   Col
             de Mig   Col de Las-Portas

Domaine de Valcros

**MEDITERRANEAN
SEA**

Paulilles

Cap Oullestrell

Côte Vermeille

Cosprons

Puig des Elmes
▲ 126 m

Col du Pere Carnère
                          Cap Castell

Puig
Giraud
285 m
▲

Banyuls-sur-Mer

Gare

Réserve

N.D.   Col de
de la Salète   las Vignes

S. Jean
La Rectorie

Castel Béar

Cap del Abeille

biologique

Puig del Mas
          ▲

Mas Paroutet

Mas
Ramonet   Col de Séris

marine

Cap Réderis

Puig d'en Rabus
181 m ▲   Col del Bast

298 m

Mas
d'Espié

Peyrefite

FRANCE

Pic Joan
457 m
▲

Col del
Barlande   Col del
            Pigné

Cap de Peyrefite

340 m
▲

Mas Nadal

Cerbère

Col de
las-Portas

Dolmen

Mas Mingou

Cap
Cerbère

Tour Carroig
(ruins) 670 m
478 m ▲   ■

Pla del Ras   Col de
             Rumpissa   **SPAIN**

Dolmen   Pic Rodona

**Col dels
Balistes**
165 m

Port-Bou

▲ Puig de Tarbaous
   629 m

Punta Clape

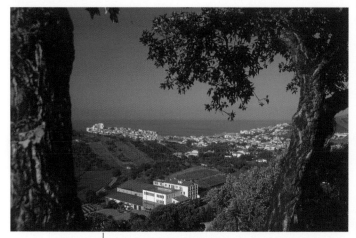

Banyuls-sur-Mer

junction. Follow a dirt road, notice a sports field on your right below and pass a house (under construction in 2003). Take a path that goes down steeply between vineyards and reach a small road. Turn left, go through a tunnel underneath the railway line and continue in the same direction. Follow a small channel and continue to a road. Turn left and walk to a junction. Turn left once more, pass a fountain and follow the road until you finally arrive at the beach of:

8.25 Banyuls-sur-Mer. Hotels, shops, cash dispenser, camp-sites, bars, restaurants, banks, railway service to Paris, tourist office (at the beach). The railway station is situated in the NW section of the village.

Internet: www.banyuls-sur-mer.com (which has a good English version). For practical information on Banyuls-sur-Mer also see the introduction to this section.

APPENDIX 1
Useful Addresses

Mountaineering Clubs

UK
Alpine Club
55/56 Charlotte Road
London EC2A 3QF
Tel: (00 44) (0)02076130755
Internet: www.alpine-club.org.uk
Email: sec@alpine-club.org.uk

Belgium
Club Alpin Belgique
129 Av Albert 1er
5000 Namur
Tel: (00 32) (0)81224084
Fax: (00 32) (0)81223063
Internet: www.clubalpin.be
Email: secretariat@clubalpin.be

Germany
Deutscher Alpenverein
Von-Kahr-Str 2-4
80997 München
Tel: 49 89 14003 0
Fax: 49 89 14003 12
Internet: www.alpenverein.de

Netherlands
Nederlandse Klim- en Bergsportvereniging (NKBV)
Houttuinlaan 16-A, 3447 GM Woerden
Tel: (00 31) (0)348 – 409521
Internet: www.nkbv.nl
Email: info@nkbv.nl

France
Club Alpin Francais (CAF)
24, Avenue de Launière
75019 Parijs
Tel: (00 33) (0)1 53 72 87 00
Fax: (00 33) (0)1 42 03 55 60
Internet: www.clubalpin.com
Email: editions.com@clubalpin.com

Spain
FEDME
Floridablanca, 84
08015 Barcelona
Tel: 934 264 267
Fax: 934 263 387
Internet: www.fedme.es
Email: fedme@fedme.es

Federacio d'Entitats Excursionistes de Catalunya (FEEC-Catalonia)
Rambla 41, Pral. – 08002 Barcelona
Tel: (00 34) (0)93 412 07 77
Fax: (00 34) (0)934 126 353
Internet: www.feec.org (short English version)
Email: feec@feec.org

Centre Excursionista de Catalunya (CEC-Catalonia)
Paradis 10, Pral – 08002 Barcelona
Tel: (00 34) (0)933 152 311
Fax: (00 34) (0)933 151 408
Internet: www.cec-centre.org
Email: cec@cec-centre.org

Federacion Aragonesa de Montañismo (FAM-Aragon)
C/. Alberada 7, 40 4a
50004 Zaragoza
Tel: (00 34) (0)976 227 971
Fax: (00 34) (0)976 212 459
Internet: www.fam.es
Email: info@fam.es

Airline Companies
British Airways: www.britishairways.com
Iberia: www.iberia.com
Ryanair: www.ryanair.com

General Tourist Information
The French Tourist Department: www.franceguide.com
The Spanish Tourist Office: www.spaintour.com
Catalonia's tourist site: www.publintur.es
Aragon tourist site: www.turismoaragon.com
Andorra tourist sites: www.andorraonline.ad and www.turisme.ad
Pays Basque tourist information: www.pays-basque-online.fr

Information on the Pyrenees National Parks
Parc National des Pyrénées Occidentales site: www.parc-pyrenees.com
Parque Nacional de Ordesa y Monte Perdido site: www.ordesa.net
Aigues Tortes national park sites: www.catalunya.net/aiguestortes and www.parcsde-catalunya.net.

Weather Forecast
www.meteo.fr

Railway Information
Eurostar services: www.eurostar.com
Other European railway services: www.raileurope.com
French railway company site: www.sncf.fr

Mountain Huts and *Gites d'étape*
All *gites* and *refuges* in France: www.gites-refuges.com
Refuges and taverns in Spain: www.refugiosyalbergues.com
There is also an excellent book, *Gites d'étape and refuges (France et Frontières)*, which contains details of 3900 huts and *gites* in France, Andorra, Belgium, Spain, Italy, Luxemburg and Switzerland. Publisher: Rando Editions. Address: 4, Rue Maye Lane – 65420 Ibos. Tel. 05 62 90 09 90 and fax 05 62 90 67 22. Internet: www.rando-editions.com. Email: accueil@rando-editions.com

Other Useful Sites
There are a few beautiful French sites that offer interesting information on subjects such as walking, flora and fauna, pioneers, gastronomy, huts, campsites, GR10 and Pyrenean Haute Route and the last Pyrenean bears: www.webpyrenees.com (this site has a list of all the Offices du Tourisme in the French Pyrenees), www.pyrenees-online.fr and www.multimania.com/pyrenees.

A fine introduction to the Spanish Pyrenees: www.pirineo.com.
Maps: www.ign.fr (the French Institut Geographique National)

Randonnées Pyrénéennes

For more than 25 years the French organisation Randonnées Pyrénéennes has been working to stimulate green tourism in the (French) Pyrenees. A long series of magnificent walking guides, which cover altogether every inch of the Pyrenees, demonstrate the unique expertise of this organisation.

Address: 1 rue Maye Lane, 65420 Ibos Cedex. Tel: (00 33) (0)5 62 90 67 60.
Internet: www.rando-pyrenees.net

CIMES (Centre d'Information Montagnes et Sentiers) is the information service of Randonnées Pyrénéennes. Walkers can address to CIMES all sorts of questions on subjects such as huts, maps, walking, climbing and canyoning. Internet: www.cimes-pyrenees.net.

The author's internet site

www.pyreneeen-online.com (in Dutch but with an English version)
email: vignemale@planet.nl

APPENDIX 2
Glossary

Aigue, aygue	water
Agujas, aiguille	sharp
Alta, alto	high
Arriu, arriou, arroyo	stream
Arrouy	red
Ayous	bilberry
Badette	tiny valley
Baix	low
Bal	valley
Barrage	dam
Barranco	ravine with a stream running through
Bat, batch, baight	valley
Borde, borda	farm, barn
Borne	border stone
Bosc, bosque	forest
Boum	small deep lake
Cabane, cabana	shepherds' hut
Caillaouas	debris
Camino	path, trail
Canal	narrow valley
Cap	summit
Carretera	paved road
Casa	house
Caserio	hamlet, farm
Choza	tiny hut
Cirque, circ (Cat.), circo	vertical amphitheatre wall of rock
Col, coll (Cat.), collado, couillade, couret, cuello	mountain pass
Cueva	cave
Coume, clot	bowl
Courtau, coueyla	place on the mountain where cattle are gathered in summer
Cresta, crête	mountain ridge
Dalt	high

301

Embalse	(dammed) lake
Embarrat	enclosed
Estagnol, estany (Cat.), étang	mountain lake
Estibe	pasture
Finca particular	private property
Font, fuente	well
Fourcat	split, forked
Garganta	gorge, canyon
Gave	mountain river
Gite	hostel, tavern
Gorge	gorge
Gourg	deep lake
Hount	well
Hourquette	steep mountain pass
Ibon	(natural) lake
Jasse	level area often used to gather cattle
Lac, lago	lake
Laquet	tiny lake
Lis	avalanche
Llano	level area, plateau
Marcadau	market
Mirador	place that offers outstanding views
Nère, negre	black
Neste	mountain river
Orri	ancient stone-built iglo-shaped hut
Oule, oulette	bowl
Pala	giant rock
Palanca	small (foot)bridge on a mountain stream
Paso	mounatin pass
Pena, punta	sharp pointy summit

Pla, plan, Pleta	level area, plateau
Pène	round large summit
Peyre	stone
Port	ancient pass (often on the French–Spanish border)
Portella, porteille, portillo, portillon, puerto, pourtet, pourtalet	mountain pass
Puente	bridge
Raillère	slope full of boulders
Refuge, refugi (Cat.), refugio	mountain hut
Riu (Cat.), rio	river
Roya	red
Ruisseau	tiny stream
Seilh	glacier
Senda	trail, path
Sente	track (created by cattle)
Serre, sierra	mountain range
Soula	sun side
Soum	round summit
Toue	ancient hut underneath a rock
Torrant, torrent	mountain stream
Tort	meandering, tortuous, winding
Tourrat	ice
Tozal, tuc, tuca, tusse	summit
Vall (Cat.), valle, vallée	valley
Vallon	tiny valley

Cat. = Catalan

APPENDIX 3 – Facilities List

	Locations (italic) and intermediate places	Altitude	Day/stage time (hrs/mins)	Intermediate time (hrs/mins)	Hotel	Bar/restaurant	Shop	Bank	Cash dispenser	Post office	Staffed hut/gîte	Unstaffed hut/cabane	Campsite
day 1	Hendaye-Plage	0m			X	X	X	X	X	X			X
	col d'Ibardin	317m		4.30		X							
	col de Lizuniaga	230m	8.15			X							
day 2	Arizkun	280m	7.15		X	X	X						
day 3	Les Aldudes	370m	5.00		X	X	X			X			
day 4	Roncevalles	930m	5.45		X	X					X		
day 5	Egurgui	850m	6.45										
	chalet Pedro	990m		3.20	X								
day 6	col Bagargui	1327m	5.15			X	X						
day 7	refugio de Belagua	1428m	9.50								X		
day 8	Lescun	900m	6.45		X	X	X			X	X		X
day 9	refuge d'Arlet	2000m	6.45								X		
day 10	Candanchu	1550m	6.30		X	X	X						
day 11	Astun	1710m		1.00	X	X							
day 12	refuge de Pombie	2032m	6.20								X		
	refuge d'Arrémoulit	2305m		5.05							X		
	refuge de Larribet	2070m	8.10								X		
day 13	cabane de Doumblas	1563m		1.15								X	
	refuge Wallon	1866m	8.20								X		
day 14	refuge des Oulettes de Gaube	2151m		5.00							X		
	refuge de Bayssellance	2651m	7.20								X		
day 15	barrage d'Ossoue	1834m	2.00									X	X

Locations (italic) and intermediate places	Altitude	Day/stage time (hrs/mins)	Intermediate time (hrs/mins)	Hotel	Bar/restaurant	Shop	Bank	Cash dispenser	Post office	Staffed hut/gîte	Unstaffed hut/cabane	Campsite
cabane de Lourdes	1947m		2.35								X	
cabane de Sausse-Dessus	1900m		3.20								X	
day 16 *Gavarnie*	1365m	5.20		X	X	X	X	X	X			X
refuge des Espuguettes	2027m		2.00							X		
Héas	1500m	6.45		X	X					X		X
day 17 cabane de l'Aguila	1900m		1.15								X	
refuge de Barroude	2373m		5.15							X		
Parzan	1100m	9.30		X	X	X	X		X			
day 18 camping El Forcallo	1650m		6.45									X
refugio de Viados	1760m	7.15								X		
day 19 refuge de Prat-Cazeneuve	2020m		4.50								X	
refuge de la Soula	1690m	6.30								X		
day 20 *refuge du Portillon*	2571m	6.15								X		
day 21 Hospital de Benasque	1800m		5.05	X	X							
refugio de la Renclusa	2140m	6.45								X		
day 22 refugio de Mulleres	2360m		5.50							X		
Hospital de Vielha	1626m	7.45									X	
day 23 *refugi de la Restanca*	2010m	7.15								X		
day 24 refugi de Colomers	2120m		3.45							X		
Bahns de Tredos	1780m		5.45	X	X							
Salardu	1270m	7.15		X	X	X	X	X	X	X		
day 25 *Alos de Isil*	1270m	9.50			X							
day 26 *refugi Enric Pujol*	2290m	7.25									X	
day 27 *refugi de Certascan*	2240m	7.15								X		
day 28 *refugi del Cinquantenari*	2438m	6.25									X	
day 29 refugi de Vall Ferrera	1940m		2.30							X		

Locations (italic) and intermediate places	Altitude	Day/stage time (hrs/mins)	Intermediate time (hrs/mins)	Hotel	Bar/restaurant	Shop	Bank	Cash dispenser	Post office	Staffed hut/gîte	Unstaffed hut/cabane	Campsite
day 29 retugi de Vall Ferrera	1940m									X		
étang de la Soucarrane	2292m	5.00	2.30								X	
day 30 refugi de Sorteny	1970m	6.15										X	
day 31 refugi de Pala de Jan	2220m		3.50									X	
camping d'Incles	1875m	7.40											X
day 32 refugi de Juclar	2285m		1.30									X	
l'Hospitalet-pres-l'Andorre	1436m	6.20		X	X	X		X	X			
day 33 refuge du Barrage des Bésines	1973m		2.25									X	
refuge des Bésines	2104m	3.00									X		
day 34 chalet-refuge des Bouillouses	2005m	7.25									X		
day 35 Bolquère	1620m		3.55	X	X	X			X			
col de la Perche	1579m	4.10		X	X							
Eyne	1560m	4.45								X		
day 36 refugi d'Ull de Ter	2220m	8.10								X		
day 37 cabane du Pla Guilhem	2265m		5.45									X	
refuge de Mariailles	1710m	7.15									X	
day 38 cabane Arago	2123m		2.00									X	
chalet-refuge des Cortalets	2150m		5.20								X		
Mines de Batère	1500m	9.15		X	X					X		
day 39 Amélie-les-Bains	220m	4.35		X	X	X	X	X	X			
day 40 Ermita de las Salinas	1080m		4.50								X	
Las Illas	550m	6.30		X	X	X	X					
day 41 col du Perthus	280m		3.40	X	X	X	X	X	X			
col de l'Ouillat	936m	6.30								X		
day 42 refuge de la Tagnarède	1045m		1.30								X	
Banyuls-sur-Mer	0m	8.25		X	X	X	X	X	X			X

NOTES

NOTES

NOTES

INDEX

A

Airline information 16
Alos de Isil 205, 207
Amélie-les-Bains 279
Amphibians 34
Arizkun 52
Astun 101
Auberge Le Refuge 144

B

Bagergue 199
Bahns de Tredos 187
Banos de Benasque 172
Banyuls-sur-Mer 246, 296
Barrage d'Ossoue 129
Benasque 139
Birdlife 35
Bolquère 260
Bordes de Moredo 205
Brèche de Roland 134
Burga 56

C

Cabane Arago 271
Cabane d'Ardané 79
Cabane d'Ardanne 76
Cabane de Doumblas 114
Cabane de l'Aguila 146
Cabane de Lourdes 129
Cabane de Sausse-Dessus 129
Cabane du Pla Guilhem 267
Camping Aneto 190
Camping d'Incles 237
Camping Forcallo 154

Camping Masia 'Bordes de Graus' 217
Candanchu 100
Chalet-Refuge des Bouillouses 254
Chalet-Refuge des Cortalets 274
Cirque de Gavarnie 87, 133, 137
Climbing gear 17
Col Bagacheta 51
Col Bagargui 71, 72, 77
Col Basabar 56
Col d'Anaye 80
Col d'Arnostéguy 63
Col d'Arratille 122
Col d'Arrémoulit 118
Col d'Arrious 109
Col d'Errozaté 66
Col d'Esquisaroy 51
Col d'Eyne 261
Col d'Hauzay 61
Col d'Ibardin 47
Col d'Inzola 47
Col d'Oraaté 70
Col d'Orgambidé 66
Col d'Orgambideska 71, 77
Col d'Osin 47
Col d'Ursua 50
Col de Baillaury 294
Col de Berdaritz 56
Col de Bimbalette 76
Col de Cambalès 114, 115
Col de Coume d'Agnel 251
Col de Curutcheta 77
Col de Formantère 278
Col de Irazako 49
Col de Jauregeberry 79

Col de l'Ouillat 290, 291
Col de la Cirère 275
Col de la Fache 120
Col de la Jasse d'En Vernet 275
Col de la Perche 260
Col de la Pierre-Saint-Martin 84
Col de la Redoute 278
Col de Lapachouaou 96
Col de Lizuniaga 48
Col de Llagastera 294
Col de Lly 286
Col de Méharroztéguy 61
Col de Mizpira 60
Col de Nabarlatz 49
Col de Nou Creus 265
Col de Pau 95
Col de Pescamou 84
Col de Peyreget 105
Col de Roncevaux 61
Col de Segalès 275
Col de Tharta 73
Col de Tirapitz 265
Col del Faig 291
Col des Anies 84
Col des Gascons 294
Col des Gourgs-Blancs 162
Col des Moines 101
Col des Mulets 124
Col du Palas 112
Col du Perthus 287
Col du Pluviomètre 162
Col du Puits de la Neige 286
Col Inférieur de Literole 136, 164
Col Lapatignégagne 72
Col Méhatzé 72
Col Priourat 287
Col Uthu 73

Coll d'Airoto 204
Coll de Baborte 223
Coll de Calberante 211
Coll de Certascan 217
Coll de Crestada 184
Coll de Curios 211
Coll de Goellicrestada 184
Coll de la Cornella 211
Coll de Mulleres 136, 177
Coll de Rio Bueno 192
Coll de Sellente 223
Collada de la Marrana 265
Collada dels Meners 236
Collade des Roques Blanches 267
Collado d'Estany de Mar 182
Collado de Causiat 100
Collado de Valhibierna 172, 192
Crête de Zazpigagn 73

E

Egurgui 67
El Serrat 232
Embalse de Campoplano 120
Embalse de Respomuso 120
Ermita de las Salinas 286
Estany de Baciver 201
Estany de Juclar 238
Estany de Sottlo 223, 228
Estany deth Cap deth Port 184
Estany Romedo de Baix 220
Estany Romedo de Dalt 220
Estany Tort de Rius 179
Étang de Couart 239
Étang de la Soucarrane 227
Étang de Lanoux 251
Étang de Pédourés 239
Étang de Pradeille 259

Étang des Bésines 250
Étang des Fourats 251
Eyne 260

F
Flowers 36

G
Gavarnie 132–137
Gite d'étape de Batère 275
Grande Fache 27, 121

H
Héas 144
Hendaye 39, 40
Hendaye-Plage 43
Hospice de France 172
Hospital de Benasque 165
Hospital de Vielha 178, 194
Hourquette d'Alans 141
Hourquette d'Ossoue 125
Hourquette de Chermentas 147
Hourquette de Héas 146

I
Ibon de Astanes 97
Ibon de Escalar 101
Ibon de Escaleta 176

L
l'Hospitalet-près-l'Andorre 242, 244, 248
La Rhune 39
Lac d'Arratille 122
Lac d'Arrious 109
Lac de Caillauas 159
Lac de Peyreget 105
Lac des Bouillouses 254, 255

Lac des Isclots 159
Lac du Milieu 159
Lacs d'Aygues Tortes 157
Lacs de Batcrabère 113
Lacs de Cambalès 118
Lago de Literola 164
Lagos de Anglios 193
Lagos de Vallibierna 192
Larrau 78
Las Illas 286
Le Taillon 27, 133
Les Aldudes 56
Lescun 39, 88–93

M
Maison Forestière de l'Estanyol 274
Mammals 33
Meson La Fuen 150
Mines de Batère 278
Mont Roig 27, 212
Montardo d'Aran 27, 188
Montcalm 28
Montgarri 206

N
Noarre 213

O
Occabé 70
Otsamunho 57

P
Parc Nacional d'Aigüestortes i Estany de Sant Maurici 31, 32
Parc National des Pyrénées Occidentales 31, 87
Parque Nacional de Ordesa i Monte Perdido 31

Parzan 150
Pas de l'Échelle 97
Paso de los Caballos 151
Passage d'Orteig 109
Petit Vignemale 125
Pic Carlit 243, 254, 257
Pic d'Anie 39
Pic d'Ayous 107
Pic d'Orhy 39, 73
Pic de Certascan 27, 219
Pic de Noufonts 265
Pic de Sailfort 294
Pic des Quatre-Termes 294
Pic du Canigou 243, 274, 277
Pic du Midi d'Ossau 104
Pic Perdiguère 17, 27, 163
Pica d'Estats 28, 226, 227, 228
Pico de Aneto 17, 27, 170
Piméné 27, 145
Pla d'Espélunguère 97
Pla de Boavi 222
Pla de Boet 224
Pla Guilhem 267
Pla(n) de Beret 199
Plan d'Aiguallut 173
Plateau de Sanchèse 81
Pleta de Llosas 191
Pont d'Amubi 79
Port d'Aygues Tortes 157
Port de Barroude 147
Port de Belhay 76
Port de Boet 227
Port de Caldes 184
Port de l'Albe 238
Port de la Peyre-Saint-Martin 115
Port de Larrau 73
Port de Rat 232

Port de Rius 179
Port de Sottlo 228
Port de Vénasque 171
Port du Lavédan 113
Portal de Remune 164
Porteille de Mourens 266
Porteille de Valmanya 277
Porteille del Caillau 266
Portella de la Grave 255
Puerto de Gistain 189

R

Railway information 16
Redoute de Lindux 61
Refuge d'Arlet 96
Refuge d'Arrémoulit 91, 109, 114, 118
Refuge d'Ayous 104
Refuge de Barroude 147
Refuge de Bayssellance 126
Refuge de Bonne Aigue 276
Refuge de la Soula 158
Refuge de la Tagnarède 291
Refuge de Labérouat 85
Refuge de Larribet 113
Refuge de Mariailles 270
Refuge de Pombie 105
Refuge de Prat-Cazeneuve 158
Refuge de Vénasque 171
Refuge de Grange de Holle 132
Refuge des Bésines 250
Refuge des Espuguettes 141
Refuge des Oulettes de Gaube 125
Refuge des Sarradets 134
Refuge du Portillon 162
Refuge Wallon 118
Refugi d'Ull de Ter 265
Refugi de Certascan 217

Refugi de Colomers 186
Refugi de Juclar 238
Refugi de la Restanca 182
Refugi de Mulleres 177
Refugi de Pala de Jan 236
Refugi de Sorteny 233
Refugi de Vall Ferrera 226, 228
Refugi del Cinquantenari 223
Refugi Enric Pujol 211
Refugio de Belagua 76
Refugio de Coronas 191
Refugio de Estos 189
Refugio de la Renclusa 169
Refugio de Respomuso 120
Refugio de Viados 136, 154, 189
Refugio El Aguila 100
Reptiles 34
Roc de Frausa Oriental 283
Roncevalles 62
Russell, Henry 127

S
Saint-Martin-de-l'Albère 290
Salardu 187, 196

T
Tavascan 217
Tredos 187
Tuc de Marimanya 204
Tuc de Mulleres 177
Tusse de Montarqué 162

V
Vall d'Aran 196
Valle de Barrosa 147
Valle de Esera 168
Vignemale 17, 27, 126, 128

LISTING OF CICERONE GUIDES

NORTHERN ENGLAND LONG-DISTANCE TRAILS
- THE DALES WAY
- THE ISLE OF MAN COASTAL PATH
- THE PENNINE WAY
- THE ALTERNATIVE COAST TO COAST
- NORTHERN COAST-TO-COAST
- THE RELATIVE HILLS OF BRITAIN
- MOUNTAINS ENGLAND & WALES
  – VOL 1 WALES
  – VOL 2 ENGLAND

CYCLING
- BORDER COUNTRY BIKE ROUTES
- THE CHESHIRE CYCLE WAY
- THE LANCASHIRE CYCLEWAY
- THE CUMBRIA CYCLE WAY
- THE DANUBE CYCLE WAY
- LANDS END TO JOHN O'GROATS CYCLE GUIDE
- ON THE RUFFSTUFF – 84 BIKE RIDES IN NORTH ENGLAND
- RURAL RIDES NO.1 WEST SURREY
- RURAL RIDES NO.1 EAST SURREY
- SOUTH LAKELAND CYCLE RIDES
- THE WAY OF ST JAMES – LE PUY TO SANTIAGO – CYCLIST'S
- CYCLE TOURING IN SPAIN
- THE LOIRE CYCLE ROUTE

LAKE DISTRICT AND MORECAMBE BAY
- CONISTON COPPER MINES
- CUMBRIA WAY & ALLERDALE RAMBLE
- THE CHRONICLES OF MILNTHORPE
- THE EDEN WAY
- FROM FELL AND FIELD
- KENDAL – A SOCIAL HISTORY
- A LAKE DISTRICT ANGLER'S GUIDE
- LAKELAND TOWNS
- LAKELAND VILLAGES
- LAKELAND PANORAMAS
- THE LOST RESORT?
- SCRAMBLES IN THE LAKE DISTRICT
- MORE SCRAMBLES IN THE LAKE DISTRICT
- SHORT WALKS IN LAKELAND
  – BOOK 1: SOUTH
  – BOOK 2: NORTH
  – BOOK 3: WEST
- ROCKY RAMBLER'S WILD WALKS
- RAIN OR SHINE
- ROADS AND TRACKS OF THE LAKE DISTRICT
- THE TARNS OF LAKELAND
  – VOL 1: WEST
  – VOL 2: EAST
- WALKING ROUND THE LAKES
- WALKS SILVERDALE/ARNSIDE
- WINTER CLIMBS IN LAKE DISTRICT

NORTH-WEST ENGLAND
- HISTORIC WALKS IN CHESHIRE
- WALKING IN CHESHIRE
- FAMILY WALKS IN FOREST OF BOWLAND
- WALKING IN THE FOREST OF BOWLAND
- LANCASTER CANAL WALKS
- WALKER'S GUIDE TO LANCASTER CANAL

- CANAL WALKS VOL 1: NORTH
- WALKS FROM THE LEEDS-LIVERPOOL CANAL
- THE RIBBLE WAY
- WALKS IN RIBBLE COUNTRY
- WALKING IN LANCASHIRE
- WALKS ON THE WEST PENNINE MOORS
- WALKS IN LANCASHIRE WITCH COUNTRY
- HADRIAN'S WALL
  – VOL 1: THE WALL WALK
  – VOL 2: WALL COUNTRY WALKS

NORTH-EAST ENGLAND
- NORTH YORKS MOORS
- HISTORIC WALKS IN NORTH YORKSHIRE
- THE REIVER'S WAY
- THE TEESDALE WAY
- WALKING IN COUNTY DURHAM
- WALKING IN THE NORTH PENNINES
- WALKING IN NORTHUMBERLAND
- WALKING IN THE WOLDS
- WALKS IN THE NORTH YORK MOORS
  – BOOKS 1 AND 2
- WALKS IN THE YORKSHIRE DALES
  – BOOKS 1,2 AND 3
- WALKS IN DALES COUNTRY
- WATERFALL WALKS – TEESDALE & HIGH PENNINES
- THE YORKSHIRE DALES
- YORKSHIRE DALES ANGLER'S GUIDE

THE PEAK DISTRICT
- STAR FAMILY WALKS PEAK DISTRICT/SOUTH YORKS
- HISTORIC WALKS IN DERBYSHIRE
- HIGH PEAK WALKS
- WEEKEND WALKS IN THE PEAK DISTRICT
- WHITE PEAK WALKS
  – VOL.1 NORTHERN DALES
  – VOL.2 SOUTHERN DALES
- WHITE PEAK WAY
- WALKING IN PEAKLAND
- WALKING IN SHERWOOD FOREST
- WALKING IN STAFFORDSHIRE
- THE VIKING WAY

WALES AND WELSH BORDERS
- ANGLESEY COAST WALKS
- ASCENT OF SNOWDON
- THE BRECON BEACONS
- CLWYD ROCK
- HEREFORD & THE WYE VALLEY
- HILLWALKING IN SNOWDONIA
- HILLWALKING IN WALES VOL.1
- HILLWALKING IN WALES VOL.2
- LLEYN PENINSULA COASTAL PATH
- WALKING OFFA'S DYKE PATH
- THE PEMBROKESHIRE COASTAL PATH
- THE RIDGES OF SNOWDONIA
- SARN HELEN
- SCRAMBLES IN SNOWDONIA
- SEVERN WALKS
- THE SHROPSHIRE HILLS
- THE SHROPSHIRE WAY
- SPIRIT PATHS OF WALES
- WALKING DOWN THE WYE

- A WELSH COAST TO COAST WALK
- WELSH WINTER CLIMBS

THE MIDLANDS
- CANAL WALKS VOL 2: MIDLANDS
- THE COTSWOLD WAY
- COTSWOLD WALKS
  – BOOK 1: NORTH
  – BOOK 2: CENTRAL
  – BOOK 3: SOUTH
- THE GRAND UNION CANAL WALK
- HEART OF ENGLAND WALKS
- WALKING IN OXFORDSHIRE
- WALKING IN WARWICKSHIRE
- WALKING IN WORCESTERSHIRE
- WEST MIDLANDS ROCK

SOUTH AND SOUTH-WEST ENGLAND
- WALKING IN BEDFORDSHIRE
- WALKING IN BERKSHIRE
- WALKING IN BUCKINGHAMSHIRE
- CHANNEL ISLAND WALKS
- CORNISH ROCK
- WALKING IN CORNWALL
- WALKING IN THE CHILTERNS
- WALKING ON DARTMOOR
- WALKING IN DEVON
- WALKING IN DORSET
- CANAL WALKS VOL 3: SOUTH
- EXMOOR & THE QUANTOCKS
- THE GREATER RIDGEWAY
- WALKING IN HAMPSHIRE
- THE ISLE OF WIGHT
- THE KENNET & AVON WALK
- THE LEA VALLEY WALK
- LONDON: THE DEFINITIVE WALKING GUIDE
- LONDON THEME WALKS
- THE NORTH DOWNS WAY
- THE SOUTH DOWNS WAY
- THE ISLES OF SCILLY
- THE SOUTHERN COAST TO COAST
- SOUTH WEST COAST PATH
- WALKING IN SOMERSET
- WALKING IN SUSSEX
- THE THAMES PATH
- TWO MOORS WAY
- WALKS IN KENT BOOK 1
- WALKS IN KENT BOOK 2
- THE WEALDWAY & VANGUARD WAY

SCOTLAND
- WALKING IN THE ISLE OF ARRAN
- THE BORDER COUNTRY – A WALKERS GUIDE
- BORDER COUNTRY CYCLE ROUTES
- BORDER PUBS & INNS –A WALKERS' GUIDE
- CAIRNGORMS, WINTER CLIMBS 5TH EDITION
- CENTRAL HIGHLANDS – 6 LONG DISTANCE WALKS
- WALKING THE GALLOWAY HILLS
- WALKING IN THE HEBRIDES
- SCOTLAND'S FAR NORTH
- NORTH TO THE CAPE

- THE ISLAND OF RHUM
- THE ISLE OF SKYE – A WALKER'S GUIDE
- WALKS IN THE LAMMERMUIRS
- WALKING IN THE LOWTHER HILLS
- THE SCOTTISH GLENS SERIES
  - 1 – CAIRNGORM GLENS
  - 2 – ATHOLL GLENS
  - 3 – GLENS OF RANNOCH
  - 4 – GLENS OF TROSSACH
  - 5 – GLENS OF ARGYLL
  - 6 – THE GREAT GLEN
  - 7 – THE ANGUS GLENS
  - 8 – KNOYDART TO MORVERN
  - 9 – THE GLENS OF ROSS-SHIRE
- SCOTTISH RAILWAY WALKS
- SCRAMBLES IN LOCHABER
- SCRAMBLES IN SKYE
- SKI TOURING IN SCOTLAND
- THE SPEYSIDE WAY
- TORRIDON – A WALKER'S GUIDE
- WALKS FROM THE WEST HIGHLAND RAILWAY
- THE WEST HIGHLAND WAY
- WINTER CLIMBS NEVIS & GLENCOE

IRELAND
- IRISH COASTAL WALKS
- THE IRISH COAST TO COAST
- THE MOUNTAINS OF IRELAND

WALKING AND TREKKING IN THE ALPS
- WALKING IN THE ALPS
- 100 HUT WALKS IN THE ALPS
- CHAMONIX TO ZERMATT
- GRAND TOUR OF MONTE ROSA
  – VOL. 1 AND VOL. 2
- TOUR OF MONT BLANC

FRANCE, BELGIUM AND LUXEMBOURG
- WALKING IN THE ARDENNES
- ROCK CLIMBS BELGIUM & LUX.
- THE BRITTANY COASTAL PATH
- CHAMONIX - MONT BLANC WALKING GUIDE
- WALKING IN THE CEVENNES
- CORSICAN HIGH LEVEL ROUTE: GR20
- THE ECRINS NATIONAL PARK
- WALKING THE FRENCH ALPS: GR5
- WALKING THE FRENCH GORGES
- FRENCH ROCK
- WALKING IN THE HAUTE SAVOIE
- WALKING IN THE LANGUEDOC
- TOUR OF THE OISANS: GR54
- WALKING IN PROVENCE
- WALKING IN CORSICA
- THE PYRENEAN TRAIL: GR10
- THE TOUR OF THE QUEYRAS
- ROBERT LOUIS STEVENSON TRAIL
- WALKING IN TARENTAISE & BEAUFORTAIN ALPS
- ROCK CLIMBS IN THE VERDON
- TOUR OF THE VANOISE
- WALKS IN VOLCANO COUNTRY
- SNOWSHOEING MONT BLANC/ WESTERN ALPS
- VANOISE SKI TOURING
- ALPINE SKI MOUNTAINEERING
  – VOL 1: WESTERN ALPS
  – VOL 2: EASTERN ALPS

FRANCE/SPAIN
- ROCK CLIMBS IN THE PYRENEES
- WALKS & CLIMBS IN THE PYRENEES
- THE WAY OF ST JAMES
  – VOL 1 AND VOL 2 – WALKER'S
- THE WAY OF ST JAMES – LE PUY TO SANTIAGO – CYCLIST'S

SPAIN AND PORTUGAL
- WALKING IN THE ALGARVE
- ANDALUSIAN ROCK CLIMBS
- BIRDWATCHING IN MALLORCA
- COSTA BLANCA ROCK
- COSTA BLANCA WALKS VOL 1
- COSTA BLANCA WALKS VOL 2
- WALKING IN MALLORCA
- ROCK CLIMBS IN MAJORCA, IBIZA & TENERIFE
- WALKING IN MADEIRA
- THE MOUNTAINS OF CENTRAL SPAIN
- THE SPANISH PYRENEES GR11 2ND EDITION
- WALKING IN THE SIERRA NEVADA
- WALKS & CLIMBS IN THE PICOS DE EUROPA
- VIA DE LA PLATA
- WALKING IN THE CANARY ISLANDS
  – VOL 1: WEST AND VOL 2: EAST

SWITZERLAND
- ALPINE PASS ROUTE, SWITZERLAND
- THE BERNESE ALPS A WALKING GUIDE
- CENTRAL SWITZERLAND
- THE JURA: HIGH ROUTE & SKI TRAVERSES
- WALKING IN TICINO, SWITZERLAND
- THE VALAIS, SWITZERLAND – A WALKING GUIDE

GERMANY, AUSTRIA AND EASTERN EUROPE
- MOUNTAIN WALKING IN AUSTRIA
- WALKING IN THE BAVARIAN ALPS
- WALKING IN THE BLACK FOREST
- THE DANUBE CYCLE WAY
- GERMANY'S ROMANTIC ROAD
- WALKING IN THE HARZ MOUNTAINS
- KING LUDWIG WAY
- KLETTERSTEIG NORTHERN LIMESTONE ALPS
- WALKING THE RIVER RHINE TRAIL
- THE MOUNTAINS OF ROMANIA
- WALKING IN THE SALZKAMMERGUT
- HUT-TO-HUT IN THE STUBAI ALPS
- THE HIGH TATRAS
- WALKING IN HUNGARY
- WALKING IN CROATIA

SCANDINAVIA
- WALKING IN NORWAY
- ST OLAV'S WAY

ITALY AND SLOVENIA
- ALTA VIA – HIGH LEVEL WALKS DOLOMITES
- CENTRAL APENNINES OF ITALY
- WALKING CENTRAL ITALIAN ALPS
- WALKING IN THE DOLOMITES
- SHORTER WALKS IN THE DOLOMITES
- WALKING ITALY'S GRAN PARADISO
- LONG DISTANCE WALKS IN ITALY'S GRAN PARADISO

- ITALIAN ROCK
- WALKS IN THE JULIAN ALPS
- WALKING IN SICILY
- WALKING IN TUSCANY
- VIA FERRATA SCRAMBLES IN THE DOLOMITES
- VIA FERRATAS OF THE ITALIAN DOLOMITES
  – VOL 1: NORTH, CENTRAL AND EAST
  – VOL 2: SOUTHERN DOLOMITES, BRENTA AND LAKE GARDA

OTHER MEDITERRANEAN COUNTRIES
- THE ATLAS MOUNTAINS
- WALKING IN CYPRUS
- CRETE – THE WHITE MOUNTAINS
- THE MOUNTAINS OF GREECE
- JORDAN – WALKS, TREKS, CAVES ETC.
- THE MOUNTAINS OF TURKEY
- TREKS & CLIMBS WADI RUM JORDAN
- CLIMBS & TREKS IN THE ALA DAG
- WALKING IN PALESTINE

HIMALAYA
- ADVENTURE TREKS IN NEPAL
- ANNAPURNA – A TREKKER'S GUIDE
- EVEREST – A TREKKERS' GUIDE
- GARHWAL & KUMAON – A TREKKER'S GUIDE
- KANGCHENJUNGA – A TREKKER'S GUIDE
- LANGTANG, GOSAINKUND & HELAMBU TREKKERS GUIDE
- MANASLU – A TREKKER'S GUIDE

OTHER COUNTRIES
- MOUNTAIN WALKING IN AFRICA – KENYA
- OZ ROCK – AUSTRALIAN CRAGS
- WALKING IN BRITISH COLUMBIA
- TREKKING IN THE CAUCASUS
- GRAND CANYON & AMERICAN SOUTH WEST
- ROCK CLIMBS IN HONG KONG
- ADVENTURE TREKS WEST NORTH AMERICA
- CLASSIC TRAMPS IN NEW ZEALAND
- THE JOHN MUIR TRAIL

TECHNIQUES AND EDUCATION
- OUTDOOR PHOTOGRAPHY
- SNOW & ICE TECHNIQUES
- ROPE TECHNIQUES
- THE BOOK OF THE BIVVY
- THE HILLWALKER'S MANUAL
- THE TREKKER'S HANDBOOK
- THE ADVENTURE ALTERNATIVE
- BEYOND ADVENTURE
- FAR HORIZONS – ADVENTURE TRAVEL FOR ALL
- MOUNTAIN WEATHER
- MAP AND COMPASS
- THE HILLWALKER'S GUIDE TO MOUNTAINEERING

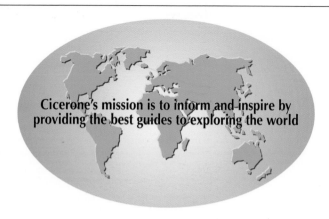

Cicerone's mission is to inform and inspire by providing the best guides to exploring the world

Since its foundation over 30 years ago, Cicerone has specialised in publishing guidebooks and has built a reputation for quality and reliability. It now publishes nearly 300 guides to the major destinations for outdoor enthusiasts, including Europe, UK and the rest of the world.

Written by leading and committed specialists, Cicerone guides are recognised as the most authoritative. They are full of information, maps and illustrations so that the user can plan and complete a successful and safe trip or expedition – be it a long face climb, a walk over Lakeland fells, an alpine traverse, a Himalayan trek or a ramble in the countryside.

With a thorough introduction to assist planning, clear diagrams, maps and colour photographs to illustrate the terrain and route, and accurate and detailed text, Cicerone guides are designed for ease of use and access to the information.

If the facts on the ground change, or there is any aspect of a guide that you think we can improve, we are always delighted to hear from you.

Cicerone Press
2 Police Square Milnthorpe Cumbria LA7 7PY
Tel:01539 562 069   Fax:01539 563 417
e-mail:info@cicerone.co.uk   web:www.cicerone.co.uk

CICERONE